IMPOLITE
CONVERSATIONS

ALSO BY CORA DANIELS

Ghettonation

Black Power Inc.

ALSO BY JOHN L. JACKSON, JR.

*Thin Description: Ethnography and the African
Hebrew Israelites of Jerusalem*

Racial Paranoia: The Unintended Consequences of Political Correctness

Real Black: Adventures in Racial Sincerity

Harlemworld: Doing Race and Class in Contemporary Black America

IMPOLITE CONVERSATIONS

ON RACE, POLITICS, SEX, MONEY, AND RELIGION

CORA DANIELS

AND

JOHN L. JACKSON, JR.

ATRIA BOOKS

NEW YORK   LONDON   TORONTO   SYDNEY   NEW DELHI

ATRIA BOOKS

A Division of Simon & Schuster, Inc.
1230 Avenue of the Americas
New York, NY 10020

Copyright © 2014 by Cora Daniels and John L. Jackson, Jr.

First Atria Books hardcover edition September 2014

ATRIA BOOKS and colophon are trademarks of Simon & Schuster, Inc.

For information about special discounts for bulk purchases, please contact Simon & Schuster Special Sales at 1-866-506-1949 or business@simonandschuster.com.

The Simon & Schuster Speakers Bureau can bring authors to your live event. For more information or to book an event, contact the Simon & Schuster Speakers Bureau at 1-866-248-3049 or visit our website at www.simonspeakers.com.

Interior design by Kyoko Watanabe

Manufactured in the United States of America

10 9 8 7 6 5 4 3 2 1

Library of Congress Cataloging-in-Publication Data is available.

ISBN 978-1-4767-3911-3
ISBN 978-1-4767-3913-7 (ebook)

For my bundles, Maya and Kaden, who teach me everyday how important the little moments truly are. —CD

For Ollie and MarMar, Mommy and I breathe our every breath for you two, even when we're using that breath to yell at you all to clean up your room or to stop teasing each other, especially then. —JJ

CONTENTS

THE INTRO

We need to talk. Those four words almost sound quaint these days. Like being asked to dance rather than grinded upon, thank-you notes chiseled out with pen and paper, getting home before the streetlights go on, or mixtapes. It is the "talk" part that does it—gives the phrase its quaint factor. That's because we don't talk to each other anymore.

Many think the art of conversation was killed by technology. That's a bit of a cop-out. Technology did indeed change *how* we talk, but if we were already engaging in truly honest conversation—where we say what we mean *and* listen to what others say—then we should be able to continue some of that even if our words are delivered differently. Instead, technology just enables the bad habits that were already forming. We were already on the road of nontalk before the text and Twitter takeover. Consider that long before we were glued to our mobile screens Hollywood was able to become dependent on the "we need to talk" line to create imaginary relationship drama in make-believe worlds because talking was already becoming something that we didn't like to do in the real world.

Everyone edits. It is part of growing up. The wonderful thing about young children as they learn to express themselves is that they do just that—express themselves. Uninhibited. They have not learned to filter yet and so say everything that comes to mind. It is why talking to a three-year-old can often flip-flop from being hilarious to embarrassing to wildly unexpected. There is a raw honesty to children-speak that us grown folks have long lost. As the parents of four children between us (all under eight years old), we each are

3

caught in this world of seemingly inappropriate honesty on a regular basis. From the "Hi, old lady" hurled across a local diner by a five-year-old to say hi to, well, an old lady to the "Mommy's fatter than Daddy" uttered matter-of-factly by the two-year-old in the backseat of the car one day. (She is.) Or even this question asked by the five-year-old while walking past a group of teenagers hanging out on the corner in the summer heat in Bed-Stuy: "Why do black people talk so loud?" (We do.)

What if we took that level of tell-it-like-it-is honesty and talked grown-up issues instead? Could we survive being so candid? That is what this collection of essays tries to do. We chose five topics—Sex, Money, Religion, Politics, Race—because those are the things polite guests are never supposed to talk about at a dinner party.

Granted, we live in a world where social networking, Twitter, Facebook, etc., has obliterated the line between private and public moments as we keep larger and larger circles updated about the big and small. It is very easy for it to seem as if we are talking constantly. But just because our private lives have become public doesn't mean that we are truly unedited. Living online also allows an unprecedented level of anonymity. So while our actions, and even our faces, are much more exposed, our words are shielded by the safety of cyber pseudonyms and anonymous comments that nobody has to claim. Never before could individuals be so involved in a conversation, any conversation—whether it be posting a simple comment or creating an entire blogging identity—without having to reveal the who behind the invectives being flung. That's not candor, it's cowardice. It's much harder to say what you mean when you have to be held accountable for those words.

You'll notice that these essays don't take on the point-counterpoint format. Although we have each contributed to the loose organization of five taboo topics we never go back and forth to each write our take on the exact same issue. This is not a he said/she said debate. Instead, each essay tackles a new idea within those general topics. For some that may sound disjointed: a kitchen-sink approach for a collection of writing from two different voices. Instead, we feel it more mirrors a natural conversation. The kind of conversation that meanders, stops, starts, gets you angry, sad, and makes you laugh. Those conversations where you start talking about one thing but end up talking about something completely different with no idea how you got there. The all-night kind of talk that lasts until the sun comes up. The best kind of conversations to have.

Since we are asking you to take this journey in candor with us, we should probably be a little more honest about ourselves. At first glance this may all sound like a lot of intellectual gymnastics between an anthropologist (John) and a journalist (Cora), an idealistic partnership that hopes to bridge academia and the street. Such professional relationships can often be anything but candid, so what's the point? But our relationship is not just professional but personal. In what is probably news to our publisher, we have had a friendship that has lasted ever since we were in high school together in Brooklyn more than twenty-five years ago (did we just admit that?). We certainly didn't go to a quaint neighborhood school that brought family and community together. It was not a place where lifetime relationships were often formed. Instead it was an urban fortress housing more than 4,000 students from across New York City, making it, at the time, one of the largest high schools in the biggest city in the country. It means we did not grow up together or come from the same place. We are also not the people today that we were then. But this shared history—we've known each other longer than we've known our spouses—is significant because it gives us a rapport that you could never get in the contrived *Real Housewives* social settings more common nowadays. Conversations of substance are hard enough with strangers; with those who you know and care about, it can get even more dicey. The stakes are higher. You argue with strangers and acquaintances, you fight with friends and family.

Perhaps we are naïve to think that most conversations today need to be more impolite. Perhaps. But without candid talk we risk, as a society, becoming stuck, whether that be in the sphere of politics, corporate innovation, or anything else.

Here's a thought: it is truly difficult to have a conversation without really listening to the person we are talking to. Not only do we no longer listen but, thanks to new technological innovations, we don't have to. Instead, we enjoy making our points so much that we only listen long enough to poke holes in other people's arguments. But that's not truly hearing them. Honest listening is really the lost art.

So let's talk. And listen . . .

SEX

CORA

Let's pray for sexually active daughters.

"I want a freak in the morning, freak in the evening, just like me . . ."

—ADINA HOWARD, *FREAK LIKE ME*

A few years ago there was this Subaru commercial that was perfectly engineered to touch any parent's heart. In the spot a father is giving his teenage daughter the keys to the car for the first time, but when he looks in the driver's seat while giving his safety speech he is still seeing his daughter as the toddler she once was. I experience the opposite effect daily. From the moment my daughter was born I've been thinking about the woman she will grow up to be. Part of this future focus is that I am an obsessive planner. I surround myself with to-do lists, buy tickets months in advance, and register for things the first day possible, always. By December 1 this past year, I had already planned out my kids' entire summer vacation, including finding *and registering* them for seven different weekly summer camps between the two of them. My husband thinks I'm crazy. What he doesn't know is the constant planning I do that he can't see. Since before my daughter could talk I have been thinking about *the Talk*, as in how will I talk to my daughter about sex. She's barely started elementary school, so our sex talks have been relatively limited so far. But that hasn't stopped me thinking. And that's mostly not because of my obsessive planning but because I'm a woman raising a future woman.

I enjoy sex.

It is amazing to me how few women can say those three words proudly, unapologetically, void of embarrassment, or even without cushioning the admission with a little humor. Perhaps the only thing I envy about men is that it is assumed that they like to get their freak on, when for women it is still something that we are supposed to whisper. Here I am a grown woman, mother of two, still married to the boy I met in college, and writing a book dedicated to candor, and of all the personal, honest, tasteless, and impolite things I've written, it is those three words—*I enjoy sex*—that make me pause at the thought of my mom reading. And if we are keeping it real, honestly, I am not sure I would be able to write those three words so loud and proud if my father were still alive.

For the record, I think about sex, I fantasize about sex, I enjoy sex. At the playground whenever I see fellow parents sporting mommy/daddy gear and exhaustion, I think about how they have also had sex. I actually find one of the best unexpected aphrodisiacs in life is to spot a family from an ultraconservative religious sect, like Hasidic Jews or the Amish, with all their children upon children in tow. Seeing all the sex that couple is obviously having immediately shames any too-tired thoughts from my mind. In fact the only good thing that came from having to endure a presidential election race with the insufferable Mitt Romney was the bombardment of family photos of his five children and his brood of grandchildren (twenty at last count), which put my sex life into overdrive. The Romney clan is clearly doin' it, and doin' it, and doin' it well.

Of course, the major flaw in my thinking is the assumption that just because you are having lots of sex doesn't mean you are enjoying it. Most people think by enjoying it, it means the sex has to be good. I come from the school where all sex, even bad sex, at some level can offer some enjoyment if you let it. I'd rather be having bad sex than, say, go to work, ditto for cleaning my house, shuttling my kids to their endless list of playdates, soccer games, or ballet lessons. Bad sex is better than the morning commute or trying to do errands with my four-year-old in tow. Where bad sex starts to lose its appeal is when it is up against other forms of enjoyment—dinner and a movie, a girls' night out, sleep. That's when our minds start to wander through all the things we could be doing that would be more fun as we wait for the bad sex to end. Still, bad sex doesn't really become bad until you've had great sex. In fact, that moment of great sex is the turning point. Before that moment of great sex, if given the choice—a year filled with lots of sex that's just okay versus a year of hardly any sex, but the sex is mind-blowingly great—I'd surely have picked lots of sex. But after that great sex moment in life it is hard to go back to okay sex no matter how much you're doin' it.

What I have realized is that, unlike some parents, I don't dread the day my daughter will have sex. That's partly why dads, like the one in the Subaru commercial, constantly infantilize their daughters because they can't bear to acknowledge their daughters' sexuality. Instead, what I worry more about is whether my daughter will enjoy sex.

That worry doesn't make me too popular at the playground. Much of the conversation in parenting circles is about how to prevent our kids from having sex, period. Whether the concern comes from our values and belief system or from a health and pregnancy standpoint or some combination, often the discussions focus on dangers and fears. Recently, I went to a meeting at my children's elementary school that dealt with talking to your kids about sex, and the speaker opened the session with: "If you have children in kindergarten they are five years away from puberty." I saw two dads bolt from the room immediately. The next forty-five minutes we were showered with various depressing statistics of the teenage pregnancy–sexual abuse–HIV/AIDS variety. Amid the fear by flurry, we learned that these days the golden rule among youth sex educators is that age ten is the new sixteen. At that *I* almost bolted from the room.

All those dangers and fears have merit and should not be dismissed. If you really want the lowdown on fearful statistics check out the Centers for Disease Control's Youth Risk Behavior Surveys (YRBS), which have become the most reliable youth sex data. The annual surveys actually monitor all risky health behavior among the nation's young people, which means you will find data documenting bike helmet use next to driving while drinking next to whether or not teenagers carried a weapon on school property in the last thirty days (this is actually a survey question that the government asks) next to questions of virginity or how many young people have had sexual intercourse for the first time before age thirteen. The data is gathered nationally, by state, and in some cases at the city level in chart upon chart for comparison. The prying eyes of the government aside, I don't want to dismiss the health risks that come when young people have sex. My problem, though, is that too often that negativity is directed at our daughters. In a recent controversial anti-teen pregnancy campaign New York's former mayor Michael Bloomberg went as far as plastering oversized posters of crying curly headed toddlers across the city to chastise teenage (black) girls to keep their legs shut. "Honestly Mom . . . chances are he WON'T stay with you. What happens to me?" The words of one ad lashed out on the side of a bus alongside a picture of a little black baby girl as I crossed the street with my own little black girl.

Of course, as parents we need to be teaching our girls *and* boys respect, responsibility, and values, all of which if we teach it right should shape their decisions of when to engage in a sexual relationship. Not educating our children about protection against STDs and pregnancy is downright irresponsible, much like driving without a license.

But as mothers we should also be teaching our daughters to enjoy sex.

It took me a long time to admit that I enjoy sex. My household was strict, and my family lived by a code of silence. It meant that uncomfortable topics just didn't get discussed. That silence ran so deep that when I got my period for the first time I didn't tell my mother. It meant that the next month when it returned I was shocked. I am embarrassed to say that in the pre–Internet era of my youth, my sex education was so lacking I had been under the misimpression that this period thing only happened once a year instead of every month. Only then did I tell my mother, not because I thought it was something she should know, but because I didn't want to have to pay for the overpriced box of maxi pads each month. Even without discussion, some things were just understood that good girls didn't do, sex being at the top of the list.

When I went off to college the one thing my dad gave me was a Bible. My husband, who unlike me was actually raised going to church every Sunday, was sent off to college with a box of condoms. We met the second day of school and finished the box by the end of the week. I enjoyed every minute of it.

To be fair to my parents, my household was not the only one— this is how we raise our daughters. When my own daughter was in the second grade a teacher cornered me one day after school to talk. It was a bit startling because my little girl is the type of student teachers typically love: smart and well-behaved. So when this teacher pulled me aside and in a hushed voice wanted to "inform" me that she thought my daughter was perhaps hanging around with the "wrong kids," I was shocked. Apparently what alarmed this teacher was that she heard my daughter utter the word "penis" during a conversation with a boy after class. The teacher had no further information for me, no idea what the conversation was about, and wanted to stress that nothing disruptive happened during class, but . . . she still "thought I should know." The parents of the boy also involved in the penis conversation never got pulled over for a hushed-tone talk. The thing is, I am sure this teacher thought she was doing good by pulling me aside because my child is smart and well-behaved, and, let's face it, a girl. But we aren't talking about when I went off to college, when good girls are sent off with Bibles and good boys are loaded up with condoms. That even today the disconnect we feel that a girl is doing something wrong by, in this case, merely uttering the word "penis," and a boy who does the same is not, illustrates how much further most of us have to go to empowering our girls when it comes to their sexual life.

I can feel the shaking heads and hear the tsk-tsks from those who think I have gone too far in my overreacting. "Your seven-year-old was caught talking about penises in school!" Here, again, my husband too thinks I'm crazy. And I must admit, my overly reflective rational self here on the page was absent that day in the schoolyard. Instead, my daughter got the stern lecture about appropriate talk and behavior in school and how I didn't want her ever to do anything in school that would cause her mother to be pulled aside by a teacher again. I might have also uttered, not too softly and definitely not at all rationally, something to the effect of "you will not play with that boy again!"

I still regret it.

———

What would Dr. Laura Berman do? I am not the daytime talk show type. I don't really have a good reason, just that I find the whole studio audience discussion on the boring side even if there are chairs being thrown. So *Oprah* was never one of my habits. People would drop names in Oprah's BFF circle like Oz or Phil or Laura, and I would have no idea who these folks were or the extent of their following. And I was fine with that. But a few years ago I was home on maternity leave with my son, getting reacquainted with daytime TV, when I caught sexpert Laura Berman on *Oprah.* She was spouting advice about talking to kids about sex that made me freeze in my remote control surfing tracks. The moment was when Berman advised the crowd to educate their teenage daughters about vibrators. Shock and awe and "oh no she didn't" squeals spread across the audience. Gayle King looked so mortified that I thought her body was going to meltify, like the Nazis in *Raiders of the Lost Ark,* right there on my screen. Berman touted a sex survey conducted by *Seventeen* and *O* magazines that found that in our discussions with our children about sex, only 35 percent of mothers talk about pleasure. She was aghast, emphasizing the only—as in *only* 35 percent. Judging from the audience's reaction I was surprised to hear that it was that much.

"You're teaching [your daughters] about their own body and pleasuring themselves and taking the reins of their own sexuality so that they don't ever have to depend on any other teenage boy to do it for them," says Berman as she encouraged the female audience to start exploring their own routes to sexual pleasure. I haven't heard Berman speak again since that very brief moment I had with daytime talk, but what made her stick in my mind was this: "When you are comfortable, that's when you can really raise a sexually empowered daughter."[1]

Unfortunately most of us are not really that comfortable.

Consider that about 75 percent of all women never reach orgasm from intercourse alone and as many as 10 percent of sexually active women have never climaxed under any circumstances (alone or with their partner).[2] How we are raised affects the quality of our sex lives. As parents we spend our lives teaching our children. Why, then, of all the important life lessons we try to teach, do we not do more to teach our children how to love their sexual side? After all, our children will always be our children but they won't always be children.

––––––

Of course Berman is not the first to bring up masturbation. Back in 1994 Dr. Jocelyn Elders made the mistake of saying what was on her mind. As the first black U.S. surgeon general, what was on her mind was children dying. So on the eve of the United Nations AIDS conference she argued that schoolchildren should be taught to masturbate to ward off STDs. The minute she uttered the *m* of masturbate she was a goner. Barely out of my parents' house of silence, in an age before reality TV when private lives were truly private, I still remember the lightning bolt of shock from hearing a person in the public eye utter the word. Obviously I wasn't alone. Elders was discarded by the Clinton administration so swiftly, it became a stunning example of just how fast government can actually move. Since then Elders still says the word "masturbate" a lot but doesn't utter the word "AIDS" so much as an excuse to do it. Protection from STDs is still one of her reasons for advocating masturbation, but pleasure is also enough. More important, she hasn't budged on the important role masturbation should play in the sexual education of our young people.

"Back then, everybody was acting like this was a word they'd never heard," Elders told *The Root* in 2011—the word being, of course, masturbation. "Everybody does it, but nobody admits to it. If everybody in Congress who'd ever masturbated in their life would turn green, then we would have a green Congress. That's true for the whole country, and other countries, too."[3]

Some fifteen years after Elders made her masturbation remark in passing (it was in response to a question), the British government started dishing out her masturbation advice to teenagers. In a sexual health pamphlet created by the National Health Service in the UK titled "Pleasure," teenagers are encouraged to exercise their right to "an orgasm a day." The "Pleasure" pamphlet was embraced by a city in northern England and circulated by local officials to teens, parents, and youth advocates. In its words: "Health promotion experts advocate five portions of fruit and veg a day and 30 minutes' physical activity three times a week. What about sex or masturbation twice a week?"

What does that say about the rest of us when a sharecropper's daughter in her seventies (Elders) and the UK (an entire nation known across the globe for being sexually uptight) are more comfortable with the sexuality of our children than many of us responsible for raising them?

———

Perhaps the hang-ups about sex that we pass on to our girls are because we, as a nation, are too romantic. I admit I have been accused of not being the romantic type. True, my husband often chides me because I'm the one who forgets our anniversary. Also my favorite genre of movies is horror, and I think sitting through a romantic comedy is worse than torture in a foreign dictator's prison. I also have a great dislike for Valentine's Day. The idea that there is a single day where everyone is supposed to get all lovey and mushy seems preposterous to me. Shouldn't a relationship filled with passion have many days like this? And if we are sentenced to only one day of passion, why would every relationship have the same day? Romance itself, at least in our modern heterosexual practice of it, seems to be a one-sided type of love. One person is actively wooing the other, often with gifts and trinkets, rather than having both sides actively engaged together to do something special for the couple as a unit. For heterosexual couples, sex becomes the most romantic gift that women can give, and thus the expectation of pleasure is given away to their partner, too. Because of the one-sidedness, our practice of romance often includes a heavy dose of fantasy. Fantasy is expected. That is what the flowers and the candles and the whirlwind are all about: "the feeling" people get that makes them know someone is "the one." It is very easy to love a fantasy—it is much harder to love the reality.

As a woman I find this all condescending because, let's face it, Valentine's Day has made a business of romanticizing women. The celebration of the holiday in the United States was, in fact, the creation of the greeting card industry, inspired by Esther Howland, who is still hailed a hero by Hallmark. Esther came across a handmade card that was part of a new British celebration of exchanging love notes on February 14. She convinced her father, who owned a stationery store in Worcester, Massachusetts, to start mass marketing Valentine's Day cards, thus introducing the fledgling holiday on a wide scale in the States. Valentine's Day and Esther's cards became such a hit here in the United States that when she sold her business, The New England Valentine Company, it was making $100,000 a year. The year was 1881. The mother of Valentine's Day, as Esther came to be known, never married.[4]

As a black woman I don't like V-day because it is the time of year when all the single-women-are-doomed stories hit the media. (Pssst, did you hear? It is easier to be hit by a truck, win the lottery, or fly to the North Pole than it is to find a husband.) In February single women are treated like a disease that needs to be cured. What's worse is that this singlehood is something that they are bringing on themselves. So the coverage is always what can be done to catch a man (the media is only interested in heterosexual love) and thus spare yourself the sentence of singlehood. When it comes to black women the scenario is even worse. (Pssst, did you hear? It is easier to be hit by a meteor, win on *Jeopardy*, or fly to the moon than it is for a single black woman to find a husband.) I am purposely not going to recycle all the stats about how hard it is for black women to marry. Instead, keep in mind that stats about SBWs should never be taken in a vacuum. Americans, as a whole, have become the nonmarrying kind, with marriage rates falling to an all-time low of 51 percent. Singlehood is the times. Against that backdrop, it should be noted that rates for black men who are not married are about the same as they are for black women, even if they don't get constant grief from moms, aunties, and the media about when they will jump the broom.

Still . . . this doesn't mean that when it comes to marriage and black women we don't have issues. One of the major differences in the single black woman pool, compared to other women, is the role of the church. And that doesn't get talked about enough.

————

I was interviewing Sophia Nelson about a manifesto she wrote, *Black Woman Redefined*, when she started preaching.

"Jesus ain't your man, he's your savior," says Nelson.

Her words shook me through the phone. A couple years later I still can't shake that moment, when I was hit with the truth and left dumbstruck. Nelson blames the rise of singlehood of highly educated black women and the lack of fulfillment many are finding in their love lives to a cycle of overdependence on the church for companionship. During our discussions it was one of the points she was most impassioned about. For me, often the only married woman in a circle of black single friends, it was affirmation for things I had been rolling over in my head. She was preaching to the choir because I too blamed the church for helping to create the single black woman class. And when I say, respectfully, that the church contributes to the single black woman class, it is not a sign that I have little faith, it is an honest look at reality.

If you start digging through our nation's declining marriage stats you will find that marriage has become a custom for the rich. It is the well-educated, well-off couples who are still marrying amid the nation's crashing marriage rates. One of the key reasons couples are delaying marriage or never marrying at all is not because of a lack of love, or companionship, or desire—it is because of economics. They don't feel they can afford to get married. (Of course, they are actually mixing up not being able to afford a wedding with not being able to afford to get married.) One of the side effects of the recent financial crisis is that college grads are starting to delay marriage because of school loan debts.[5] When you see marriage through an economic prism the lower marriage rates for black and Hispanic couples begin to make more sense. The crisis is not a crisis of values, as it is often portrayed—it is a crisis of economics. The desires to get married have remained the same across races for decades. That is why Nelson's look at professional single black women is significant because this is the class of women that are truly going against the trend. And that is why for black women—who go to church regularly more often than any other women or group of people period[6]—the role of the church cannot be overlooked when talking about relationships.

Nelson sees the issue as one of companionship. That is why her "Jesus ain't your man" comment is hard to shake. She argues for more balance for our faith-filled lives, warning against being more concerned with what we think He wants that we no longer live the life that we want. Nelson blames the rise in singlehood of highly educated black women and the lack of fulfillment that many are finding in their love lives to a cycle of an overdependence on church for companionship. In *Redefined*'s survey of black men, 51 percent believed that professional black women's devotion to religion can interfere with a relationship's intimacy. Black professional women surveyed discussed "having to choose between their commitment to God and their standards for men," implying that one would have to be compromised in a relationship. A majority of professional black women (66 percent) reported that they would rather be alone than enter into a relationship with someone who is below their standards for the sake of companionship. "We need a healthy intersection of faith and humanity and sexuality," insists Nelson.

For me I don't see it as an issue of companionship but more of an issue of romance. Celibacy is a romanticized notion of Faith. There is an increasing amount of scholarship that is looking at how modern society has a much more conservative view of sex than the Bible intended. In her recent book *Unprotected Texts: The Bible's Sur-*

prising Contradictions about Sex and Desire, Jennifer Wright Knust, an ordained Baptist minister and a professor of religion at Boston University, argues that the Bible's teachings on sex are not as absolute as Americans often suggest. "When it comes to sex the Bible is often divided against itself," writes Knust.[7] With that she argues that some exceptions can be found on its teachings against premarital sex. It is just one of the things in the Bible that can be both forbidden and allowed. The key is if we accept that the Bible is a complicated text with multiple layers and insights, then we should also embrace the notion that there could never be an absolute view of its teachings. That would be too simplistic and instead we need to respect the Bible's shades of gray. Writers like Knust argue that sex in the Bible is easy to find if you have the training to look. My concern with celibacy is it is only possible if the pleasure of sex becomes removed. But even if you believe that the primary purpose of sexual intercourse is to procreate then shouldn't creating life, making a baby, be enjoyable?

Sophia Nelson, a church-going woman who comes from a family of preachers, tells me: "You can have a healthy sex life and be a godly woman."

And that is the point.

Black women have allowed the church to shape their sex lives. It hasn't stopped us from having sex (so on some level we must accept the Bible's shades of gray) but instead it creates a foundation of sexual contradiction, guilt, and dishonesty that can be suffocating. This matters because our hang-ups about sex are *related* to our singlehood. That doesn't mean that black women are causing their singlehood. It is not something we are bringing on ourselves and it is not something that is up to only us to resolve. But, it is hard to build a strong partnership with someone if you don't understand yourself. Sexual desires are part of that. There is nothing wrong with that. It is time that we realize that sexual intercourse is not only a gift for our partners but a gift for ourselves. And that is a lesson that every woman, regardless of race, should embrace.

I was off the market by the time the hook-up culture was embraced by young women. At first glance I was excited to hear that young women were aggressively acknowledging and indulging their desires. But about the same time that this supposed sexual revolution was taking hold I started getting "the question" from young women. The how-did-I-find-a-mate question. Sometimes it was cloaked in the form of career chitchat. When I'd talk to journalism students, the women would ask me if the field was family friendly. That would then often spill into a discussion of snide comments about the lack of relationships on campus and the fear that families would never come. I once had a student of mine thank me at the end of the semester for being an "inspiration." I wish it had something to do with my journalism, but her next breath explained it was because I was married with two young kids. In circles off campus when I would meet young women the questioning would be more direct. Once at a book club dominated by young black women I got more questions about how I found a black husband than I did about the book I was there to talk about. After the constant questions from those younger women about mate catching, all I could think was that despite all this hooking up, women were still not having great sex.

As I write these musings my daughter is only seven. Can I imagine the day when I will be talking to her about specific sex toys? Probably not. But I am hoping for the day when I talk to my daughter about how there is no right or wrong way to enjoy sex. Everyone has different turn-ons and things that make them feel good. She should never feel pressure to try something with her partner that she does not want to but she should also not feel embarrassed or ashamed by the things that she wants to explore and do, either. A sexual relationship is the most intimate connection you can have with a partner and that should be cherished. Great sex stimulates your mind, body, and soul, right down to your curling toes. You can't get there without respect, respect for yourself and respect for each other. And yes, dear, you are supposed to enjoy it.

In the meantime, forget white dresses, I will be praying my daughter has enjoyed an orgasm before her wedding night.

JOHN

There's a conspiracy to hypermasculinize black boys.

My fathers are a blur. Both of them. Just in slightly different ways.

My stepfather showered me with all kinds of generously overblown praise for getting good grades in elementary school, but he was pretty quiet when it came to just about everything else. We hardly shared any *Cosby Show*–like heart-to-hearts. A fatherly version of the strong and silent type, he didn't have many actual conversations with my siblings and me. It was more like he gave us orders and assessed the speed and virtuosity of our responses to them. I wouldn't have opted for such a strict parent (had I invented my own, which I did fantasize about from time to time), but he was effective at producing at least one of the results that relatively poor parents so want for their children: upward social mobility.

A high school graduate, he spent his entire professional career as a dietary aide in New York City hospitals, stamping dates on labels for patients' food supplements, placing those labels on their corresponding plastic containers, and then carrying metal trays of that stuff around to patients in his wards. My mother, who married him just before I started kindergarten, also worked as a dietary aide before she went back to school at night and earned her BA in sociology from Touro College. After that, she became an adult caseworker for social services in the city. Neither of them came from money or had a fancy education, but they were able to see some of their children move more assuredly into the middle class, including one son who has become a lawyer and another, me, who writes books and teaches at universities. My sister chose a life in the arts, as a gospel performer, and the fact that she isn't starving for her craft probably says something right there. Though that sister still lives "at home" with our mom, it is not the cramped Brooklyn apartment that we grew up in but a suburban house in a fairly quaint part of northern Jersey, and it would be easy enough to construct a white picket fence around it if anybody wanted to.

My mom is still a caseworker, though she'll be retiring soon, and my stepfather, long divorced from her and living in the same Canarsie housing project where I lived with my family from second grade through high school, spends part of his days tethered to a dialysis machine.

Because we didn't really talk all that much when I was a child, I find it hard to chat with him now, and I feel guilty about that. I do. I remember his birthdays, but I almost never call. I should, but I don't know what to say. Where to start. His commitment to making sure that I did well in school played a pivotal role in my life. I know that. I wouldn't be a tenured professor now without his efforts. And I've told him so, but his fathering style was so autocratic and menacing, so disciplinary and severe, that I probably haven't quite forgiven him for how terrifying he seemed to me as a child. His style produced real results, no doubt, but always with the specter of mild violence stalking somewhere nearby.

"Bring me the belt," is all he'd say, once he'd decided that a particular infraction had crossed some line that demanded immediate corporal redrawing. Or, he'd just instruct me to "lie down" if he was already wearing a belt. "Lie down" meant position yourself atop the nearest available horizontal surface posthaste, either a bed or a couch or even the armrest of a particularly sturdy chair, all depending on where the declaration was made. These moments were most chilling, I think, because he never looked steam-coming-out-of-his-ears angry. It wasn't like he would go ballistic and lash out in a rage. It was always a verdict unassumingly reached. Measured and methodical. A plain and antiseptic weighing of the situation. Then the decision:

"Lie down." Something about it might have felt more humane, more human, if he'd just lost control a little, even once, if the entire thing were more emotion-riddled and frenetic. Instead, he would give me a few almost mechanical lashes with a leather strap across my butt or my back or the back of my legs (I never knew the location or the amount of lashes to come) and then it was done. All over. That was that. It hurt like hell, mind you, but there was no yelling, no loss of control, except occasionally from my bladder. It all seemed strangely calculated and contained—and so much more enigmatic as a consequence.

My biological father is a different kind of enigma to me, starting with the fact that I don't even know what he looks like. There are a lot of ways I could find out, but I don't bother, which is its own weirdness, I suppose. The last time one of my mother's sisters took me to visit him, the last time he and I met, I was still in college, and he was living or visiting (I'm not sure) the same East Harlem apartment that his mother, my paternal grandmother, has occupied since I was a baby. I would end up shaking his hand and patting the head of his other son, a brother I didn't know existed before that moment and someone who would friend me on Facebook more than fifteen years later, which was the next time we'd have any contact.

I don't remember much about my first father. Nothing tangible or articulatable. Mom left him for my stepfather when I was still a toddler, and I had no contact with his family afterward. I don't even remember that summer visit, not with graspable detail. And I didn't actually get to see his face that day either. He was a literal blur.

When my aunt brought me to meet him during the summer after my first year at Howard University, I was working at a Burger King in Canarsie, trying to earn enough money for a new pair of glasses. I'd broken mine into two taped-together halves that I was too embarrassed to wear in public, so I went to meet him without them. But my eyesight has long been so bad that the world in front of me is barely more than splotches of lights and darks without prescription lenses. So, when I went to meet him, to reconnect, after so many years, I couldn't see a thing. It was all out of focus, just bleeding colors and their accompanying sounds. I squinted as best I could, without trying to draw too much attention to it, but that didn't make much difference.

My biological father was only eighteen when I was born. Or maybe seventeen. I can't exactly remember, and I haven't looked at my birth certificate in a while. He had my name though, John Lester Jackson, which was so striking the first time I read that document. The "Lester" always sounded ugly to me for some reason, which is why Cora, my coauthor, still loves to work my nerves by calling me "Lester" whenever she possibly can. But seeing it on that birth certificate brought home the fact that it was a part of my name. My name. I liked that. And my stepfather rightly surmised, midway through high school, that I would put my full name on just about everything I owned or had to profess as mine ("John Lester Jackson, Jr.'s marble notebook") partly out of a desire to mark space between the two of us, to assert my difference from him in a passive-aggressive (or maybe just passive) way. He didn't do anything more than make note of the fact, just once, and then never brought it up again. As long as I was doing my schoolwork, he'd let me have my relatively tame form of rebellion.

But that summer in 1990 is the last time I "saw" my biological father. Almost twenty-five years ago. I don't know where he is now or what he's been doing all this time. I only have that faint image of him in the back of my head, blurred beyond recognition. I can close my eyes and smell the apartment, imagining myself standing there, only a few feet away from him, but I can't make out his features—though my aunt made a point, during that visit, of saying, several times, how much I looked like him.

Growing up, I assumed that my stepfather had made my mother promise to keep my biological father away, to cut him and his kin off completely. Since I felt fully integrated into my stepdad's wider Trinidadian clan, I didn't miss out on having an extended family. And given the fact that we didn't spend a ton of time in deep conversations, we certainly never talked about the Jacksons I'd left behind. Not a word.

The one thing that I do remember my stepfather bringing up as a topic he wanted to make sure he broached with me was homosexuality. He didn't obsess about it, but I can recall one particular exchange. It was memorable mostly because he made a point of sitting me down and presenting the entire thing as a planned and purposeful event.

I was about thirteen or fourteen at the time. And if I had the language in my mental Rolodex back then, I would have probably described it as an intervention. Kind of. His point was that there are gay people in the world, all over the world, even in our very neighborhood, and my job was to stay away from them, especially older gay men, who are dangerous and sick. Any questions?

He might have used the word "pedophile," but I could be making that part up. He definitely did say "faggot," and more than a few times, though matter-of-factly and without all the venom I'd heard that word laced with whenever kids used it on the playground or in school. This little sit-down was a preemptive measure, and though I don't know what prompted it (maybe a news story he had watched or something overheard at work), I nodded that the message was loud and clear.

What was so striking about that very short lesson, why I remember it to this day, was its theatricality. The purposeful and pointed intensity of it. This wasn't something he voiced in passing as it popped into his head (like "boy, never go down on a woman, because she won't respect you after that," which he offered up while we were headed out the door to shop for shoes I could wear to my junior high school graduation). The homosexuality discussion, though short (four or five sentences from him, some head nods back from me), was something planned out. He had given it thought. This was a father-son moment.

What is it about raising black boys that makes homosexuality seem like such a monstrous threat? Are black men especially afraid of raising gay black boys? Is that what prompted my stepfather's uncharacteristically prearranged talk with me? Do fathers read it as a commentary on their own masculinity? Gay apples implicating the trees they've fallen from? And is one of the responses to that concern an overinvestment in hypermasculinity? In producing fighters, gang-stas, warriors, hustlers? Anything but "faggots." Is raising a pimp or potential womanizer better than finding out that your boy wants to be a "princess" in the school play? Or in real life?

When comedian Dave Chappelle walked away from his hit TV series several years ago, he tried to explain the decision in different ways, and one of the factors he brought up more than once was the pressure he was getting from producers and executives to dress in drag for a skit. He didn't want to do it, and they were making him feel like he wasn't being a team player for refusing. They kept pressuring him, Chappelle claims, and he started to feel like their investment in his donning a dress and wig seemed bizarrely out of proportion with the skit's value to the show. There was something weird, he thought, and irrational (and maybe even conspiratorial) about everyone's commit-ment to his foray into comedic transvestism. Why did they so badly want him to dress up like a woman? Was it part of the conspiracy to destroy black boys by giving them images of femininity to emulate?[8] Flip Wilson had done it. Martin Lawrence. Eddie Murphy. Jamie Foxx. It was a black comic's rite of passage. Why? Were they attempt-ing to produce gay feelings in black males, or at least to make them more comfortable with being effeminate?

But dressing in drag isn't the same thing as, say, kissing another man on camera. That's the ostensible deal breaker for the black male entertainer. Do you remember Will Smith's very early movie *Six Degrees of Separation*? He played a black gay hustler, and his character was scripted to have an openmouthed kiss with another man. Smith consulted Denzel Washington and other black actors about that scene, and they supposedly advised him against doing the kiss on-screen, which might have been the kiss of death for his career. Black audiences, they argued, would have a hard time getting over it. So the kissing scene in that movie includes a very awkward cutaway, so you don't actually see any lips or tongues touching at all—the back of a head obstructing our view. The actual kiss, quite plausibly, a simula-tion. But was it still not quite enough? Is that part of the reason why there are so many rumors on black gossip websites these days about

Will Smith being gay and Jada being his beard? And there is always "new proof" that he, or she, is stepping out with some secret gay lover.

The last few years, I've been conducting anthropological research with a few different religious and political groups that proselytize on Harlem sidewalks, and I've heard a lot of speculation about the impact of gay imagery on the psyche of young black boys. This is only a very small portion of the black folks that Denzel was warning Will about. And many of them would have been more suspicious about a transvestite skit than Chappelle was. I even heard rumors about transnational corporations genetically engineering foods to change young people's sexual orientation from straight to gay. Some of the people I spoke to claimed that homosexuality was "non-African," a strictly European invention, something found in ancient Greece (full of white people) but not ancient Egypt (home of storied and heterosexual black kings and queens). Homosexuality was sometimes equated with cultural genocide. The more black boys are turned gay, they argued, the fewer black babies are born. And that, some proclaimed, is the plan. More than a few people declared that this was all a kind of underground racial warfare. Homosexuality needed to be shunned, they stressed, because it jeopardizes the very future of the race. I don't believe that either of my fathers would have gone quite this far, though my biological one did live a few blocks from where I heard those arguments.

In response to this genocidal threat, black men are supposed to lambaste homosexuality as a scourge on the race and beat back any forms of effeminacy that might promote homosexual proclivities. The sexist, hypersexualized, and violent gangsta is an explicit rebuke of all things gay.[9]

Part of my point is that there might be a link between this demonization of homosexuality and the social vulnerability of black boys and men. Since we don't want queers, we overcompensate by creating the would-be thugs that society readily stigmatizes, imprisons, and kills as social pariahs.

Of course, blacks don't corner the market on homophobia, and although some studies find black Americans more conservative than other racial and ethnic groups on the topic, it would be unfair to single out black people as exceptionally antigay. Even countries like Jamaica, which are notorious for their homophobic public discourse and ordinances, shouldn't be fetishized as some kind of exception to the rule of wider societal acceptance. Just recently, Zimbabwe's infamous leader Robert Mugabe made a joke about beheading gays in one of the country's newspapers, calling homosexuals "worse than pigs, goats and birds" and arguing that US and international attempts to link foreign aid to the nation's formal acceptance of homosexuality "seeks to destroy our lineage."[10] This is a version of the "homosexuality is non-African" argument, just moved from ancient to contemporary times. But the black diaspora doesn't monopolize state-sponsored homophobia. Look at Russia's newest laws against promoting gay lifestyles in front of impressionable young Russian children. And is that much different from the Boy Scouts of America fighting to keep gays officially banned from its ranks? If anything, I would argue that many American fathers, regardless of ethnic or racial background, share a special concern (whether they act on it or not) about the prospects of raising gay sons—of raising any gay children at all, but especially sons.

———

Trayvon was Tracy Martin's son.

When the George Zimmerman verdict came in, I was in Cape Town, South Africa, touring with a low-budget documentary film that I helped produce, *Bad Friday*, about the history of state violence against Rastafari in Jamaica. South Africa has recognized same-sex marriages since 2006. It was the first country in Africa to do so. But it is also famous for its high number of publicized attempts at "correcting" homosexual females through rape. The nation's constitution protects gay rights, but authorities are believed to do much less than they could in their efforts to stop these orchestrated attacks.[11]

South Africa was a surreal place to be when the Zimmerman verdict came in. There was little talk of Trayvon in the South African media, but the crew from America and Jamaica touring with the film (about twenty of us altogether) was disheartened and depressed by the verdict—and by the fact that we were so far away from all the grassroots responses to it. I kept thinking about Trayvon's father that week. Both identifying with him and wondering how much he might be like either of my fathers.

The verdict brought us down, but Cape Town's beauty buoyed our spirits a bit, though we had been warned not to let the breathtaking views of its mountain ranges and coastline lull us into forgetting that South Africa was a very dangerous place, full of brazen and ruthless criminals, young black men who were brutal and well-armed. But its violence has a clear social map, and the black gangsters, the rough-necks, have places they inhabit, places where they belong, and those places tend to be far away from the everyday lives of most white and well-off South Africans.

South Africa polices the geographical line between its haves and have-nots. America does, too. Ask Harvard University professor Henry Louis Gates, Jr. He knows, and he isn't even a roughneck, at least not in any typical sense. He might be academia's version of a gangsta, but that's still different from street gangsterism, the differ-ence between vicious wordplay and actual gunplay, between knowing about it and being 'bout it 'bout it.

I bring up Gates because he helped create national headlines a few years ago by getting himself arrested in Cambridge, Massachusetts, for verbally lashing out at a police officer intent on questioning him as he entered his own home, a residence that the officer didn't believe Gates owned. President Obama was even asked to comment on the incident (calling the arrest "stupid," in perhaps his last candid racial comment as president), and the commander-in-chief ended up orga-nizing a much-lampooned "Beer Summit" at the White House to sit down with the policeman and the professor over drinks. It was all just a silly mix-up, the caption to their photo-op was supposed to read, a one-in-a-million case of mistaken identity. What are the chances that such a misunderstanding could have escalated in this way? There's probably a higher probability of lightning striking that famous Ivy League professor.

When he yelled at that cop, Gates was expressing outrage at decidedly unsaid—but ubiquitous—racial and spatial expectations. And Trayvon Martin would have been quite familiar with them. As would his father. And both of mine. And any of the black South Africans I met on my trip.

Racism has always meant nonwhites shouldering extra kinds of public scrutiny, like blacks and coloreds walking around with special passes in South Africa whenever they left their townships, but it is only since the 1960s that racists in America have no longer been able to carry their racisms around unapologetically. We live in a world, thankfully, where racism can't speak its own name, at least not in the bright light of day, not without some reprisals. Not even in South Africa. This isn't to say that unrepentant racists no longer exist, only that any whiff of explicit and undeniable racism will find the perpetrator asked to resign from office or paraded around the public sphere for collective rebuke and ridicule. The wrongheadedness of certain takes on Trayvon Martin's murder pivots on this point, echoing the destructive links between hypermasculinity and black vulnerability.

As some see it, Zimmerman would only have been guilty of murder, if at all, had he slipped on a white Klan suit before taking his shot. Or maybe if he had been caught on videotape chasing Martin down the street and screaming "Nigger!" at the top of his lungs. Anything short of that kind of clichéd notion of racial animus is supposed to take racism completely off the table as a legally and socially potent explanation for the tragedy, which meant that there was an incessant hunt for the "smoking gun" of explicit racism. People carefully scrutinized the 911 call for any of racism's magic words. When they couldn't find them, some read "punks" as a plausible euphemism, which it certainly could be. (Zimmerman probably would have known better than to call Martin by a racist epithet in a call to some anonymous 911 operator.) However, this is exactly the worst way to think about how we might make sense of Trayvon's murder, even if state prosecutors put many of their own eggs in that basket. Other points and themes better ground any attempt to think through this senseless killing—and the jury's verdict.

For one thing, Martin could only look out of place to Zimmerman because it is normal to assume that a young black boy in a hoodie probably doesn't belong in a relatively comfortable suburban neighborhood. Zimmerman and the Cambridge cop who stopped Gates were playing the percentages, and most of the time (because "hypersegregation" keeps black residents out of white neighborhoods), they both would be right.[12] We live in a world where we can safely bet on a lot of social experiences and outcomes—on people's places in society—based on skin color. And we do that all the time. Obama's stint in the White House is a victory for racial inclusion in America, but it is still the exception that proves an opposite rule. The Obamas in the White House is the lightning strike, not the end of America's racial storm.

Racism is alive and well whenever blacks and whites can do the exact same things and end up with markedly different results. A white teenager in a hoodie wouldn't automatically be deemed an outsider and a "punk" in Zimmerman's neighborhood without other incriminating evidence to stoke the flames. And that teenager would be much less likely to end up dead for his athletic attire, though I think some might emphasize Martin's oft-invoked "hoodie" a little too much. He would have been in trouble with or without it (just ask Gates).

Black academics are very good at dressing well and cultivating particularly nonthreatening—even performatively effeminate—forms of public masculinity. If not, they would find it much more difficult to succeed in the academy. Across racial lines, confidence is sometimes read as arrogance. Being knowledgeable means being unteachable. Passion is hostility. I've seen it. So, black male academics soften their personal styles, their gestures and body postures, purposefully or not. Or it might just be that the ones who can't tone down their hypermanly vibe simply interview their way right out of the most prestigious posts. But none of that helped Gates during his altercation. And how much more difficult to negotiate exchanges with "the law"—even to survive them—when all the accoutrements of black masculinity's most threatening traits are visible from the start: the bravado, the thugged-out stare, the unpredictable "cool pose."[13] How much more threatening when you are not trying to make white people feel comfortable? Or when you don't have the ability to pull it off no matter how much you might try?

None of this is meant to let Zimmerman off the hook for killing Martin. But it shouldn't let the rest of us off the hook, either.

We sleep well at night by pretending to live in a fully meritocratic world where people get what they deserve—that is, when affirmative action doesn't unfairly disenfranchise whites. Anything else is a freak accident. Society's version of getting struck by lightning. There are no miscreants calculatedly raining bolts down on our heads. It is just dumb luck. Or lack of effort.

Martin's death is significant because it reminds us that some kinds of mistaken identity are systematic. They actually aren't innocent *mistakes,* not really. If anything, they are desperate attempts to correct the mistakes we think we see when people aren't sticking closely to our preconceived notions of racial possibility, when they aren't simply locked in their predictable social places. That's precisely why Zimmerman followed Martin. And the surveillance couldn't have surprised the boy. Even as a teenager, he would have been used to it, so much so that it is extremely unlikely Zimmerman's paranoia alone would have prompted Martin to physically attack his accuser. He might have hurled some choice words Zimmerman's way, maybe the same ones Gates used on that Cambridge cop, but young black men who are committed to challenging everybody who assumes they don't belong somewhere would find themselves fighting all day long.

Obama punctuated his response to the Zimmerman verdict by saying that he could have been Trayvon Martin thirty-five years ago. He could have been mistaken for an anonymous and threatening black man who didn't belong. In truth, were it not for the prophylactic and retroactive protections of class privilege, which only go so far, Trayvon Martin is Obama right now. (And some right-wing pundits put a symbolic hoodie on the president every chance they get.)

———

Trayvon Martin is also Hector Pieterson.

Only a day after the Zimmerman verdict, I found myself mesmerized by images I saw in Soweto at the Hector Pieterson Museum, named after the thirteen-year-old boy who was killed in 1976 when he and his schoolmates protested the South African government's attempt to force them all to learn their school lessons in Afrikaans, a language that they didn't know and which felt to them like one colonialist imposition too many. It wasn't the most oppressive apartheid mandate, but it was the final straw. Pieterson was just a young boy who happened to get killed by a policeman's bullets during the start of the protests. It could have been anyone. Any of the children. They weren't gunning for Pieterson in particular. He just happened to be in the line of fire.

Martin wasn't explicitly protesting apartheid's pernicious proscriptions, but he also just happened to be in the line of fire, a line that cuts across America's historic color line. It was a mistake, but a systematic one, which isn't really a mistake at all.

And what does any of this (my seemingly off-topic rant about Martin, Gates, Zimmerman, black men with designated places in the world) have to do with the question of homosexuality and black boys? Nothing. And everything. Racial profiling, structural racism, is indifferent to sexual orientation. But there is something telling about how easily the likes of George Zimmerman can read a young black teenager as a threat, an ungenerous reading in cahoots with the investments that many fathers have in raising manly men. When my stepfather was sitting me down and talking about the perils and pathologies of homosexuality, he was faintly laying the foundation for an approach to black manhood that would never be read generously from across the racial tracks. If anything, it would provide the behavioral pretext for the kind of pathological fear and suspicion that Zimmerman used to justify pulling the trigger on a defenseless young teen. When I was a teenager, I often felt defenseless, especially when standing in my stepfather's shadow. But I was also defensive.

Some of the most insensitive and unfair conversations we ever have are the ones we have with ourselves, and I remember calling my biological father a "faggot" at least a couple of times. Not out loud. In my head. He must have been soft, I thought. Weak and spineless, the stuff that being a "faggot" was supposed to imply. It took me a long time to start unlearning this formulation of things, to even imagine that it might warrant unlearning, but as a kid I kept thinking, how else could I make sense of the fact that my "real" father had let another man take his son away from him? That's what I thought. That's what I said. "How could I ever love a person like that? How could someone who does that ever love himself?"

We all witness things that we can't quite explain and don't really understand but that put seemingly disparate ideas together in uncanny ways. Ways we can't forget. Like when I was sitting in a barbershop about a year ago, and I heard another patron or one of the other barbers (my glasses were off, so I couldn't see a thing or make out who was speaking) say that Trayvon Martin looked a little "sweet" to him the first time he saw the youngster's photo on the news. Sweet was a euphemism. He said it a few times. And then he asked if other folks saw it, if they knew what he meant. Nobody else said they did. But I remember pondering, what would it matter (in terms of the news coverage and the public outcry of support from the black community) if he were *sweet*? In ways that only a novelist would dare take up, probably—sadly—quite a bit.

MONEY

CORA

We're not movin' on up.

"It's becoming conventional wisdom that the U.S. does not have as much mobility as most other advanced countries. I don't think you'll find too many people who will argue with that."[1]

—ISABEL V. SAWHILL, ECONOMIST AT
THE BROOKINGS INSTITUTION

We like to think of ourselves as a nation of strivers, up-from-the-bootstraps kind of folk. The reality is we are a nation of salesmen. How else can you explain our blind faith in the American Dream? Despite the evidence against it (and there is a ton) we still believe that hard work is all you need to propel yourself to the top of the ladder no matter how low a rung you may start on. That only in America one could be raised in a log cabin and grow up to be president. Or, rather, in America one could still move from log cabin to the White House. The pitch is so powerful that the world's most vulnerable continue to flood our borders each day to get a piece of that dream. Perhaps the biggest proof that we are such good salesmen is that when faced with the reality that many of us are not movin' on up, we, as a nation, still don't stop believing.

Because of that, most will never believe me when I say that American mobility is a myth, perhaps the greatest myth of all time, bigger than Zeus, fairy godmothers, and Santa Claus. Still, even the most conservative of studies conducted in the last five years conclude that

39

America has less mobility and greater income inequality than other developed nations around the world. Period. In the words of journalist Michael Moran, who helped write a series of stories for the GlobalPost that compared the level of inequality in American cities to those around the world, it means: "In today's America the children of the rich will very likely get richer, poor kids will probably remain so, and those in the vast middle class will be challenged, even in two-income households, to just tread water."[2]

I know, I know, facts seem to have little power over good marketing but here goes:

More than 40 percent of Americans raised at the bottom fifth of the family income ladder remain stuck there as adults and 70 percent remain below the middle, according to the Pew Economic Mobility Project.[3] That level of being stuck at the bottom is greater than even in Britain (30 percent), infamous for its impenetrable lines between classes. (They do have queens and royal palaces after all.) In fact, one recent study found that, despite our nation's reputation of meritocracy, just 8 percent of American men at the bottom actually do rise to the top fifth compared to 12 percent in Britain.[4] (Mobility studies typically examine the plights of men so they don't have to bring gender bias into play.) Of no surprise, black folks have it worst. African Americans are not only more likely to be stuck at the bottom, but also more likely than any other group in the United States to fall from the middle in a generation.[5]

It should be noted then when talking about economic mobility— the ability to move up the ladder within your lifetime or across a generation—there are actually two kinds: absolute mobility and relative mobility. Absolute mobility means the change of income over time. Relative mobility measures the change in class of a person or where they rank in the income distribution of the society as a whole. In terms of absolute mobility the United States is doing quite fine. According to the Pew research 84 percent of Americans have higher income, when adjusted for inflation, than their parents did at the same age.[6] That said, Pew also found that despite the rise in income there has been very little movement up the economic ladder. Pew researchers explain this in the best real-world talk I've heard so let me borrow their metaphor: it is as if we are all standing on the same moving escalator. We may each be going upward, but everyone remains in the same position compared to each other. That is upward absolute mobility. What we also need is for that person who walks up the moving escalator to pass those standing—that person would be experiencing relative upward mobility. Pew cautions that for mobility discussions to matter you need to consider both, and their research does that. It is hard not to agree with that balanced view. Still, I think relative mobility is really at the heart of what most of us are imagining when we think about the American Dream. For folks still stuck at the bottom, those still struggling in the middle, and the majority who still never make it to the top, by any measure, having some more extra dollars in our pockets compared to our parents doesn't really matter that much. Life remains the same. Like being able to upgrade your parents' log cabin with a flat screen and some nice curtains but still not being able to afford to actually move out on your own.

The Gini index is what economists use to measure income inequality. A hypothetical Gini coefficient of 0 means everything is equal, and a coefficient of 100 would mean that a single person has all the wealth in a nation.[7] The most recent coefficient for the United States is 47. That is a level of income inequality higher than virtually every developed nation in the world, according to the Organisation for Economic Co-Operation and Development (OCED), a Paris-based international organization of countries founded in 1961 to promote economic progress. In fact, according to OCED, the only developed nations with worse income inequality than the United States were Chile, Mexico, and Turkey. Income inequality in the United States has soared to its highest level since the Great Depression.[8] If you look at the Gini coefficient, the depth of America's income inequality is more startling than many of us realize. For example, Bridgeport, Connecticut, has the same level of inequality as Bangkok, Thailand.[9] The GlobalPost did an interesting series of articles where they matched U.S. cities to cities across the globe based on their Gini coefficients. The distance between the rich and poor in Los Angeles is comparable to Beijing, China. The inequality found in Topeka, Kansas, rivals that of Nairobi, Kenya. And Fernly, Nevada, which is outside Reno, has the same level of income inequality that you would see in New Delhi, India. Yet as much as we might point our fingers at China, Africa, and India, the income inequalities within our own borders often go ignored. Except, of course, if you're poor, then you know life sucks no matter where you are in the world.

Why does income inequality matter? There is a growing amount of evidence that shows countries with significant levels of income inequality, like the United States, also have the lowest levels of economic mobility, like the United States. If you think of the ladder, it is harder to climb up the ladder when the rungs are farther and farther apart. In typical rankings of world mobility the United States falls behind most of Europe and Canada. Typically the only Western nations to fare worse than the United States when it comes to mobility are Italy and the United Kingdom; both nations are also plagued with high levels of income inequality. In 2012 economist Miles Corak, a bit of a hero in mobility circles, crunched the numbers and looked at a wider scope of countries and found that Japan, Singapore, and Pakistan could also be added to the list of societies with more income mobility than the United States. Who knew that the American Dream could be more of a reality in Pakistan than Kansas?

Why are we still believing?

I was reminded just how strong that belief in the dream is shortly after President Obama's 2013 State of the Union address. Most people may remember the speech for the dramatic "deserves a vote" climax at the end when he tried to shame House Republicans for not wanting to bring gun control legislation to a vote in the wake of the tragic school shooting in Newtown, Connecticut. Sharing with the nation the tragic shooting of Hadiya Pendleton, a fifteen-year-old majorette who loved Fig Newtons and lip gloss, who was killed one mile from Obama's Chicago home a week after returning from performing at the president's second inauguration, Obama looked into the gallery at Hadiya's parents, Nate and Cleo, and told the chamber: "They deserve a vote!" Hadiya's parents managed to keep their composure as they stared back at the president. That moment of unimaginable strength of two grieving parents shamed Congress and the political games they play better than any speech could. As if empowered, Obama continued: "Gabby Giffords deserves a vote. The families of Newtown deserve a vote. The families of Aurora deserve a vote. . . ." Clips of that section of the speech dominated the airways into the next day.

For me it was another passage of the speech that continued to ring in my ears:

"Tonight, let's also recognize that there are communities in this country where no matter how hard you work, it's virtually impossible to get ahead. Factory towns decimated from years of plants packing up. Inescapable pockets of poverty, urban and rural, where young adults are still fighting for their first job. America is not a place where chance of birth or circumstance should decide our destiny. And that is why we need to build new ladders of opportunity into the middle class for all who are willing to climb them."[10]

There is something powerful about a sitting president of the United States during the State of the Union telling the nation that the American Dream is broken. Despite the nation's attention to the emotional gun control appeal, much more time in the speech was actually devoted to the nation's stalling mobility. Starting from Obama's call for universal preschool to his proposal to raise the minimum wage, it was the effort to shrink income inequality, not control gun violence, that actually contained concrete proposals to work toward. Asking for a vote, after all, is really just the minimum of expectations.

Two days after the speech, I was sitting down with a college journalism class to discuss media coverage of the State of the Union. One student in the room was puzzled by the mobility section of the speech, which, admittedly, I had brought up, in part to stop the "deserves a vote" noise that was dominating the discussion. "Shouldn't we be striving for higher than just the middle class?" she asked. She couldn't understand why Obama had focused on entry into the middle class rather than the top of the ladder. When I tried to explain the stickiness at the bottom and the stalled economic mobility of the moment I could see her eyes starting to glaze over.

"So he is mainly just talking about poor people," said the college student who could not see below her (black) middle class starting point. "But don't poor people want to get to the top? No one wants to stop at middle class."

She looked at me baffled.

I looked at her baffled.

Now, to be fair, this student was not the brightest in the room, or any room that I have been in, so the idea of metaphor may always be above her literal mind. Forget about understanding a belief system that if we raise those from the bottom we move an entire society. But there is something about her literal take of the president's words that makes a point. While exact definitions of the American Dream vary, researchers find some core themes emerge for most everyone: freedom to accomplish anything you want with hard work, freedom to say or do what you want, and that one's children will be financially better off.[11] So, yes, the dream was always about moving from the bottom to the top. The fact that, despite the horror stories of out-of-work grads and crippling college loan debt, this student and others in her generation still cannot imagine a world where that dream is not a possibility, speaks to how powerful that dream is. Likewise, for those of us, like myself all the way up to President Obama, who get upset that the dream is no longer *always* possible. Our outrage is also a sign of how strong that dream was for us. It is hard to get upset over something that you never thought was a possibility.

In 2009, during the height of the Great Recession, Pew pollsters found that our faith in the American Dream was so strong that 8 in 10 Americans still felt it was possible to get ahead despite the worst economy in a generation.[12] The faith in getting ahead was just as strong among lower-income, less-educated, or unemployed Americans. The fact that this belief held true regardless of race or class and despite a near unanimous consensus among Americans that the economy was doing poorly (94 percent described the economy in negative terms) led even the pollsters to call the results "striking".[13] The American Dream—the belief that hard work will lift you up— seems to be the one thing that all Americans believe in.

In 2011, when Pew went back to check on the public's perceptions of the American Dream and mobility as the nation emerged from the recession, pollsters found that although Americans were more pessimistic about their own personal circumstances their faith in the American Dream as a whole was still not shaken. The 2011 poll found that less than one-third (32 percent) of Americans rated their own financial situation as "excellent" or "good" (down 9 points in just a year, and down 23 points since the recession started in 2007).[14] In addition, only 47 percent of Americans still believed that their children would have a higher standard of living than they themselves enjoyed. Still, despite all that pessimism about their current situation, the dream endured. When asked what is the most important factor for a person to move up the economic ladder, 91 percent of Americans say hard work. Considering that according to the poll most of us thought our own financial situation at the time was struggling, then if hard work really is the pixie dust, it makes you wonder why we all didn't just work a little harder to lift ourselves out of it.

It has always been amazing to me how much we, as a nation, dismiss the impact that our parents have on our future. Sure, those of us with good home training will thank our mamas at our moments of great success. But we never really give our parents the credit that they truly deserve. Proof of this is how Americans, perhaps more than any other society, seem to underestimate how much our parents' wealth contributes to our own success. This is what we are saying when 91 percent of us say hard work alone is the biggest factor in our success. That sentiment was made blatantly clear during the 2012 Republican Convention when an offhand remark by Obama trying to explain government's contribution to society's success inspired the "We built it" response theme for the convention—"We" being small business owners and "it" being their businesses. Much was made about the partisan-colored glasses needed for a phrase like that to make sense. However, that kind of bootstrapping belief system where the individual becomes the most important ingredient in success is not a partisan trait but an American trait. That is where the hard work of the American Dream stems from.

There is some debate over the exact origins of the "pull oneself up from one's bootstraps" metaphor. Some of the earliest documented references, according to discussions at the American Dialect Society, trace it back to the 1830s when the phrase starting popping up in popular writings. (Others are not so convinced, pointing to a story about Baron Munchausen, a folktale creation that was first put to paper in English in the late 1700s.) Interestingly, what isn't under much debate is that originally the phrase was meant to imply an impossible task. Boots literally used to have loops, known as bootstraps, which allowed people to hook their finger to pull their boots on. So the idea that someone could actually lift themselves by their own bootstraps was understood to be preposterous. In one early reference the idea that someone could believe in the possibility was dismissed as being as silly as say "sitting in a wheelbarrow to wheel himself" while another reference equated it to trying to "get rich by taking money from one pocket and putting it in the other."[15] In 1862 the *Chicago Tribune* scoffed: "The hopeful individual who expects to raise a weight vastly beyond his strength, belongs to the same class of fools with great expectations, as he who promises to lift himself by his bootstraps." Linguist Ben Zimmer—who has traced the phrase's history (finding all of the previous examples)—argues that the metaphor's connotation didn't shift to a possible task until the early twentieth century. By 1927 an article in the *Times* of London, under the headline "The Bootstrapper," alluded to both aspects of the phrase's history, characterizing the concept of self-improvement as an American belief while also using it as an example of utter American stubbornness because of the obvious impossibility of being able to accomplish such a thing.[16] Despite the origins (or international mocking), the shift of the phrase has had everlasting effects. The idea of lifting oneself up from one's bootstraps is not only believed as a possibility but proudly American.

It is why election-season politicians stumble over each other to spread their bootstrapping roots, often stretching the metaphor and their own history as far as the public will allow. When writing about the bootstrap mythology on his blog, Gromykobreakfast.com, blogger Andrew Gauthier points to a priceless *Daily Show* skit during the

2004 Democratic Convention that made fun of the constant boot-strapping claims of politicians during the convention. Of course, that was the convention where Illinois senator Barack Obama described to America how his father "grew up herding goats." To which Jon Stewart turned to Stephen Colbert, then the chief political analyst for *The Daily Show,* for some insight. Colbert offered that because of his own bootstrapping history he could relate, declaring: "That's why I believe in the promise of America, that I, the son of a turd miner, the grandson of a goat ball–licker, could one day leave those worthless hicks behind while still using their story to enhance my own credibility."[17]

What is overlooked when we take the majority of the credit for our success is the safety net or cushion that our parents provide. How far we go in life is directly linked to where we come from. That doesn't mean that it is a determining factor, but it is definitely a contributing factor. The extent of our parents' wealth determines what neighborhoods we are raised in and thus what schools are available. Children who grow up going to good schools typically continue on to college, the better schools go to the better colleges. And the rewards continue to follow. A four-year-college degree is the single biggest contributor to upward mobility.[18] Our parents' wealth also determines what level of choice we have once we become adults because it affects the amount of debt we have and amount of debt we will have. We are living in an era where the levels of college debt are now often seen as crippling for new grads, but for those of us without cushions it always was. The size of your cushion affects every financial choice you make from the type of jobs that you might consider to where you can afford to live. Most important, your level of opportunity expands with the size of your cushion. Not having to worry about constantly slipping financially gives you options and allows free choice. It is much easier to take chances—start a business or follow a dream—when you know those decisions, even if they fail, will not cripple you. Of course, that does not mean that those of us without cushions can't create the next big idea. But there is a confidence that comes from always knowing free choice that is hard to measure. As proof of the limitless possibilities of American hard work we used to hold up Henry Ford and now we hold up to Mark Zuckerberg. Both success stories are something that as a nation we should be proud of. That kind of innovation, genius, and yes, hard work, should always be celebrated and should inspire. Still, rarely noted is that Zuckerberg comes from a family of affluent Northeast physicians, while by contrast Ford was a farmer's son.

Nancy DiTomaso, a professor at Rutgers Business School who wrote *The American Non-Dilemma: Racial Inequality Without Racism*, was curious about why there was still this pesky black-white wealth gap if we had fixed that ol' discrimination thing with the civil rights movement. Although she thought she was getting to the bottom of racial inequities, she ended up revealing a lot about the economic inequalities that are tied to race. DiTomaso was inspired by her classes of mostly white students where year after year she saw students who believed in civil rights, were against discrimination, thought equal opportunity was the standard for fairness, and felt people should be rewarded for their effort. Their commitment was genuine and yet we still have a nation of racial inequality. So, with academic zeal she traveled across the country, focusing her research on the job histories of whites starting with first jobs back in high school. She found that 99 percent of the people she talked to got 70 percent of the jobs in their lifetime through some kind of help from family, friends, or acquaintances, in terms of getting inside information, having someone use influence on their behalf, or someone who could actually offer them a job or an opportunity. What ends up happening is that despite everyone's good intentions, because of the segregated social lives that most people exist in, those advantages keep getting passed around the same circles, perpetuating the same inherent inequalities. Talking to NPR's Michel Martin, DiTomaso said:

> One of the things that I came to understand as I was doing this research is that when we talk about issues of racial inequality we so often frame it primarily in terms of whites doing bad things to black people or non-whites. And we think about the job market as whites denying jobs to blacks and to other minorities. But the research that I did found that most people get jobs because

whites are helping other whites get jobs, as opposed to trying to keep blacks out of jobs—at least in the post–civil rights period. And that difference is very important because discriminating or excluding people from jobs is illegal. But helping friends or family members or acquaintances get a job is not illegal.

DiTomaso is trying to change our frame of reference for how we think about racial inequality: "Instead of thinking primarily about discrimination and racism, to call attention to the extent to which people use favoritism or advantage—essentially, unequal opportunity instead of equal opportunity—as ways to get jobs and to position themselves for decent lives."[19]

In fact, so ingrained is the cushion, that in discussions about fairness and inequality, although virtually everyone polled got their jobs through some kind of help, when DiTomaso asked people directly what contributed to their current life status or situation people talked about how motivated, persistent, and hardworking they were. Only 14 percent admitted that help of any form was a contributing factor. And that's the point.

The safety net that parents provide doesn't necessarily stop after one generation. Our parents' wealth can directly affect our own children's lives from the subtle to the overt. If your level of college debt is on the low end thanks to your parents, you will be able to afford to buy a house at an earlier age and start building your own wealth sooner, setting the foundation for a more comfortable and stable life for your own kids. (That would be the subtle effects of your parents' wealth on your children.) If your parents help with the down payment on your first house, or contribute to private school tuition, or cosign a loan for a car, all would be more overt effects of their wealth. No matter what the extent, that cushion matters. It helps ensure you don't slip and gives you the foundation to move up.

———

My husband and I are both climbers on the escalator. We've been lucky to experience not only absolute mobility but relative mobility.

Still, when my husband and I pulled off the miracle of buying our home (not in the best school district) we were still paying off our college loans as well as the loan we had taken out to pay for our wedding. My dad, a lifelong renter, did not live long enough to have dinner in my home. When he passed away the year before, we were already in the process of looking but I was keeping the search a secret, hoping to surprise everyone. One of the moments of my day when I still think about my dad the most is when I pull out my house keys and open my front door.

Despite our success, my husband and I live every day knowing we have no cushion. As much love and support as our family provides, there really is no one who could afford to bail us out financially if times get rough, no one with enough disposable wealth to help us with a mortgage payment if things get tight. We are the ones that the economists talk about who can slip back. (Downward mobility has become so common that now 1 in 3 of all Americans raised in the middle class fall out of the middle class as adults.[20]) When I pick up my kids from the good school they go to, far away from our home, I often think about how they may never understand what that means—life without a cushion or the fear of slipping. Then I think about how many of the fellow parents also picking up children in the schoolyard don't know what that means, either. And I am reminded how lonely the schoolyard can be.

It seems that the American Dream burst in 1971. It was also the year I was born. The writer in me feels that there must be some kind of storytelling gift in that connection, but the pessimistic New Yorker side of me screaming "I knew it! I knew it!" prevents my mind from finding a way to take advantage of that gift to tell the story. Apparently upward mobility was not only still possible but accelerating in the 1950s and 1960s. Since then, most economists agree, it has gotten harder and harder. There is no clear consensus on why. Some blame globalization and the decline of unions, others blame tax policies (oppressive or unbalanced) or government regulation (too much or not enough), technology, a gap between productivity and wages, and of course, the rise in income inequality.

Really, the reasons why are as diverse and plentiful as there are minds thinking about it.

That there is consensus about the threat to the American Dream between the Right and the Left is often overlooked amid all the shouting and tantrums. The sides agree that there is a threat. This consensus was well documented by, of all places, the Heritage Foundation, the conservative think tank. A recent Heritage report, *Defending the Dream,* offered:

> Leading Republicans and Democrats frequently appeal to the vanishing American Dream in their speeches. Progressive journalists, union leaders, and conservative pundits all worry that the American Dream is slipping away. The Heritage Foundation calls its entitlement reform plan Saving the American Dream, while activists Van Jones and MoveOn.org named their organization Rebuild the Dream. In June, liberals hosted a "Take Back the American Dream" conference at the Hilton in Washington, DC; two months later, conservatives hosted a "Defending the American Dream" summit at the same hotel.[21]

Where the Right and Left disagree is in what that threat is. That is because the sides define the dream slightly differently. The Right sees the American Dream only as the opportunity to rise from rags to riches. The Left sees the Dream as the actual ability to rise from rags to riches. It is opportunity vs. results. This allows both sides to embrace the threat to the American Dream rhetoric and continue shouting. (Tellingly, the subtitle of the Heritage Foundation's *Defending the Dream* report is *Why Income Inequality Doesn't Threaten Opportunity.*) For both sides, though, at the heart of this Dream is mobility.

It is why even some of the nation's most conservative voices are having a tough time overlooking the evidence of our lack of mobility. During the Republican primary debates former U.S. senator Rick Santorum of Pennsylvania repeatedly talked about the need to increase economic mobility, admitting that mobility in parts of Europe is better than in the United States. The *National Review,* a conservative standby, ran a story in November 2011 under the headline "Mobility Impaired," where it discussed the cracking of the American Dream. The Tea Party (which launched a Restoring the American Dream bus tour during the last presidential election) anger against Washington stems from a belief that spendthrift government is blocking the ability of the average person to get ahead. Even former Republican vice-presidential candidate Paul D. Ryan, who maintains that overall mobility remains high, has been heard admitting that the United States may lag behind when it comes to mobility from the very bottom.[22]

This brings us to the quote in the *New York Times* from Isabel Sawhill, an economist at the Brookings Institution, which opens this essay. It is worth repeating: "It's becoming conventional wisdom that the U.S. does not have as much mobility as most other advanced countries. I don't think you'll find too many people who will argue with that."

So why argue? Hard work is *not* all that matters. Instead of debating it anymore, let's start with the *conventional wisdom* that mobility is a myth. Now what?

It means that our lack of mobility is the beginning of the discussion not the end point.

Maybe if we start treating economic mobility as the exception that it is instead of gambling that things will get better in the future we will start focusing on making things better for how we are living now. That means policy should focus on making sure that everyone can, at least, live comfortably just where they are no matter what rung they might be on.

Instead of putting all our focus on a dream, let's think about the meaning of American Reality. As a nation, what do we consider the acceptable standard of living for Americans? Or maybe not the standard *of* living but, rather, our standard *for* living, and I know I am getting metaphorical. But what are the economic standards for American life: a job for ourselves + a house for our family + food on the table + schools for our children? Like asking for a vote, it really is not asking for that much.

Despite how much we cling to the Dream our wants never reach as high. In that same 2011 Pew poll that revealed how tied we are to our faith in hard work, when it also asked what is more important, financial stability or moving up the ladder, 85 percent of people chose financial stability. If that is true, then it is about time we decide what is the standard for stability. Because most of us are just not going to climb.

This acceptance in American Reality instead of being governed by a Dream does not mean that there won't be movement. There will always be outliers. (That's why economic policy that ignores the poorest doesn't make the best sense, because you miss the outliers.) But that's the point: movement is the exception. So let's figure out how to make life acceptable today. Then, if the Dream is still important, let's do the hard work to create a society where this Dream is actually the reality. If we can do that, then that's something we all can proudly pump our fists over and boast: We built it!

I must admit that part of me is afraid that I have set my expectations too low. This is a sticky issue for me, because as much as others put their faith in the importance of hard work I put mine in the importance of high expectations: high expectations of others and for ourselves. I can't count the number of times that I have preached that the solution lies in raising our expectations. I may have started talking about the cultural dysfunction that plagues us when I blamed (low) expectations (as I argued in my last book *Ghettonation*), but now I realize that you don't really need to define the problem at all. Raising our expectations can be part of *any* solution. It is also, in true bootstrap mythology, something we can do ourselves. John (my coauthor) thinks I should clarify here that I am not pointing fingers at just some of us. As a social scientist he is worried that some might push me into the classic bootstrapping mistake of blaming the "victim." I don't think I need to provide much clarification, though. Raising expectations starts in our homes, on our block, in our neighborhoods, across our country. And I won't ever back away from believing in the significance that expectations hold for all of us. Because of that, I do want to clarify that I argue the importance of focusing on making today better even if tomorrow has to wait, with caution and a little fear. You never know where your words will end up and to what use. But then I started thinking about what policy could look like if we truly did embrace a concept of American Reality and aim for today.

If we think about improving today, then we should start with our workplaces. Whenever someone asks me why I got into business journalism, implying it is an odd fit for the social issues I often seem most passionate about, I remind them that we spend more of our waking hours at work than we do at home. Our workplaces are where any kind of societal change needs to start. Better housing, better health care, better education all start with better wages.

Workplace reform often focuses on issues of race or gender. Research studies focus on the stubbornness of discrimination. The media loves to obsess about women's work choices as if there is a choice for most women. Instead, if we really want to change today, we need to focus our workplace reform on the needs of working mothers. I know that sounds incredibly self-serving coming from a working mother of young children. And because of that perception, now is perhaps the only moment of my life where I have wished that I were a white man so that the focus could be on the message instead of the messenger. But, consider that we live in a nation where the majority of mothers are employed outside the home. Many of these mothers work full-time. Two-thirds of mothers are bringing home at least a quarter of the family's earnings. And 4 in 10 mothers are either the sole breadwinner or bringing home as much or more than their partner. Those numbers have increased steadily every year since at least 1967.[23] Truth is, most women in the workplace are mothers or will become mothers. Even those women in the workplace who may not be biological mothers often still end up caregivers—mothering another family member's child or mothering their parents, making them just as much mothers as those who wear the title by our traditional definitions.

Much is often made of how women have changed the workplace, but that is not only old news it never was news since women were always working. Sure, the nature of the jobs that women hold has indeed undergone a transformation, but that change is often mistaken as a beginning rather than a phase of a continued history of work for women in this country. Even the 1950s' image of the traditional family with the husband as the sole breadwinner was a myth. The reason some (white) families could afford a stay-at-home mother was the government was subsidizing families. According to historian Stephanie Coontz, cochair of the Council on Contemporary Families, 40 percent of young men starting families in the 1950s were eligible for veterans' benefits. These benefits allowed working-class men to get an education or training for middle-class jobs and then allowed them to buy homes. It is the ultimate cushion. Added Coontz: "The federal government then paid 90 percent of the costs of massive highway projects that opened up suburbia to home buyers and provided blue-collar workers with jobs that paid a family wage. Today's families receive far less government support, even though job security and real wages are falling."[24] It means the stay-at-home mom is always the exception.

Therefore, by focusing our workplace reform efforts on the needs of working mothers, we improve the realities of our nation's families today and thus society tomorrow. Yes, it is the lift-the-lowest-rung-to-lift-all-boats point of view that my young journalism student couldn't grasp after the State of the Union.

What would a mothercentric policy look like? What should it look like? Simple: it starts with quality, affordable child care. That is the only way to ensure that our work pays rather than parents paying to work. It should be a cause that every politician stands behind if they value family. No other reform that affects work matters if parents can't afford dependable, flexible care for their children when they are at work, no matter what time of day they have to work (shift workers, like restaurant workers, often have the added burden of finding child care that is flexible to meet their unpredictable and unconventional schedules). According to recent research from the U.S. Census Bureau, the cost of child care has risen dramatically since the 1980s when inflation is accounted for. The average cost of child care ranges greatly from state to state from about $4,600 a year in Mississippi to almost $15,000 in Massachusetts. However, in more than half the country, or thirty-six states, the average annual cost of day care is higher than a year at state college. And no matter what state you live in, as well as Washington, DC, day care for two children (a baby and a four-year-old) is more expensive than the average cost of rent in that state for a year. My home state of New York is the least affordable state when it comes to child care where parents of school-age kids pay on average $11,000 a year to have their kids watched for the few hours after school until they return from work.[25] The fact that child care is virtually absent from the political debate is a sign that we would much rather talk about family values than do something that values families.

From there our policy to better today would mean we would need a living wage not a minimum wage, paid family leave so we can take care of our babies and our parents, health care for the sick and preventive care for the healthy (not only can illness stop you from working and earning an income, but anywhere between 17 and 62 percent of personal bankruptcy claims are due to overwhelming medical bills), and payment equality that is not an act. I would also include quality education for our children no matter if they are rich, middle-class, or poor as something to improve upon today. Most see education for its future benefits, to ensure that our children will be able to find jobs tomorrow, but there is always a generation of our children looking for jobs today.

At the beginning I worried that urging the focus on today instead of tomorrow was lowering my expectations, even giving up on the hope of mobility. But, looking at the To-Do List for Today, I realized if we as a society can do that for ourselves, if we could see that list as an obligation for all our citizens, that would be the highest of expectations.

And you thought I wasn't a dreamer.

JOHN

Watching TV is better than listening to jazz.

When some black people dream the American Dream, they probably have a jazz soundtrack playing underneath the images they conjure up in their heads, but I, for one, hate jazz music. That's right, I said it. I *hate* jazz. So much, in fact, that if jazz were a living, breathing human being (and not an African American musical genre birthed in the American South during the early twentieth century), it wouldn't want to meet up with me in a dark alley somewhere. Or if that hypothetically walking and talking musical form were already being pounced on and pummeled by a manic and muscular (and equally anthropomorphic) hip-hop in that same alleyway, I would just turn around and walk away. And I wouldn't feel the slightest twinge of guilt, justifying my inaction by telling myself that we all might just be a little better off if jazz got its ass kicked.

And it doesn't bother me that some people would interpret my hostility as narrow-minded, or even as an example of racial self-hatred. How could a black person—a black academic, no less—not genuflect to the sacredness of jazz as a quintessentially and authentically African American cultural practice? It is racial blasphemy, or another case of airing dirty laundry in mixed company. But I don't care. I want to lead the anti-jazz movement as far as I can take it.

I'll try to explain some of my hatred for jazz in a minute, but first I want to mention why that hate is relevant to a book about having impolite conversations on controversial topics.

If you'll remember, almost as soon as President Obama appointed Eric Holder as the country's top prosecutor, Holder called Americans "cowards" and lobbied for a new national dialogue on race and racism. Just the year before, in my book *Racial Paranoia*, I argued against any new demands for a "conversation on race" in the United States. As a social scientist, I spend a lot of my professional time studying social differences, including racial ones, so it isn't necessarily in my own self-interest to try to put the kibosh on race talk, but some of Holder's righteous indignation over Americans tiptoeing around race needs unpacking—and for reasons that hover closely to the central theme of this book.

America's racial conflicts don't stem from the fact that we talk too little about race. We talk about it all the time. We have race-talk diarrhea, which is why some people (mostly, though not exclusively, white people) feel like we talk about it too much. "Enough already," many people cry. "I'm not a racist, and blacks shouldn't blame racism for their problems." Or they play the ethnicity card: "My grandparents were immigrants. And they had it just as hard. But they didn't complain. They pushed on and made something out of their lives." We've all heard these laments before. Although we may not always have very deep or empathetic things to say about race, we invoke it constantly, almost by rote.

The biggest problem with these ongoing conversations, however, isn't just *what* we say, it is *who* we are saying things to. In fact, what we say is always determined by whom we are talking to. And in an American context, if we are talking to someone from another race about race, we are usually talking to strangers or pretty close to it.

There are actually two very vibrant conversations about race going on in America all the time: one within racial groups, which is usually a version of preaching to the choir, and a second kind, halting and politically corrected for public consumption, which tends to take place between people of different racial groups who know each other in mostly superficial ways. These are the two kinds of discussions we have never stopped having. And Holder's point was that they are both too easy—that they are both cop-outs.

We don't need two parallel and disconnected conversations about race, insular dialogues that allow people to reinforce their preconceived notions. We need one common discussion, where we can speak to people who will sometimes challenge our assumptions not just second them. Genuine and effective talk about race and racism requires friendly antagonists not just amen corners.

Unfortunately, Holder's provocation seems to stop there. And that's not nearly enough. We need to address a second issue, in many ways an even more intractable one.

Mere strangers don't talk, not really, at least not in anything other than ephemeral and ineffectual ways. They might banter about the weather or last weekend's football game, but that's not the kind of talking about race that will suffice, even if a particular stranger might inadvertently say something at some point that resonates and sticks with you.

Talking is a *means* not just an *end*. It helps to forge relationships, potentially strong and deep ones. That actually should be the end-game for all this talk about race talk. Not just the cultivation of one multiracial *dialogue* for the sake of streamlining public discourse, but the creation of one intimate and interconnected *America,* a place where people actually speak with one another despite differences of race and ethnicity, of opinion and ideology.

The United States of America is still spectacularly segregated: where and with whom we live; where and with whom we go to school; even where and with whom we worship. All are disproportionately determined by race—or by other factors that create racially significant outcomes. And Americans' most intimate and personal social networks are at least as segregated and apartheid-like as the places where they live, learn, and pray, if not more so.

So the issue isn't that we don't talk about race, it is that we only tend to talk about race with people who look like us and share many of our assumptions, at least most of the time, which explains why, say, blacks and whites in America can examine the same evidence in the Rodney King police beating, or the O. J. Simpson murder trial, or the case against George Zimmerman and come out on opposite ends of the opinion spectrum, significant majorities of both races seeing those things in diametrically opposed ways.

But without getting into a "chicken or egg" discussion (about whether we don't talk across racial lines because we know that the other folks don't agree or we don't agree because we don't take the time to venture across the racial tracks), the fundamental point I want to make is that those two things are inextricably related: what we think about the world and who we interact with (in really meaningful ways) while we traipse around in it. And the stakes start to get really high when we are talking about serious topics with people we really know and love, with our closest friends and family, people we've had relationships with for many, many years.

And this is part of the reason why my jeremiad against jazz warrants mention in this book. Because my coauthor, whom I appreciate and care about very much, one of my oldest friends in the world, happens to have a brother, her only brother, who is a professional jazz musician and is thoroughly committed to his craft. At her wedding one of her brother's compositions was featured prominently during a teary-eyed moment of the ceremony. The funeral for her father (an artist also deeply connected to jazz) was held in Manhattan's famed "Jazz Church," and instead of a formal service there was a jam session at the altar. So, this isn't merely idle or academic talk. It could be read as a kind of personal attack on the people Cora cares most deeply about. Even fighting words. And that's why we don't want to talk about race and racism in any real way. Forget about a hot-button issue like that one: even just criticizing a musical genre that is no longer particularly popular can land you in hot water, or come off as offensive, which is only a big deal if you care about insulting the person you're talking to.

Ironically, it is sometimes much easier to be polite with strangers. You give them a smile or your seat on a bus and move on. For most people, it is probably a little harder to be impolite to someone you don't know, especially when you're standing right in front of them. We can all do it online, shielded by anonymity's too-tempting cloak. But it is harder face-to-face. It seems egregious and unnecessary. Why bother? If someone does something to upset and offend you, then all bets are off. But otherwise and for the most part, only genuine ass-holes practice impoliteness in any consistent way vis-à-vis the general public.[26] We end up saving most of our face-to-face impoliteness for the people we know best, because they can take it. Because they will sometimes be willing to take it. And we don't often feel the need to keep up appearances or watch our p's and q's around them, which is, in some ways, a kind of backhanded compliment. So, I don't mean to offend you, Cora, or to attack one of your brother's central passions (and even his very livelihood), but let me explain why jazz sometimes makes me sick.

My disdain for jazz is steeped in two things, and neither of them has to do with mid-twentieth-century European scholars (the "Frank-furt School") who dismissed it as a homogenizing and dehumanizing handmaiden to fascism.[27] I might let it take an ass whipping in an alley, but I wouldn't prosecute it for crimes against humanity. Not quite.

My first criticism might sound like sour grapes, but it is just an aesthetic preference. Since I'm not a musician myself, I always pay more attention to vocalists than to virtuosic instrumentalists, to crooners over drummers, saxophonists, and trumpeters. I like listening to lyrics, to the explicit stories being told in songs, which is part of what draws me to hip-hop. Hip-hop is all about the centrality of "the spoken word," the significance of stories and storytellers. I like a funky beat as much as the next fan, and it is certainly a part of "the talking drum" tradition, but when I listen to hip-hop music, I'm following the rhetoric, privileging the poetry. The rest, for me, is secondary.

For jazz purists, that is my initial sin. I'd prefer to hear Louis Arm-strong sing rather than blow his horn just about any day of the week. Nina Simone, Arthur Prysock, Ella Fitzgerald, and Billie Holiday are towering figures in jazz, with huge and loyal followings, but the Miles Davises and John Coltranes and Thelonious Monks define that music's canonical core, especially for would-be connoisseurs. And my second gripe is with those very aficionados.

At its most pretentious, jazz music sometimes gets used to justify pompous brands of social sifting, a snobby elitism that easily serves as a class-coded policing of African American culture. To appreciate jazz is to join the black in-crowd. It is supposed to indicate a kind of social seriousness. When jazz-loving comedian Bill Cosby started going after poor blacks a few years ago for being their own worst enemies (for being lazy and shiftless and giving their kids weird names), he was really just making explicit the class critique that had been implicit in his hit TV show's obsessions with jazz music and musicians in its subplots all along. Poor blacks might have watched those episodes, but they didn't get the subtle class-based critique. So, he has started to go for the jugular.

If it has become increasingly commonplace to attack one's political opponents for "class warfare" in contemporary electoral politics (labeling them antipopulist "vulture capitalists" or anti-American "socialists"), the subtler versions of these accusations and assaults have always been played out on the terrain of cultural politics, through critiques of what other people wear, eat, and listen to. And jazz has long been a key weapon in that battle.

No other music, the claim goes, can hold a candle to jazz's essential (and even existential) distillation of African American angst and aspiration, but it is a definition of African Americanness that pivots on social status, on class differences. If the blues demands respect for its straightforward and vernacular profundities, jazz is supposed to add a learned and well-heeled dose of proficiency to the mix. And neither jazz nor the blues get maligned these days nearly as much as that other "race music" known as hip-hop, which is still occasionally invoked as "the anti-jazz" and dismissed as barely music at all—not to mention getting implicated in actual alley fights all over contemporary urban America.

In the not-so-distant past, jazz musicians like Wynton Marsalis and music critics like Stanley Crouch were the most vocal proponents of jazz's qualitative difference from (and superiority over) hip-hop. Crouch has mused publicly about the "retarding effect" of hip-hop, a genre that, according to him, takes relatively little talent—and that profits from the public denigration of black people.

From a posh perch at the world-renowned Lincoln Center, Marsalis once dismissed hip-hop as little more than "a safari for people who get their thrills from watching African Americans debase themselves, men dressing in gold, calling themselves stupid names like Ludacris or 50 Cent, spending money on expensive fluff." These were heightened (but only slightly) versions of how members of the African American culturati's older generation characterized what's wrong with hip-hop's too-easy conflation with blackness. It is the language of class warfare without any talk about changes to the tax code or the proper social role of capitalism.

This idea of a battle between jazz and hip-hop is just one version of class warfare within black America, and it pivots on the longstanding compulsion for a "politics of respectability," which is the idea that black people should put their best foot forward in front of white people so that they don't embarrass "the race." Authentic blacks are supposed to be austere, strong, silent, and disciplined, nothing like the Stepin Fetchit caricatures of black people first made famous in early-twentieth-century American media (at just about the same time that jazz went viral).

Jazz is a black, middle-class response to the threat of racial inauthenticity, a trump card rejoinder to the equally problematic assumption that urban poverty is the only thing that legitimately comprises African Americans' social realities. And this is true even if the black middle class is unable or unwilling to sustain jazz music anymore, which leads to discussions (at least in Spike Lee's movies) about the extent to which jazz has become "white music," something supported mostly by white audiences not black ones, complete with its own PBS documentary series by Ken Burns. Cora even admits that at some of her brother's gigs, he would be one of a very few black faces in the entire club, playing music or listening to it. I have a sneaking suspicion that not a single black person in America really likes jazz. They just say they do, mostly because they think they're supposed to. So, they smile and pretend and even purchase a few CDs for their personal collections, just to sustain the ruse. But I don't buy it. I'm not convinced. And by the way, classical music operates in a similar

way vis-à-vis class in America. But at least it is called *class*-ical, an
honest indication of its pretentions. And jazz is kind of like *classical-
in-blackface*. So maybe we should rename it *bourgiecal*: music for
bourgie black folks. Make things more explicit.

Most Americans can't read music these days. Not well. They are
a lot like me on that front. They might know the basics (which I
got from Ms. Gabey's Glee Club, grades 3 to 6), but they don't fully
understand the instrumental intricacies of art forms like jazz. Of
course, there are still a few people who are trained as instrumentalists and who appreciate that kind of sonic storytelling. So when
they hear music on the radio, they don't just focus on the words.
The instruments are their tour guides. But fewer and fewer people
can speak that language with much sophistication, even if they act
like they can. Some of jazz's biggest fans are just poseurs. They can't
elaborately dissect a jazz tune or scene like, say, Ralph Ellison could,
who famously claimed to have learned "the discipline and devotion to
his art," writing, from watching jazz musicians in Oklahoma City.[28]

I've been thinking a lot about jazz lately, but not because I've been
listening to it. I've been watching it. Not in a club; on-screen.

HBO's *Treme* is an object lesson in a different definition of jazz
music's social realities. Given the ratings-worship of contemporary
TV executives and their less-than-stellar track record of producing
hour-long dramas with substantial African American storylines,
Treme, the series about post–Katrina New Orleans, probably wouldn't
have been possible unless somebody at the cable network agreed with
Spike Lee's take on the music's current clientele: lily white. HBO
prides itself on being better than regular network TV, which is part
of the reason why it was even willing to take a chance on a show like
Treme, a series that wonderfully challenges some of jazz music's elitist
pretensions.

David Simon, a 2010 "MacArthur Genius" and creator of HBO's
critically acclaimed *The Wire*, conceived of *Treme* with veteran TV
writer/producer Eric Overmyer. Like *The Wire*, *Treme* is a tale of
class, race, and the harsh realities of contemporary urban America. It
is a story about the traumas of everyday life in the wake of a disaster,

about the frighteningly fine line between human resilience and frailty. It is also quite clearly about jazz music, jazz at its most material, mystical, and magisterial. It is a version of jazz that outstrips the ways that some middle-class blacks wield the music as a class-sharpened sword.

Treme is a post-Katrina lamentation, a chronicling of how New Orleans residents, black and white, new and old, attempt to drag themselves, their loved ones, and their grizzled city back from the brink of annihilation. The characters are political to a fault—all of them. Their politics differ in large and small ways, but just about everyone seems to wear them, quite conspicuously, on exposed and frayed sleeves. All of it is about the politics of race and class, and their intersection. And about the politics of music itself.

There's Albert Lambreaux, the "Black Indian" elder played with scalding intensity by Clarke Peters, police detective Lester Freamon from *The Wire*. Single-minded in his obsession with carrying on his community's spectacular rituals and public displays, Lambreaux is an anchor to a slowly receding past, one in need of active and adamant recuperation. At one point, he is also squatting in a storm-damaged home and completely broke. As a counterpoint to the asceticism of Lambreaux, Wendell Pierce, another *Wire* alum, plays philandering trombonist Antoine Batiste, a struggling artist who chases gigs to keep food on the table for his newborn child and live-in baby-mama, Desiree, played by Phyllis Montana LeBlanc, whose poetic performance was one of the most noteworthy parts of Spike Lee's documentary about New Orleans after Hurricane Katrina, *When the Levees Broke*. Batiste is trying to do right, and his strivings (sometimes successful, sometimes not) are easily the most troubling and endearing aspects of the story. Khandi Alexander's no-nonsense rendition of Ladonna Batiste-Williams, Batiste's ex-wife, has her spending much of the show's first season fending off his miss-you-now-that-you're-gone advances and searching for her missing brother, a metaphor that attempts to capture the ease with which many poor New Orleanians found themselves lost in "the system," even before those levees failed. Batiste-Williams enlists attorney Toni Bernette (Melissa Leo) in her search, and Bernette eventually finds out the worst, and not too long before her own husband, Creighton, John Goodman's pitch-perfect personification of left-wing histrionics (replete with an unforgettable YouTube rant against George W. Bush), allows his own personal frustrations (including writer's block on an overdue book manuscript, with which I identify all too easily) to get the best of him.

But the show is most centrally about the music itself, jazz, and *Treme's* attempt to use real musicians along with seasoned and award-winning actors usually means that the differences between those two groups (in terms of actorly believability) is sometimes pretty conspicuous. But that is more than compensated for by the power of the musicians' sincere and invested self-presentations. The entire show can be read (between the lines of its explicit narrative logic) as a careful lesson in jazz music and culture.

It isn't just a throwaway statement to declare that jazz is a character in this series. Every episode showcases various subgenres and musical styles and includes several cameos from respected local and international artists. And then there are those long musical interludes. It is unfair and misleading to call them interludes at all, since that would imply that they are little more than bridges between more substantive scenes. To interpret the lush and lengthy musical performances this way is to misread them entirely. They are ends in and of themselves, the story's melodramatic machinations a mere excuse for luxuriating in these sovereign symphonies. Each episode is "about" the music itself, the ostensible story lines of politics and romance, bravery and debauchery, trauma and triumph, narrative means to decidedly musical ends. Of course, for the sake of full disclosure, I must admit that I have fallen asleep during more than one of these nuanced and well-choreographed musical romps, especially when there is no singer to guide me through to the other side. Even still, I love the idea of such seemingly self-indulgent televisual musicality, even if I wouldn't necessarily have been above fast-forwarding past one or two of them on any given Sunday evening.

Aside from *Treme's* unabashedly powerful fetishization of music itself (and all fetishes aren't necessarily bad or dysfunctional), the other wonderful thing about the show is that its muse, its raison d'être, jazz, is not completely Wynton Marsalis's jazz. Not by a long shot.

Whenever Albert Lambreaux's son, Delmond, appears on-screen, I think of Wynton Marsalis and his powerful perch at Lincoln Center. Delmond, played with a kind of piercing blankness by Rob Brown, is a relative superstar in the larger world of recorded jazz. He has an authentic New Orleans pedigree, but he spends far too much of his time in a different world, a Marsalis-like world. That isn't to say that Delmond can't go home again. He does, even if somewhat grudgingly. And he clearly respects his father's lifestyle and assessment of musical mastery, which is one of the reasons why he cuts an album with him, but Delmond's Madison Avenue polish gets little traction in a place like *Treme*. He is little more than a glorified outsider; his version of jazz proficiency has lost its grit. His dad might even fear that it has lost its soul.

New Orleans takes pride in its occult-filled mythology, but a soulless, zombified jazz music just won't do. The jazz of New Orleans is supposed to have too much life in it for that. And as people like Crouch and Marsalis know, jazz in New Orleans can be a decidedly seedy thing, as much of a working-class endeavor (for the likes of talented hustlers such as Batiste) as a middle-class phylactery. These may be amazing musicians, and they dress up rather nicely for prestigious gigs at swanky venues, but they are "the people," regular people, with little patience for aristocratic pretense. To be "down in the Treme," as the show's theme song opines, is an unequivocally lower-class position, one that requires everyday struggles for survival—and that was even before the rupture of Katrina in 2005.

According to many media scholars who study contemporary Hollywood, shows like *Treme* radically alter the way network stories get told. They keep upping the ante in terms of the nuanced and complicated narrative arcs that screenwriters juggle.[29]

A colleague of mine, scholar Elihu Katz, has wondered aloud about TV's potential demise. He asks if we are currently witnessing "The End of Television." Katz's point is not just about the quality of what's being broadcast today, but if we did, in fact, focus on content alone, we'd probably have to say that TV is far from dead. It has probably never been more alive in terms of the complex stories it tells, especially with offerings like *Treme*.[30]

Granted, television is a mixed bag, and quite a bit of it seems derivative and uninspired these days, but at its best it can sometimes outdo Hollywood, even the latter's most impressive cinematic fare. And I say this as a filmmaker and an enthusiastic film watcher.

For one thing, the complexities of character development that one can witness over a TV show's entire season dwarf the best films' attempts at cramming subtlety into two-hour portrayals. *Treme* as a feature-length movie might work (in the hands of a wildly inspired director), but the slow ooze of Creighton's self-destruction or Ladonna's second-season rape would be so much less powerful once predictably squeezed into a single motion picture's second act (at about page 60). TV allows storytellers to take more chances than Hollywood filmmaking can afford. And we really get to know the characters, to notice their changes over time, and to miss them when they're gone. *Treme* has introduced several fascinating characters, including jazz itself, and each new season promised to allow them all ample time to meticulously unfurl.

Treme used its focus on jazz to comment on race in America today, a kind of meditation on racial difference and on the many ways in which blackness and whiteness share a complicated history in the South, even "the new South," and even one as singular and exceptional (in terms of its particular racial story) as New Orleans. If jazz music can tell us something about how class conflicts and racial tensions play themselves out, *Treme* seems to also imply that the music isn't reducible to these social and political issues, not in its final instance, even if the entire context within which its melodies circulate is as politicized, racialized, and class-gutted as New Orleans has become since Katrina. In that sense, *Treme*'s hyperrealist portrayal of a gritty Big Easy seems, ironically, almost utopian, as though it imagines that the objective artistry of musicians and their music, if taken seriously, might just be enough to keep the waters from rising next time around. So, the show does, at one level, definitely believe much of the hype about jazz, and I tend not to buy such wishful claims, but *Treme* makes me want to love and appreciate jazz music—at least a little bit. But I can only do that because it tries to push jazz's social snobbery and classist proclivities far from center stage.

The problem, however, is that *Treme* is the outlier. And it is just a TV show. In real life, too many people use jazz as a way to lift their noses above the populist fray. But then again, as *Treme* demonstrates, jazz musicians themselves, people like Cora's brother, almost never do that. Ralph Ellison didn't do it. Ethnomusicologist and jazz pianist Guthrie Ramsey doesn't do it.[31] Sometimes, the fans who don't actually play any of this music are often the worst culprits of such sonic snobbery—and that's regardless of whether or not those fans are really bona fide, card-carrying members of anybody's comfortable middle class.

RELIGION

JOHN

Is Twitter the new religion?

I'm only a lukewarm believer and backsliding practitioner when it comes to worshipping at the altar of Twitter.

I get the draw. It feels like an incredibly modern way to "communicate," almost godlike speech: to everyone, all at once. "Behold, everybody I know, I am eating dinner at my favorite restaurant. Wait, I shall send you a photo of the appetizer." The lure of this new super-duper loudspeaker is understandable, but I keep thinking that it isn't quite for me, and not just because I would like to believe, in a self-glorifying way, that I don't have a particularly strong God complex.

My resistance to sliding into the unbridled celebration of all things Twitter shouldn't be written off as a generational thing. It isn't just because I'm the virtual equivalent of an old fart in "social media" years, though that is also true. There's something about the unprecedented speed with which we've flung ourselves into the expanding Twitterverse that screams Faustian pact to me, a lopsided contract with some evil genius. As many others have complained, we might be leveraging some precious things—our privacy, true intimacy—for the sake of immediate gratification.

As a young kid, I was fixated on the idea (first introduced to me by a third-grade teacher) that one of the keys to success is "deferred gratification." I even loved the sound of the phrase, its literal phonetics. Of course, the budding academic in me would be intrigued, such highfalutin words for a simple notion: disciplining yourself enough to put certain things off for later, not satisfying some tempting and immediate desires right now for potentially bigger and better long-term goals. The phrase also stuck with me because it reminded me of my own childhood version of what religion was all about: deferring gratification like crazy.

There were all these fun things I wanted to take part in as a child, activities that my Seventh-Day Adventist upbringing summarily precluded, Saturday morning cartoons first and foremost. Saturday was the Sabbath in my household, which meant we weren't supposed to work or play. It was a day for reverence and reflection on the mercy and power of God. It was our day for churchgoing and Bible reading. Unfortunately, Saturdays are also the days reserved especially for childhood entertainment. The entire week is organized around that fact, which meant a plethora of tempting alternatives to the mandates of Seventh-Day Adventism. But part of how I tried to defend myself against the lures of earthly want—like sneaking into the living room and turning on the television early Saturday mornings, before everyone else got up—was by thinking about the gratifications to come when I reached that ultimate goal, living with Jesus after he returned to claim his faithful and take them up with Him to "the land of milk and honey."

The deacons and deaconesses who took such good care of me back then, who looked after this young church member (baptized and reciting memorized Sabbath School "mission stories" in front of the entire congregation by age thirteen), would probably cringe at the above formulation of things, at the idea that following God's word was about deferring happiness. There is direct gratification that comes from doing His will, they'd say. Joy isn't deferred. The delight of following Jesus's example should be immediate and intrinsically fulfilling. And that made sense to me, too. But when I thought about those *Justice League* cartoons, or, even worse, Saturday afternoon kung fu movies on channel 5, it still felt like deferral to me. In many ways, that is part of what my SDA upbringing taught me to develop, a pointed ability to put some things off for later. Not all the time and 100 percent. I sneaked peeks at *Super Friends* some mornings (on mute!), and I feel like I found a way to catch *The Five Deadly Venoms* on TV about 20,000 times, simulating its martial arts movements with friends over the subsequent weeks. But I understood the lesson learned by putting off some of my petty desires until the sun set on Saturday evenings. It even felt like a small little accomplishment. A mini victory, of sorts. Religion was a central venue for teaching me (imperfectly, to be sure) some small respect for self-control.

And I don't invoke religion lightly here. It seems the perfect analogy for many of the contemporary functions of new and emergent social media. Twitter and Facebook and LinkedIn and Instagram (and all the others that are probably already out there but would effectively be less hip once someone like me knows they even exist) are examples of a kind of modern-day religion. They reflect some of our profoundest current beliefs about the world and our place in it.

We are used to worshipping celebrity, and we still do that—either fawning over Lady Gaga and Tom Cruise or hoping to take our own home videos viral, trying to gain our fifteen minutes (or 1,000,000 views/hits) of fame. The amazing thing about social media like Twitter is that they vacillate, effortlessly, between idol worship and star-gazing, on the one hand, and solipsism/self-promotion, on the other. We follow other icons, other gods, yes, but we also declare ourselves would-be gods at the same time. Why else would we send our most intimate details to hundreds, even thousands, of (mostly) strangers or acquaintances recast as "friends" (and, tellingly, "followers") unless we were trying to join some cultish group—or lead one? We provide people with information about the tiniest minutiae of our everyday lives and idle thoughts. And even this is about celebrity, about the fact that we all have a chance, we hope, to be chosen as the next big thing.

Twitter isn't necessarily competing with traditional religious organizations for members or donations, but it might be useful to think about how social media act as a kind of "civil religion" these days. It has a quasireligious tint to it, providing one central version of *the* moral foundation for contemporary American and global culture. Social media offers up the basic logic for understanding our interconnected world and the relationships we forge with one another in it.

Virtual spaces like Twitter and Facebook organize those relationships, giving them meaning and determining their impact on our lives.

Thinking about social media as a kind of religion begs the question, what is religion? This is a deceptively easy thing to ask, but very difficult to answer, at least satisfactorily. Our answer depends on whom we are talking to, whose religion we're talking about.

Anthropologists don't all agree on any one single best definition of religion, though we do have some versions we invoke more often than others. One answer is to cast religion as a fundamental way that social groups organize their responses to existential questions about life and death. Why are we here? How did we get here? What happened to the people who were here before us? And when will it all end, if at all? (No wonder all our essay titles in this religion chapter ask questions.) This isn't to say that all religions necessarily take these questions on to the same extent—or in any exclusive sense. Clearly, science would also imagine itself in the "questions of life and death" business.

And there are probably versions of what we might call "religion" that would find this categorical definition ill-fitted to their exploits. There isn't really a universal definition of religion, not even one that would privilege belief in the supernatural as some kind of ultimate characterization, or specific rituals and practices as uniformly present. But I do think that one sweet spot for questions about what religions are—and what they do—could be glossed with a placeholder linked to existential angst and inquisitiveness.

Linking religion to its larger cultural context (to other things people do, think, and say), while also looking at beliefs across cultures, anthropologists think about religions as cultural concoctions that we pretend are anything but merely cultural.

Anthropologist Clifford Geertz gave anthropology one of its most famous definitions of religion in the mid-1960s. He described religion as "(1) a system of symbols which acts to (2) establish powerful, pervasive, and long-lasting moods and motivations in men by (3) formulating conceptions of a general order of existence and (4) clothing these conceptions with such an aura of factuality that (5) the moods and motivations seem uniquely realistic."

Religions allow us to answer the big questions with an air of definitiveness and certainty that would otherwise be hard to muster. The ones that we'd need a lifeline to answer on game shows. Or the cognitive power of crowdsourcing with the studio audience. In a subsequent essay, I provide a discussion of what "culture" is, and religion, for an anthropologist, is only a particularly powerful and deeply felt example of culture. Religion is an attempt to answer all the most important questions in life. To understand the impossible.

At the same time, this is hardly the only thing that religion is responsible for. And in many ways, the other functions of religion are even more interesting.

James Baldwin tried to define religion during his 1961 trip through Israel: "(And *what*, precisely, is a religion? And how dreary, how disturbing, to find oneself asking, now, questions which one supposed had been answered forever!) But one is forced to ask these kindergarten questions . . ." To some people, Baldwin included, religious beliefs feel a little threatening, and not just for the lives and wants of nonbelievers. "For the word 'religious,'" he continues in his October 8 journal entry from that same trip, "I read 'tribal.' Is it not possible to hope that we can begin, at long last, to transcend the tribe?"

Social media is less a transcendence of the tribal logics that might inform religious groups and more a reconfiguration of the tribe's basic attributes.

Religion is one of the ways in which we police ourselves. We monitor ourselves for potential threats to the social order. Religion is a way of determining how we protect the group from forms of antisocial behavior. This isn't to say that religions can't sanction antisocial acts. They can be made to do that, too. And all the time. But that's only because they intend to provide a compelling list of actions that are allowable and not, as well as rationales for those determinations. This is obviously where the rubber hits the road on long-standing debates about things as different as terrorism (suicide bombings, etc.) and abortion. Self-policing begins with self-inspection, which is one of social media's most fascinating features. Not only does it blur the line between public and private life, between what's appropriate to share with the world and what you should be ashamed to let your mama find out about you. Social media makes us complicit in our own surveillance. We are responsible for giving people access to our every move, sometimes literally. I first got spooked when someone told me that one of the Twitter apps I was using, when I started experimenting with tweets (because the publisher of my last book thought it could help to get the word out about the book's release), basically made me GPS-trackable to everyone else on Twitter. The idea that we share our daily whereabouts and thoughts with whoever might have a computer gives them access to portions of our lives that were (thankfully) much less public and visible before.

Philosopher and public reformer Jeremy Bentham famously wrote about the "panopticon" as one particularly effective prison design. In prisons built on that model, the prisoners were always visible to a centrally located (and effectively invisible) prison guard. They were always on view—the guard provided with a kind of godlike view of every inmate. The logic of Twitter and Facebook and other new social media is panoptic in a similar way. They allow us to position ourselves into view for all the world to see. Whether we see them looking at us or not, we have to internalize the fact that they could be watching. The Internet itself gives providers access to our every keystroke and website visit—and in ways that big-data crunchers can use to predict what we might want to buy. Social media platforms allow a larger public to have access to our ever-shrinking backstage lives, even when we also self-consciously simulate some of our backstage antics with that wider audience in mind.

This panoptic view is a little different from Bentham's, especially since it makes us all guards and prisoners at the same time. We can watch and be watched, spy other people's avatar-selves while putting our own on public display. Philosopher Guy Debord would describe this scenario as a "society of the spectacle," our authentic lives replaced by their "mere representation," by the cold and inescapable passivity of blankly staring while being stared at. For him, this is a dehumanizing face-off. It comes at the expense of true interaction and social engagement. Of course, there is a lot of activity (or at least a lot of very active typing) required for tweets, Facebook updates, and all of that, but Debord would warn that these are still obstructions to genuine human contact. He even went so far as to argue that advertisements and other forms of media marketing are like religion, giving media "consumers" (and he was most concerned about us all being turned into nothing more than consumers of products and visual spectacles) a sense of "fervent exaltation," which he considered somewhat comparable to erstwhile social responses religious believers of that old-time religion would have had to divine "miracles." Cultural critic Jean Baudrillard characterized our contemporary world as a "simulacrum" of reality, a mirage that replaces our ability to actually live life. It is the simulation of living without any real life to ground it. Maybe reading all of these French philosophers is what has me so anxious about Twitter, but I do think that there are a few uncanny ways that new social media's logics pivot on the kinds of investments that my Adventist upbringing also would have linked to religious beliefs and practices.

For instance, there is the way that Twitter and other social media sites traffic in assumptions about their own ostensible omnipotence, their seemingly unstoppable social and political might. Whether the Twitter faithful are using the platform to launch campaigns against brutal African strongmen, to let the rest of the world know about their corrupt governmental regimes, to create a flash mob somewhere, to pressure authorities into bringing a case against high school football players who have sex with drunk teenage girls, or just to tell people about their newest book or CD, Twitter is imagined to have almost boundless social and political power. Many people put their faith in the seemingly unlimited possibilities of social media.

Part of social media's power—as what I'd call a kind of postmodern deity—is linked to its omnipresence. The ubiquity of social media is another thing that likens it to religion. It is everywhere. It seems to have access to just about everything. And this was before Wikileaks. No matter how removed the village or how prestigious the post, someone is sending out a tweet or reading one. And those tweets are being retweeted. Or scrolled across the bottom of a CNN newscast. There is nothing beyond the purview and province of social media's gaze. It is the Jehovah of twenty-first-century life. Or at least its Santa Claus.

The other thing about social media is its purported omni-benevolence, another important theme in many descriptions of religion. Sure, there are bad people online. Pedophiles stalking children and snarky tweeters who hide behind the relative anonymity of user names. But that is a problem of evil people, not an indictment of the medium itself, at least for its most die-hard users. Social media can only bring good to the world. Connections to "friends" here, an uplifting and inspiring aphorism there. The kind of sometimes gushing commitments to the ultimate social good of online connections was traditionally reserved only for the reverence of deities.

Omniscience is another important trait in delineations of religious investment. Anything you want to know, you throw out into the great ether known as cyberspace. This is the ultimate in crowdsourcing, all the knowledge and know-how of the world right at your fingertips. In the early twentieth century, French sociologist Émile Durkheim was making the case that religious belief was a reflection and expression of social life, a way to reinforce social norms and expectations. Of course, societies couldn't imagine that they knew it all, so they imbued supernatural beings with that power. Social media users are not shy about conceding that kind of all-knowing power to the massive social networks they have access to online. Or an ill-advised N-word, offered up in relative private, goes viral in ways that demonstrate new media's all-seeing power.

This might not work for every religion, but there is certainly a confessional aspect to some of them that would be familiar to many new media users. Either you confide in a priest, or you take your requests for forgiveness straight to the deity through prayer, admitting your darkest and most dastardly secrets. There is an equivalent confessional aspect to social media that shouldn't be downplayed. We disclose so much, to so many. And it isn't just folks like former congressman Anthony Weiner who overexpose themselves.

Social media is the contemporary place, par excellence, for fellowship. That is a very religious-sounding word, at least in Christian contexts, which is why I use it purposefully here. Because it makes self-professed secularists a bit antsy. Fellowshipping speaks to the ways in which believers are supposed to commune with one another. People used to attend churches or synagogues or mosques for rich and long-standing fellowship. Now their church is Twitter. Or Facebook. The digital images of Instagram. These sites represent virtual forms of ongoing communion, people bond with one another and with the media platform itself. Fellowship is a word that was always just co-opted by Christianity anyway. "Sharing in common" is the Latin. And sharing in common is what we do online, social media sites taking the term back with a vengeance.

There is also a kind of self-righteousness to some social media advocates, people who champion these platforms with the zealousness of religious converts. How could anyone who really wants to be a part of the world choose *not* be on Twitter or Facebook, they ask. These folks look at nonusers with the combination of contempt and pity usually reserved for nonbelievers. Even if they don't actively proselytize, there is a way that being on Twitter simply gives you the kind of hubris that comes with believing that you have access to an unshakable Truth. And it can make you difficult to be around, annoying, self-centered. Like I care about your new article or blog post. I'll click on the link, of course. And maybe even read some of it. But the clicking and reading are more of a compulsion than any kind of concession to the legitimacy of the imposition—or the sense of self-importance it demonstrates.

When I tried, fleetingly, to be active on Twitter (which I might have to try again, admittedly, once this book is out and we are lobbying to get more than just family and friends to care), it was difficult for me to justify (to myself) sending links out to my own writing. I did it, but it felt weird. Like everything was about hawking my "brand," though the self-promotional push of it all usually had to be denied and downplayed, no matter how disingenuous the gesture. But divulging little personal (and ostensibly noncommercial) tidbits and daily updates didn't seem any better. I know nobody cares. And if they do, there is probably another, deeper problem that they need to address—and not sublimate into an obsession with other people's inane cyber offerings.

It was—and still is—fun to trawl through other people's tweets and Facebook posts, especially the catty and confrontational and controversial ones, so long as they aren't directed at me. And some folks are particularly masterful at the well-wrought and provocative tweet. It can be so entertaining. But that's usually because they don't care that what they've written is wildly inappropriate, though it can still sometimes get them in hot water, fired from their real-world jobs, or even, in extreme cases, banished from the site altogether—excommunicated, literally, from the kinds of communion taking place in our newest mega sanctuaries of global communication. As far as I'm concerned, the question is, what are we believing when we tout the powers of social media? What does that tell us about who we are and how we are re-creating our social worlds? I want to believe that the future is all rose petals and perfect harmony, a global village of milk and honey paved by the circuitry of new media platforms. I want to be a keyboard-thumping member of the church of Twitter, but I can't help but feel like its immediate gratifications go against the elegance of that one claim that my third-grade teacher and Adventist upbringing conspired to convince me of a long, long time ago.

CORA

Can a nation still have faith if it has lost its hope?

I admit it. I am definitely a glass-half-empty kind of gal. Some act like pessimism is a bad word, a character flaw that we shouldn't embrace. I am not ashamed of my downside leanings. Foreseeing the worst possible outcomes not only keeps me prepared for life but constantly motivated to overcome life. In fact, there should be a better word for what half-empty thinkers like myself feel rather than pessimism if only because no one wants to listen to a pessimist. Too often optimism is mistaken for happiness, and thus displaying anything else is seen as psychologically dysfunctional. Instead, I think seeing the downside of things is being grounded in reality. Not being crippled by your own pessimism (or optimism) is what makes us truly healthy.

Because I see the world through this lens, from the moment Barack Obama took the oath of office for the first time, I've been waiting for the hope to die. It is hard to remember now with the barrage of scandals and negative press, depressing economic news, and the heavy clouds of disappointment dripping from pundits' lips, but there was a moment when the majority of voters were downright giddy over the possibility of a President Obama. That is, after all, how he was elected, twice. I started teaching college journalism part-time the spring semester of 2009. My first day of class was the day of Obama's inauguration. I had forgotten how deafening the "liberalism" of college campuses can be. However, even then it was amazing to me how different the excitement was on campus compared to the excitement that morning when I left my home in (Do or Die) Bed-Stuy, Brooklyn. In New York's largest black neighborhood there wasn't a storefront window that was not covered in Obama signs. More popular than the Obama Hope posters that made a splash across the nation, in Bed-Stuy were various posters with iconic images of Obama, Malcolm X, and Martin Luther King Jr. floating together that refused to let the neighborhood forget the history of the moment. Perhaps as a result of that weight, in Bed-Stuy on Inauguration Day 2009 it felt almost as if the neighborhood was holding its breath. There was a stillness. In contrast, on campus that day the excitement seemed more like a high. My pessimism would not allow me to relate to the level of giddiness around me, nor could I believe it could ever be sustained. Highs, after all, are by definition an artificial happiness. Back in Bed-Stuy you couldn't forget the history; on campus it already felt like history had passed and folks were moving on to the after-party.

The scene four years later at inauguration time was a lot different. In Bed-Stuy the Obama-Malcolm-Martin posters from 2009 were still hanging, a little frayed at the edges. On campus, Obama bashing had become sport. Where before I had to rein students in with their Obama enthusiasm, now I was finding students who felt it their obligation—as students—to constantly be critical of the president even if they ultimately still claimed to be a supporter, a Democrat, an Obama voter. It was June 2011 when I knew for certain that the hope was dead. I was walking in Brooklyn's Prospect Heights neighborhood, a diverse community known for its melting-pot liberalism. At my son's preschool in the neighborhood I once got lectured by a parent for feeding him Cheerios from General Mills for breakfast. I'm not sure if she was more upset about the unrecycled packaging the Cheerios came in or the inorganic grains my son was ingesting. But I pushed her over the edge when I defiantly admitted I poured regular store-brand milk over it, too. It was in this neighborhood, down the block from my son's preschool, that I saw my proof. "Obama Sucks" was spray painted across the pulled gates of a storefront window. Any type of graffiti these days in New York City stands out—we did that in the 1980s. But to see that message spray painted there in that neighborhood stopped me cold, despite my pessimism. It would be like covering your windows with Yankee banners in the heart of Boston. No one would dare. I immediately took a picture of the "Obama Sucks" graffiti and texted it to John with the message: "It has begun."

I bring all this up not because I want to delve into politics and voting patterns—too much has already been written about the youth vote and Obama. (Part of what was missed by the media in the doomsday discussions that President Obama's declining support of the youth vote would cost him reelection was that the youth vote doesn't have to be white. Obama's declining support was with white voters—regardless of age. So, yes, among young white voters, like my students, support had dropped and approval ratings continue to wobble. But the Millennial generation is by far the most racially and ethnically diverse generation we have, so if anyone bothered to speak to all those brown faces they would have found a much different picture of the youth vote.) Still, what interests me more than politics is the mood. Because even though the majority of the young people (like my students) ended up voting the same way in both elections there was definitely a change in mood. Some dubbed it pessimism. The economy and disappointment in politics supposedly had made our young people pessimistic about life. As a pessimist I don't agree. What I saw spread across campus was more negativity than pessimism, which isn't the same thing. Just because you prepare for the worst, as we pessimists do, does not mean you don't have hope that it will not happen. Negativity, however, is more the loss of hope. It got me thinking about the slight difference in the excitement after the 2009 inauguration that I couldn't put my finger on then. I realized now it had to do with hope. In Bed-Stuy the restrained calm over the neighborhood that day was because hope had been fulfilled. On campus the "now what" cloud in the air was the first sign that the hope buzz had already started to burst. By 2013, the negativity was able to thrive because hope had died.

After the 2012 election the political scientists started their obsession with crunching numbers. A Harvard survey a year later of voters under thirty found that "faith in most major institutions—with notable exception of the military—has declined over the past several years."[1] The pollsters blamed the hyperpartisanship and gridlock of Washington for killing young people's "idealism." The survey concluded: "Unless the discourse in America changes, from the top-down, all of us will suffer and the nation will lose a generation of the best and brightest citizens, voters and public servants the world has to offer."[2] Trey Grayson, the director of Harvard's Institute of Politics, told the press that the survey had experts worried that the lasting effect on this generation of voters will be that their cynicism about government and politics will turn into "a negative attachment that may be hard to overcome."[3]

Other number crunchers came out with similar findings. One Young World, a global youth leadership summit that attracts visits from Desmond Tutu, Kofi Annan, Bill Clinton, Jack Dorsey (Twitter founder), and Bob Geldof (the Irish activist-singer behind "Do They Know It's Christmas?," the original charity single for aid to Africa), concluded that America's youth were more "pessimistic" about the future than those of the rest of the world. Only 29 percent of young Americans agree with the statement: "I feel very positive about my country's future."[4]

The statement about the future of our country that the One Young World folks used to gauge pessimism struck me. What they were really asking about was hope. To not feel "positive" about the future is to have no hope that things will get better. Seventy-one percent of America's youth no longer had hope.

Rather than limit its inquiry to politics, the One World folks attempted to see how deep that hopelessness was entrenched. So they asked about faith. They discovered that fewer than half of America's young people agreed that their faith is "a guiding force" in their lives, versus 64 percent of young people around the world, including in China. (I'm not really sure why the One World press release summarizing American responses singled out China for some questions, but it did. In many cases it made it seem as if they were using China as an explanation point. Not only is the entire world doing X but even

China is, too! Only 64 percent of young people around the world said faith is "a guiding force," including China!)

When we think about the impact of the Hope generation, we too often limit those discussions to politics. But that is shortsighted. That's where the Harvard folks went wrong. Instead, the Hope generation's most lasting influence may be more of a spiritual one. Can a generation without hope still have faith?

——————

The number of Americans who do not identify with any religion is rapidly rising, according to the Pew Forum on Religion & Public Life. Pew dubs them "nones." Today one in five Americans are religiously unaffiliated, the highest it has ever been since Pew started polling on such issues. This number has grown by 25 percent just in the last five years to 33 million Americans. Much of the growth is coming from young people. One-third of adults under thirty are religiously unaffiliated. More significant, Pew also found that young adults today are much more likely to be unaffiliated than previous generations were at a similar stage in their lives.[5] So blaming it on youth doesn't apply here.

Of course, just because you are not affiliated with any religion doesn't mean you don't have faith. In fact, two-thirds of the "nones" say they believe in God, with one in five claiming to pray every day. Although some may find this hard to imagine, personally I am a believer, because I have seen it. My father was a man deeply committed to his belief in God and faith and prayed regularly while never being a member of an organized church. I think his resistance to organized religion was actually because his faith was so strong. For him when faith is pure there was no need to soil it with someone else's interpretation. With my father as inspiration I often think that confusing religion with faith is one of the biggest mistakes we make in our spiritual thinking. Your faith can be very strong without ever going to a formal house of worship, just as your membership to a house of worship does not guarantee that your faith is true. When we act as if one requires the other—as in faith requires religion or religion requires faith—we belittle individual belief systems including our own faiths and religions. I am particularly sensitive to diversity of faiths, because my parents were of two different religions. While my father was a proud Christian, my mother was an equally proud Jew. She would never consider herself religious—in her mind that was for my dad. But having grown up Jewish in the South emboldened her faith, even if she doesn't admit to it. So it is never something she denies or takes for granted.

When it comes to matters of faith I definitely take after my father in that I am a woman who has faith but I choose not to worship in a formal house. For me one's faith does not have to be confined to a house—it is how you live. When I went off to college, one of the biggest adjustments I had to make was sitting down at the dining hall table for dinner and watching people eat without blessing their food. It was so engrained in my upbringing that my first dining hall dinner with a group of four students, strangers who would eventually become like family, I was frozen, actually concerned about the repercussions of eating at a table that was not blessed. Interestingly, that group that I ended up breaking bread with—two practicing Catholics, an AME Methodist, and an observant Conservative Jew—turned out to be some of the most observant students I came across over the next four years, never missing Sunday mass, temple, or church service, which stood out on our elite northeastern Ivy League campus, where religion was often hard to find. The point is, our belief system should not be judged by what is on the surface but what is in our soul. I had no right to make assumptions of my dinner companions, just as others have no right to do the same with me and the "nones." Only you know how true your faith is and how that faith informs your decisions in life. And if you truly have faith it shouldn't matter at all what is going on or not or how in the souls of others.

The rise in "nones" is interesting because it is a sign of our changing faith story. For instance, for the first time in history the United States does not have a Protestant majority in part thanks to the "nones."[6] Within the ranks of the unaffiliated the number of atheists has also been rising rapidly to include more than 13 million self-described atheists and agnostics, nearly 6 percent of the US public, the highest it has ever been since Pew started polling on such issues.[7] Perhaps not surprising, much of this increase is among young people. There are now 386 atheist student clubs across the United States, among those 48 of them are in high schools, up from just 12 high school atheist clubs less than three years ago.[8] Some have argued that the rapid rise in atheism makes it one of the fastest growing "religions."[9] Beware of assumptions when trying to figure out who all these atheists are. Black folks have a history of prominent atheists stretching back to Frederick Douglass. The civil rights movement is often remembered for the advocacy of the black church, but there was a significant population of black thinkers at the time who were drawn to atheism precisely because they couldn't believe that a God would allow such injustices to be waged against black people. Labor leader A. Philip Randolph came up with the idea for the March on Washington and stood by Martin Luther King Jr.'s side during the "I Have a Dream" speech, all while being a committed atheist. Langston Hughes was a very loud doubter of religion and so was Richard Wright. And who could forget Lorraine Hansberry's character Beneatha, the aspiring doctor in the partly autobiographical play *A Raisin in the Sun*: "God is just one idea I don't accept. . . . It's just that I get so tired of Him getting credit for all the things the human race achieves through its own stubborn effort. There simply is no blasted God! There is only man—and it's he who makes miracles!" Today, by many accounts, the African American atheist community, although still a minority, is growing significantly with outspoken atheist bloggers (Godless and Black, TheBlackAtheist, Black Woman Thinks), active Facebook groups, and black atheist organizations, including African Americans for Humanism, Black Nonbelievers, and Black Atheists of America, that now have meetings in almost every state. The biggest, African Americans for Humanism, which was founded in 1989 and has sixteen affiliate chapters across the United States, has boldly waged a billboard campaign across Dallas, New York, and Durham, touting black atheists during Black History Month.

While you can have faith without religion, what about faith without hope? There I think things get a little more complicated. By definition faith is the belief in something that you don't have to see, don't have to prove. Unfortunately, our understanding of faith has become a bit clouded, because typically those that speak out the loudest like to equate faith with the belief in their God, but the truly pious recognize and respect that there are all different forms of Faith and Gods. Meanwhile, hope is the desire for something to happen. On some level faith is the dismissal of the reality we can see, while hope is the desire for a new reality. Most assume that the two are connected—that you need one with the other. I think it is easier to see that hope needs faith. If you are wishing for something then you also believe that it can happen. Wishing is hope and believing is faith. It took me a little longer to see that faith also needs hope.

Although I teach college journalism, I am not a professor like John. Partly because my teaching is a part-time gig but mostly it is because I am a journalist through and through. My world is not campus—it is just a place I visit. It means when I am around young people on campus I still feel like I am looking in, reporting, and constantly comparing what I experience there to the real world, where I spend most of my week. I teach on a campus where the overwhelming majority of students are white and middle-class, and I go home to a neighborhood that is still majority black and lower- to working-class (even as it is starting to gentrify). I used to marvel at the contrast. And then one day I realized I wasn't marveling as much anymore. I started noticing that my students were sounding a lot like the guys on my corner. The two groups may use different slang and cadence, but the moods had merged. It was the hopelessness. Not that there wasn't good cause. This generation of young people is experiencing record unemployment and debt. According to the Center for American Progress, the slow economic recovery has hit America's youngest workers especially hard, and while the unemployment rate has fallen from its peak, more than 10 million young people under the age of twenty-five are not fully employed. My students are not immune. The unemployment rate for the youngest college graduates is 7.4 percent—twice the unemployment rate for college graduates in their thirties and early forties, who experience an unemployment rate of just 3.4 percent.[10] More disturbing, 5.8 million Americans ages 16 to 24, or 1 in 7 young people, are what economists dub as disconnected or not engaged in school or working, according to Measure of America, a project of the Social Science Research Council. That includes any type of training program or part-time work, too. While the disconnected technically may include some who are unemployed and searching for a job, because you have to be unemployed for at least a year to be considered disconnected, this group mostly covers those young people who have dropped out of the labor force entirely, giving up their employment search even if they want a job. In other words, 5.8 million young people are that hopeless.[11]

It occurred to me: when the Hope generation lost its hope, it was getting a dose of what it feels like to be black in this country. Or more specifically, what it feels like to be a young black underclass man in this country—those guys on my corner, or any corner in Black America—where being disconnected is a way of life. While the Measure of America 1 in 7 figure made national headlines, deeper in the report was another figure: the disconnected rate for young black men now stands at 1 in 5 not engaged in school or work. (Latinas were the next worse off, with the disconnected rate hovering slightly better than 1 in 5.)[12] Depending on what study you look at, that rate of disconnected black men has hovered worse than the 1 in 7 youth figure for more than a decade.

———

The connection between hopelessness and the inner city is not new. Cornel West is probably the most outspoken on what he sees as the nihilism that plagues Black America. Since then the concept has been so internalized that it serves as a stepping-stone for empowerment discussions even if we don't realize it. The thinking has manifested itself into the focus on black men as the way to uplift the community. The most recent was a *Newsweek* cover story under the headline "The Fight for Black Men." My pessimist side thinks "fight" is perhaps language too strong to describe the mode of Black America now.

Sometimes I think the biggest problem we have today is black folks have forgotten how to fight, but that is another conversation (see my Obama essay about complacency in the Politics chapter). However, I did find the focus on black men by such a mainstream media outlet interesting. It was an illustration of how mainstream the nihilism argument has become. As a result there are a lot of policies and programs, big and small, trying to "fix" black men. I say "fix" because it feels to me that often this help starts from the viewpoint that black manhood is some kind of disease that needs curing. I feel the same way when I see commercials for birth control pills that boast of the added benefits of virtually eliminating a woman's period, as if our menstrual cycle was a defect that we needed to be freed from. The same often goes for black men.* When we focus exclusively on one segment of a community as a way to uplift, we ignore that a community is made up of interlocking relationships—families. You can't just focus on one (family) member. Instead of acting as if black men are the cause and thus the solution of a community's issues, why not respect the community as a whole and focus on the family that it is.

Newsweek's cover story took readers on the depressing journey from slavery to Jim Crow to the War on Drugs and incarceration disparities. Personally I'm not a big fan of this type of victimhood journalism because it treats the problems of one community separate from the problems of the nation. Instead of our issue, all of us, it becomes their issue, whoever they are at the moment. (See John's Haters essay in the Race chapter.) Regardless, the underlying conversation in the *Newsweek* story was really the hopelessness pervasive to different degrees across the Black community. (In an interesting example of the crossover between hopelessness and faith, the author of the *Newsweek* cover story, Joshua DuBois, is not a journalist by training but a spiritual advisor to President Obama and the former head of the president's Office of Faith-Based and Neighborhood Partnerships, where he was known as the "pastor-in-chief.")

---

*Professor John tells me that this is called "the deficit model" of black masculinity and that it has a long academic history in the social sciences.

The response to the *Newsweek* cover was predictable. Believers nodded their heads and talked among themselves, agreeing loudly. The loudest nonbelievers ignored the piece, which was even easier than usual to do, since the "Black Men" cover ran barely six months after the print version of *Newsweek* stopped hitting newsstands. Economics forced the eighty-year-old magazine to be demoted to a purely digital format that, honestly, is struggling to be heard. This combination left reaction to the "Black Men" cover primarily online, ripe with its anonymous vitriol. Most people online were tired of what they saw as black boohooing. The story's emphasis on slavery as the root of all things that have gone wrong really didn't help much either. (The slavery angle particularly irked RLLEIGH, who forty-five minutes after the story went online posted a lengthy angry response in the comments section that stood out for its *lack* of racial slurs and grammatical mistakes. "It's pitiful how much energy the black community engages in trying to excuse the circumstances they have created for themselves," RLLEIGH opened. He then went on to emphatically stress how neither he nor his daddy nor his granddaddy nor his granddaddy's daddy nor his granddaddy's daddy's daddy owned slaves, which led him to end with something most of white America has come to agree with: "I for one am over it and done with it." The online cheers were deafening.) What is interesting about the *Newsweek* cover is that no one needs convincing of this hopelessness anymore. Our faith in it is that strong. Even the bombardment of backlash and hate messages in the comments section did not doubt the hopelessness factor of black men—they just didn't care.

My belief in the hopelessness has nothing to do with faith. I know it is there because I see it every day. I see it when I talk to people in my neighborhood who never venture out of our corner of Brooklyn, even though we are a short subway ride to Manhattan, where millions of visitors manage to venture to from every corner of the world. I see it from teenagers who get congratulations for surviving to eighteen. Or from young people who live for today because tomorrow may not come. I see it from the jobless (both those who were once employed and those who were never employed) who have retreated to the margins because they have no hope that they could ever find work. And I see it from the guys on the corner who have given up, otherwise they wouldn't always be on the corner.

That's the problem with hopelessness—it becomes self-destructive. That is why it is easy for so many not to care. As long as it is happening to them and not me it's all good. When I was a kid I remember the myth was that you could not dream that you are dying. The schoolyard logic went that if you are psychologically sound, you could never allow yourself to die even in a dream. So if in your dream you are falling out a window before splattering on the pavement your imagination will save you somehow—perhaps you grow wings in your dream or you turn into another person at the last minute or even wake up. The reasoning behind the myth was that our self-protective fight for life is so strong that it persists even in our dreams. My logical mind knows this can't be true, but I find the idea of such a mighty survival instinct comforting anyway. Now if you do a Google search about dying and dreams, you'll find the current myth around the schoolyard is not about whether or not it is possible to dream that you die but *when* you do indeed die in your dream will you then die in real life. Apparently that survival instinct is not as powerful as we thought it was. Now we are actually destroying ourselves in our dreams, too.

I spend a lot of time thinking and writing about our self-destructive behavior. Of course, no community has an exclusive claim on destroying themselves from within. That kind of stupidity crosses race and class lines. (If only that point could be shouted from the rooftops for all to hear like the Muslim call to prayer.) So while every community regardless of race or class can be ghetto, the difference is your race and class will determine how much that self-destructive behavior will entrap you. In addition, outside forces—deliberate or not—can never be dismissed for how they contribute to the downfall of a people. Often it is the outside forces that create the environment for the self-destructive behavior to develop and flourish. You can't blame one without the other, but it is what we do to ourselves that is an easier fix. Life is tough, in part because there are forces that can and will keep you down. There is no reason your own behavior should ever make it easier for the powers-that-be to stop you from climbing. I am old school (give me Aaron Hall and Guy over Robin Thicke any day) so this is something I tell my kids all the time. It is how you raise black children who will not just survive but succeed in the face of isms and obstacles. In fact, in our polite world I know me and my husband's parenting can sometimes sound harsh. For instance, my four-year-old loves to say things are unfair. If his older sister is swimming on her own and he's stuck with a floatie: No fair! If he isn't the first to get something, anything, from his toothbrush to a treat: No fair! If Daddy gets a bigger portion of rice at dinner: No fair! No fair! No fair! Such is the motto of a preschooler. For every No fair, my husband always tells my son the same thing: Life isn't fair! Upon hearing my husband's words, some parents turn their noses up at the playground as if we killed the tooth fairy. But then after each "life isn't fair!" we watch my son figure out how to overcome the situation. Learning to swim early, making sure he gets on line first for everything from his toothbrush to a treat, finishing his rice and asking for seconds so he can "get as much as Daddy." Interestingly, I recently caught myself giving the don't-make-it-easier advice to the white middle-class young folks in my classes. When you've lost hope it is easy to become self-destructive. It means I have students who give up. Not in the normal bad student sense but more of a worldview sense. They begin to accept that the obstacles they face today are (admittedly) bigger than recent generations might have faced, but they make the mistake and assume there is no way to overcome. Like the guys on the corner.

Even if our survival instinct is not strong enough to penetrate our dreams I still think the schoolyard myth from my youth was on to something. If you think about it, truly self-destructive behavior, the kind that comes when you have lost hope, can only be possible if there is no faith that life could be better.

———

What does society without faith look like? Atheists often point to Sweden or Norway and act like they have found a secular utopia. But those are countries without religion—that does not mean that they are people without faith. Because our faith is individual, the beliefs in something that cannot be proven, some argue that even atheists have a kind of faith. Their faith that there is no God can be just as strong and unwavering as those whose faith is certain that a God exists. Instead, if you are looking for a community that is truly without faith, you'd have to look at our inner cities, at the corners. That is where our hopelessness has become dysfunctional, which is a better sign that faith has been lost.

Black folks are often mistaken for the most faith-filled flock. But that is because we do religion more than anyone. Every major study finds that African Americans are markedly more religious than the US population as a whole. A 2009 study by the Pew Forum on Religion & Public Life found that nearly 8 in 10 African Americans, or 79 percent, said religion is very important in their lives, compared with 56 percent of the general US population. More than half of African Americans reported attending religious services at least once a week. Some scholars credit the historic importance of the black church—both politically and socially—to the hold that religion plays in African American lives. But even African Americans who don't go to traditional black churches still manage to out-church the rest of the congregation. Pew found that "across a wide variety of religious groups, black members are more likely than members of their faiths overall to say religion is very important to them." For instance, African Americans who are members of evangelical Protestant churches are significantly more likely than evangelicals overall to see religion as very important in their lives (89 percent vs. 79 percent). The difference is even greater among members of mainline Protestant churches. More than 3 in 4 African American members of mainline churches say religion is very important in their lives, compared with about half of all mainline Protestants. But again we have to keep in mind that faith and religion are two different things. We have seen plenty of godly men (from wife-beating ministers, embezzling pastors, and molesting priests) who do things that could only be possible if faith is wavering. So Black America has religion. Black women have religion.

Still, regardless of how many of us fill those pews on Sundays (or Saturdays, like John's former SDA flock), that doesn't mean a lot haven't still lost faith. That is the only way I can make sense of the nonsense that we are allowing to happen in our backyards. We no longer have faith that life could be any other way.

———

Perhaps it is my pessimist side that I see a world without faith every day. But I still believe it is my pessimism that personally makes me strong—preparing and overcoming. One of the proudest moments of my career was actually when I was still in grad school and my National Reporting professor, a very bigwig in the field who at the time was head of the Pulitzer Prize committee, pulled me aside about halfway through the semester for a heart-to-heart. He was holding a profile that I had written for class about Dr. Mindy Thompson Fullilove, who was doing groundbreaking research on AIDS and urban communities when it was still considered a gay disease. President Clinton had just named her to a national AIDS commission, and for some reason that I will never figure out, she gave me her first press interview after the news broke. That was my moment. Despite the National Reporting moniker of the class, no one else had managed to profile a national figure for the assignment, so I went into the meeting cloaked in young cockiness, waiting for what I was sure would be glowing praise. My professor did do some praising before the "but." "You do great work *but* . . ." and then his words I have never forgotten. "You do great work, but you seem to only write about African Americans. You are too good a journalist to stifle your career like that." Honestly, before that moment I hadn't really noticed. The beauty of a National Reporting class, I felt, was that anything going on in the nation was up for grabs. Besides the Fullilove profile, I can't remember any other stories that I wrote for a class twenty years ago, but I do remember thinking at that very moment how odd it was that the Fullilove piece was what pushed this professor to reach out with concern. All I could think of was, here was a profile of a national figure whom the president of the United States was talking about and newspapers around the country were scrambling to write about, and all my professor saw was a story about a black woman and so that made it less important. I never stopped writing about black folks. But the lesson I took away from that chat did prove to be the most important of my graduate experience: As a reporter it is my job not only to uncover stories but to make sure every reader understands that if we are indeed the world, then every story is also about them. Because RLLEIGH, who ranted "I for one am over it and done with it" in the *Newsweek* comments about the "Fight for Black Men" story, missed the point. When you have a segment of the population this large that is disconnected or disengaged, that has lost hope *and* faith, that is not a black people problem—that is an American problem. It means our nation is not living up to its potential.

I do find myself with an optimistic notion. Maybe now that a generation of white middle-class young folk have gotten a taste of what it feels like to be black in this country it will finally force everyone to care. I hope.

JOHN

Are black people still overchurched?

Sociologist E. Franklin Frazier once wrote passionately and pointedly about the claim that Black America was "overchurched," overrun by storefront operations, powerful mainline denominations, smooth-talking sermonizers, jack-legged preachers, and a whole lot more. This was the 1960s—just as black churches and their leaders were getting themselves mobilized as powerful institutional forces during the height of the civil rights movement. The question of whether or not blacks were overchurched was meant to hint at the idea (made famous by social theorists like Karl Marx) that religion is an "opiate of the masses," that it depoliticizes believers, keeping them docile and obedient to the powers that be.

And in certain circles, Christianity was considered particularly narcotic given its central role in Western justifications for transatlantic slavery and racial segregation. By some accounts, it is one of the major reasons why black people seemed unnaturally willing to accept their second-class citizenship (and before that, no citizenship at all) for so long. This unflattering characterization of Christianity was precisely why Islam offered itself up as such a powerful and urgent politicoreligious alternative to black folks in the 1960s. When Malcolm X and the Nation of Islam stood-in for the more confrontational (and less nonviolent) wing of the antiracism movement, they were riding a wave of assumptions about how and why Christianity could never free oppressed people, especially not with its talk of "turning the other cheek" and loving thy neighbor unconditionally. America had been a Christian nation for the entire time its citizens reveled in treating their fellow human beings as chattel (not lovable neighbors), and these Christians interpreted the Bible as an explicit ally in their white supremacist cause. Christianity, Malcolm X and others argued, had always been part of the problem.

But there is also a long history of political protest and activism fomented by religious devotion all across the globe, attempts at translating sacred beliefs into antiracist social and political practice, including Christian beliefs. In the United States, abolitionists used biblical passages to challenge the moral legitimacy of slavery. Anthropologist Roger Lancaster chronicles the place of "liberation theology" in Latin America to specifically demonstrate how incomplete and inaccurate any portrait of religion would be if it painted its subject as little more than an apolitical justification for quietism, conservatism, or socially reactionary ideologies. Religion, he argues, has long greased the wheel for progressive and anti-exploitative agendas, serving as a catalyst for radical political change and social justice.

Of course, you can't tell the story of America's civil rights struggle in the 1950s and 1960s without giving African American Christianity a major part to play in that tale. Historians have documented the many ways in which Christian doctrines (espoused with poetic vigor by the likes of Martin Luther King Jr.) and Christian institutions (as sites for planning nonviolent actions, assisting activists during protests, and disseminating key information to movement participants) served as the backbone of the mainstream civil rights movement. The black church seemed far from just an opiate by then.

Whether or not African Americans today are as religious as they were when Frazier wrote, or during the activism of the 1960s, whether or not they regularly attend churches as much as they once did, black people still pray an awful lot. At least the ones I know. And maybe more than just about any other group, especially if we are talking about public displays of piety. Praying at restaurants and cafés and stuff. It has long struck me as a little weird, but also amazingly common, even among black folks who don't otherwise seem particularly prone to broadcasting their religious commitments far and wide. They still pray—often quite publicly. And this is part of a larger trend.

We all know that black entertainers seem much more likely to thank God in public, right there on the red carpet, or when they are picking up some prestigious statue on stage: "I want to thank my Lord and Savior Jesus Christ, the most important person in my life. Thank you, Jesus." When Jesus gets mentioned, it is usually before any talk about agents or spouses or children or anyone else who helped them along the way, which makes sense. Might as well start at the top.

And it doesn't matter what the award is for. I'm sure that when black porn stars win awards for Best Blowjob or Hottest Three-way, they start their speeches the exact same way, with a public declaration of their faith: "Thank you, Jesus, without whom none of this would have been possible."

Even hip-hop artists known for lyrics about killing people, drug dealing, and sexual violence make a point of praying on their albums. DMX, for one, has entire songs that are simply prayers to God—in between bouts of paranoia, unremorseful gunplay, celebrations of drug dealing, and all kinds of graphic tales from his relationships with the ladies. And those interstitial prayers, truth be told, sound pretty heartfelt to me. Genuine. And DMX isn't nearly the only rapper who would make a point of thanking God or Jesus when he accepts his BET Music Award or Grammy. These entertainers are usually dismissed as hypocritical or even bizarre for doing so, but they are probably just a particularly egregious example of how much black people feel comfortable with (and invested in) testifying to others about their religious beliefs. They aren't hypocrites, they'd say, just honest enough to admit that they aren't angels all the time.

I think about this whenever I go out to lunch with my black students, either with graduate students or undergraduates, because of their disproportionate propensity for praying before we break bread. And by this point, I know to just assume that most of my black students will probably want to do so. Usually not in a very dramatic, let's-all-hold-hands-while-I-sermonize kind of way. More often, it's a subtle silence, five or seven seconds max, eyes closed and head bowed, before they come right back to our conversation, as though there had been no pause at all.

I am used to older black people breaking into prayer before meals, which made the practice seem like a generational thing to me. As one gets older and progressively frail, more years behind you than in front, it might make sense to start prioritizing conversations with God. One might be thinking more about mortality, wondering what comes next, doubling down on the belief that there is more life waiting on the other side of this one. I could see the entire thing even being a bit of a preoccupation at that point, and praying over a public meal might be the least of its manifestations.

But when I became a professor, I was surprised that so many of my young black students did it: prayed over their food in restaurants. The first few times this happened to me, students pausing to pray before our lunch meeting somewhere, I ended up suspended in mid-conversation, a fork or sandwich bite already in my mouth. I was caught so much by surprise that I didn't know the most appropriate way to respond. Clearly, I would stop talking, since I was usually, invariably, in the middle of some longwinded sentence, but was that enough? I experimented with all kinds of alternatives. Bowing my head right alongside them, with or without an apology. The apology, by the way, would have been for the fact that not only was I ostensibly a heathen who ate without giving thanks beforehand, but also because I realized, just about immediately, that sometimes someone would dip into a prayer extra quickly to make sure that they covered my eating with their entreaties, trying to begin before I got too far along—since they saw me reach for my fork. I had forced them into a rushed prayer. And after the first couple times of being surprised by student prayerfulness, I never again spit the food out of my mouth as part of my embarrassed response.

Once or twice a student has even asked me to take her hand, or just assumed I would do as much when both were extended, palms up, far enough across the table for me to grasp them. I find that the guys almost never do this one, usually choosing to pray without any bodily contact.

I am used to praying at particularly significant occasions—holidays and large family gatherings. Or whenever I visit my mom's house and stay for a meal. Those prayers would all be out loud, mostly succinct offerings aimed at expressing thanks for the food we were "about to receive" and for family in general. Amen. And that was different from the marathon prayers we would have during church services when I was a kid—or when we visited and prayed for the sick and shut-in as part of our church-based community service. Those were all inside the believer bubble where everyone was praying. We'd also do the "moment of silence" kind of things, which looked much more like the lunchtime pauses that my students sometimes take. But those were always moments one could prepare for—things to be expected. They were programmed into the ceremony. It was even announced ahead of time: "Let's have a moment of prayer for X." Then we could all bow our heads in unison. No surprise. No rush. No food spitting.

By now, of course, I readily expect prayer from my black students over lunch. I anticipate it. So much so, in fact, that I usually take notice on the rare occasion I have a first lunch with a student who doesn't pray. They are such a rare breed. Someone should probably study them.

Far more common are the black students who pray over, say, sandwiches and fries with their smiling professor. Sometimes, if we are really having an interesting conversation before we sit down to eat, it'll take me a few minutes to realize that I am effectively holding them hostage as they politely wait to eat until they can figure out a relatively inconspicuous and unobtrusive way to get their silent prayer on.

But I am also getting better at not just waiting on some of my students to say their premeal prayers, but instead explicitly prompting them to do it. "Do you want to pray?" I'll ask, smiling. And nine times out of ten they do, though I fear that a small proportion of those might be professor-pressured into doing it. Hard to tell.

I've gotten so confident that I can also just casually wait for students to make their moves. And they have so many different styles: the preemptive prayer, the head drop between clauses, the explicit request for a pause. Once, I waited so self-assuredly that it prompted a student to ask me if I wanted to do the praying *for* both of us, which I did, stage-whispering a few lines to God in a crowded Burger King.

If my students are in any way representative, I have one question: Why do black folks seem to pray so much more than everyone else? And what are they praying for? Even if my students aren't representative of anything except relatively elite black college kids, the basic question still stands: What's all this public praying about? Don't they see that just about nobody else is doing it?

I usually just end up doing what anthropologists sometimes do whenever we have questions. We ask other people to help us answer them. So, I asked my students. What were they praying for when they were at the lunch counter with me? Was it just about the food? Did they stick requests about other things in there, too? Maybe some major familial issue? A financial problem? And why did they feel the need to do it in public? Could they anticipate ever not doing it? Even more, did they do it around their white professors, too? Did they even go out to lunch with white professors? I feel like I almost never see that. And if they do get taken out to lunch by a white professor, where do those profs take them? Realizing that it is easy for me to get off-track, when I did query them, I stuck to the prayer thing as much as possible. And most people just told me that they'd never thought about it. That they had been praying over meals—any and all meals—for as long as they could remember.

"The real question," as one student playfully (and seriously) answered, "is why, if you grew up 'in the church,' you don't? That seems strange to me. What self-respecting black person raised in the church doesn't pray over food?"

I laughed. She did, too. But she actually wanted an answer.

"I'm shy," I finally said, "so I don't really try to draw extra attention to myself when I'm out in public. That's probably why I became an anthropologist, too. Because I prefer to listen to other people, to draw the attention to them—and off of me."

"And prayer is about drawing attention to God. So you should be all into that."

"Maybe if God were actually at the table," I said playfully. "And people saw something other than me looking like I'm talking to myself like a crazy person."

"That's it," she responded. "That's it! He's at the table. And people can see Him when they see you acknowledge His presence."

Another of my students swore up and down that any time he had ever asked God for anything in prayer he'd gotten it. "Every single time," he assured me. "God answers prayer."

With that kind of track record, I wanted to ask him to ramp up his requests a bit. How about cures for some diseases or even just a few years of world peace?

But then he reminded me that the answers come in God's time. Not his. So sometimes it can take a while, and his job is to be patient, to have faith. To know that the prayer is already answered, even before he sees the response. Even before he'd ever asked the question. God will also answer a different, better request than the one being made, he added, even if the supplicant isn't yet able to formulate it.

I always find folk theories on prayer very provocative, but science is also taking a crack at the subject. I've tried to keep up a little with some of this science on prayer, from the field of neurotheology, which examines how prayer might rewire the architecture of the brain, to randomized experiments on the actual impact of intercessory prayers on sick people. I could read those all day, whether they disprove the null hypothesis or not. I find prayer just fascinating. Everything about it, even if I don't do it nearly as often as my mother would like, or as my upbringing in the church should have inculcated.

I even taught a class a couple of years ago called "Spiritual Communication," which was something like "Introduction to the Anthropology of Religion" meets "Introduction to Communication." We examined some of the ways in which various societies think differently about how human beings can speak to sentient beings other than humans, such as angels, gods, demons, fairies, saints, and the dead. Although particulars differ from culture to culture, sanctioned and socially shared assumptions about humanity's ability to contact superior—or just radically different—entities is almost universal. And prayer is one of the most obvious examples of how some religions operationalize talking with God.

Part of me realizes that I don't pray as much as I could because it always feels a little bit like an act of desperation. Like you have given up on all your viable options and are just chucking up a Hail Mary pass into the end zone of life because you've exhausted all your legitimate moves. In many ways, that's the most and least anthropological way to think about prayer. Anthropologists who study religion, at least traditionally, often aren't themselves believers of the religions they study, and so their job is to be respectful of people's beliefs even as they try to make sense of them, using categories and concepts that might seem very foreign (and even offensive) to the believers themselves. In that context, it wouldn't be far-fetched to imagine that some mobilizations of prayer could be compellingly thought of as a way of keeping hope alive in spite of the fact that all reasonable courses of action seem impossible. Hope produced by hopelessness.

To detractors, praying is part of the problem, especially if it dissuades people from actually going after what they want. Like that old joke about a religious man drowning in the ocean, praying for God to save him, and waving off the rescue boats that pass by (as he waits for God). You pray instead of taking initiative and getting what you want. In the political context, it would mean praying to God for a new ruler, or just for the mean ruler to die (or turn over a kinder, gentler leaf), instead of taking up arms to fight back against despotism. It is the political equivalent of pathetic.

But if there is no way to fight and win, one doesn't want to lose faith completely, and prayer can keep the candle burning just a little bit longer. If anything is possible with prayer, there is always a chance of that last-second reprieve. Of a mini miracle. Prayer becomes that other "art of the possible"—and even of the impossible, at least potentially.

Of course, people who pray don't think of it as desperate. Or even an art. And they would be right, too. Prayer incorporated into your everyday life becomes just another part of your daily routine, a routinized act no more or less noteworthy, in some ways, than brushing one's teeth or walking the dog. Praying over lunch is no more dramatic than unfolding your napkin and placing it on your lap. That ritualistic incorporation of prayer into everyday life isn't the same thing as someone desperately getting baptized on his deathbed and praying with the minister or priest as he sees that bright light fast approaching.

Again, none of this is to say that blacks actually pray any more than whites do. I'm thinking of Cora's praying Yale classmates freshman year. And I'm sure if I hung out in white evangelical circles I would see many more displays of public prayer than whatever I glimpse of my students and other black folks in Philadelphia. I'd also probably see more of it if I were teaching at an evangelical college, which is part of the point. Academics, even seemingly religious ones, tend to be much less explicit and open about their religious beliefs (especially at elite and secular institutions), since being religious is often read as irrational and even silly in a world where the scientific method and reasoned analysis are kings. Think of the cottage industry that Christopher Hitchens, Bill Maher, Sam Harris, and others have helped to perpetuate that is organized completely around dismissing religionists as—at worst—crazy and dangerous. Even if my white colleagues are more religious (on some objectively verifiable scale) than any of my black students might be, they know not to broadcast that fact in the coffeehouse across the street from campus. It makes me actually think that something very empowering might be going on with these young black students who get the memo (about not carrying their religions on their sleeves within a certain radius of their university) and summarily disregard it. That does seem amazing to me, inspiring even.

But I still feel like I never know which version of things, powerful or pathetic, seems the best description of those who are young, prayerful, and black these days. In truth, I'd probably assume they are a little bit of both those things, which is aptly human. Besides, given all the craziness we see ourselves doing to one another in the world today, I can understand why somebody would think that *if we ever needed the Lord before,* as the gospel tune goes, *we sure do need Him now.*

POLITICS

JOHN

I could be a Republican.

Right-wing think tanks periodically complain about the number of registered "Democrats" in American universities. Full disclosure: I'm one of those registered Dems. By some counts, there are as many as five or six card-carrying Democrats for every one "Republican" in the humanities and social sciences. The concern is that these kinds of lopsided numbers produce an institutional bias against conservative opinions within academia—and against those scholars who hold them. Republicans, some claim, are actually being discriminated against. Nobody talks about it, they say, but it amounts to systematic intimidation and intolerance. Instead of complaining, most conservatives who overcome all the odds and make it into the academy supposedly just keep their political beliefs to themselves. Any hint of their R-word affiliations will get them demonized by liberal colleagues—and potentially attacked in student newspapers run by the undergraduates those liberals have already brainwashed.

Those on the "left" respond by suggesting, only half-jokingly, that most Republicans simply aren't smart enough for the academy. Or maybe they are too smart for it. Too smart to sign on for the relative poverty that a "life of the mind" often entails—instead, opting for jobs in the finance industry doing things like manipulating derivatives (at the entire planet's peril). Of course, there are many more Republicans in some academic fields than others. They probably give Dems a run for their money in disciplines like economics and political science. These are fields dominated by white men. They are also the most highly paid in the social sciences, as well as the most respected in the larger political and social world. President Obama has something like a football team–sized group of "economic advisors" that he consults on a regular basis, but he would probably be impeached if he had the same number of anthropologists or sociologists on retainer. Those two academic fields tend to have more women and minorities in them these days, and they are less uniformly committed to statistics and the methodological holy grail of random control trial experimentation.

I'm an anthropologist, and a person of color. And I got away with taking very little math in college, which is part of the reason why I'm an anthropologist and not an economist, but maybe I should change my political affiliation anyway. Why not be a Republican? Even just for a couple of years. What would I have to lose?

I know that some people might ask why I would want to affiliate with a political party that seems committed to discouraging African Americans from voting. But no matter how much more difficult they make it for African Americans to cast their ballots, it would still be hard for their newest—and unabashedly self-serving—antivoting regulations (penned and poised even before the Supreme Court's recent gutting of the Voting Rights Act) to disenfranchise me personally. Sure, Pennsylvania's Republicans would probably love to suppress the turnout in highly Democratic Philadelphia, where I live. Granted, the poor people of color across the country that they are trying to keep from the voting booths share some of my political positions. But maybe I could change those positions—at least some of them. It might be fun to see how "trickle-down economics" feels for size, to embrace it, to champion "small government" at all costs. But first the party would have to meet me halfway on some things, too. That would only be fair.

Like, what are we, me and my new Republican allies, going to do about the Tea Party's ascendency and all of their creepy "take back America" stuff? I can't help but think that some of them, a good percentage, want to take it back from the likes of me. And they seem to mean this literally. Guns already purchased (preferably without background checks) and ammo procured for the occasion. I have to admit, though, that far from taking America away from anybody else, I sometimes feel like I've only ever gotten a chance to gently rub some small portion of it from time to time, and always under the watchful eyes of its real owners.

But I might just be able to do this Republican thing, especially since I actually appreciate the initial spirit of the Second Amendment as Thomas Jefferson and the other founding fathers seemed to imagine it. I know what it is trying to defend against. It was a gamble, their notion of a democratic nation; who knew if it would work. Or for how long. More than 200 years hence, the jury seems to be in on whether this thing can work, at least as well as any of the other political alternatives. Besides, I don't trust my fellow citizens enough to think that I am in less danger with them armed than without. If I had to choose, especially given the unbridled xenophobia that usually seems to accompany populist and antigovernment sentiments of any and all kinds, I would probably want to make it more difficult for Americans to buy guns under the cover of darkness, without any restrictions or oversight (let them "bear arms" with knives, spears, and ballpeen hammers instead), and take my chances with governmental tyranny. There are purer versions of democracy to be sure, including those that would have 300,000,000 people occupying every crevice of the country. But I'll have to ask David Graeber more about how that would work the next time I see him. Could he really imagine us not being stuck with our watered-down and lobbyist-riddled incarnation of things?[1]

If I were a Republican, I would have to push back hard against the radio demagogues and antisocial types who use it as a ruse for other things, like selling their latest screed about how all Democrats should be drawn and quartered. Or about Obama's latest conspiratorial cover-up that is unprecedented in the history of all politics the world has ever known. I'd be a Steve Schmidt or Michael Steele Republican, more reasonable than not, even when trying to do my duty and tow the party line as a TV pundit. I remember when Steele was heading the Republican National Committee (RNC) (before they ran him out of there) and he made national headlines for agreeing with the claim that African Americans like himself, in positions of power, have "a slimmer margin of error" in America. Steele included President Obama in that category, which was met by a swift dismissal from the White House press secretary. That was nonsense—not even a Democratic White House could let that proposition stand. And it was unfathomable that Steele would endorse such a position, which is only one of the reasons why he was removed from his RNC post. Slim margin, indeed!

Of course, some might ask why I'd want to cavort with folks who seem to tolerate me, at best, and actively seek to marginalize me by some reasonable characterizations of things. Fair question. Well, for one thing, I buy the argument that having some serious black Republicans—who aren't bat-shit crazy—keeps the Dems more honest, but I'd have to tweak their Republican platform a bit, take out some of the fat and nonsense, even as I'd commit to backing various policies I've always found unappealing.

School vouchers? Cool. Let's do it. For everyone. We've already given up on public education for our major cities and the poorest Americans who live there. Why not just make it official and end public education completely? The slow bloodletting going on in places like Chicago and Philadelphia and just about every other big city in America is absurd. As I write this, Philadelphia is contemplating the idea of reducing each of its public schools to just a principal and a shorter roster of teachers than they have now. No security guards. No office staff. No nurses. Or did we get rid of them last year? Our kids' public school has started teaching all their grades "Singapore math," which tries to provide students with grounding in the intuitive logic that links the most basic mathematical ideas to the most advanced ones. Maybe we should make sure that state legislatures get retrained in this new system, too. Then they might be able to determine the logical outcome of all these draconian cuts to public education.

The GOP has already won the public school battle. And in spades. Many wealthy Americans are in the suburbs with their decidedly better-financed public schools—protected from the poor by the higher cost of living out there. And the wealthier urbanites, including the gentrifiers, huddle in a couple of good public schools or pay the mini college tuition it takes to send their kids to private ones.

I know that charter schools have a mixed track record, but let's do it. What the hell! Charter schools for everyone. It is part of the underlying orthodoxy: faith in the market as a social cure-all. Clearly, I believe in market forces. Heck, I even want to create a market for racial epithets (see the next chapter's "Nigger, please!" essay). But that has to mean that we first demonstrate our commitment to a fully inclusive version of the marketplace.

And if I were a Republican, I would probably do far less lionizing of Ronald Reagan than is the fashion these days. Cora and I both came of age in the Reagan era. And for better or worse, I probably owe the fact that I've never had a single puff of pot in my life to the "Just Say No" brainwashing of Nancy Reagan. That and the relative asceticism of a childhood in the Seventh-Day Adventist church: back then, no Christmas trees, no wedding rings, no movie theaters. Certainly no alcohol. So there were plenty more things to rebel against before I ever got to illegal drugs. But I am not a huge fan of Ronald Reagan. In fact, I still have nightmares about Lee Atwater and George H. W. Bush huddled over a spotlighted table in a dark and smoky war room coming up with that infamous Willie Horton ad in 1988. I know it wasn't an ad for Reagan's campaign, but since he was the incumbent at the time, and Bush was his vice president, he doesn't get a pass as far as I'm concerned. So, I am doubly suspicious of Reagan—both for the role his administration played in damping down my experimentation with marijuana and for Reagan's complicity in race-baiting politics. Instead, I'd be a reconstructed Lincoln Republican. I know Lincoln's stance on slavery was, as much as anything else, a calculated means to a federal end, but it was a good means. Even if slavery's days were already numbered because of changing global economic realities, there were still so many folks on the wrong side of history with that one. It did take some fight. And it meant saving the country from all those citizens who would rip it asunder to keep their slaves.

As a Lincoln Republican, I would be willing to stop taking it so personally when other Republicans spit all of their rhetorical vitriol at our first black president. It always strikes me as such a razor-thin cover for racist backlash. Racism with the tiniest layer of plausible deniability. You know black people and R-E-S-P-E-C-T. We kill people over feeling disrespected, don't we? And this unleashing of utter contempt and disrespect for Obama implies contempt and disrespect for all the country's darker citizens. If Obama is not qualified to be president, it is because he would never be qualified—and for reasons that only a magic fairy could fix.

Obama being deemed unqualified for his office always strikes me as a much more high-profile version of the assumptions that guide most of America's lucrative professions. In academia, the default assumption for many detractors is that if you're not a white male you couldn't possibly be qualified for your post. You must be an Affirmative Action baby.[2] You must not be as good as your white colleagues, who obviously got their jobs through pure, unadulterated merit. It is a powerful fantasy. Merit is always seasoned with structural and interpersonal bias. Who you know. Who knows you. Whenever I would write a particularly "controversial" post, back when I was blogging for *The Chronicle of Higher Education*, it would often be met with the categorical dismissal of affirmative action. I was only blogging for the *Chronicle* because of affirmative action. I didn't earn it (ostensibly, not as much as the other, whiter academic bloggers on the site). The same people who don't think Obama is qualified to be president are the ones who don't find it at all strange that blacks and Latinos are predominantly the people cleaning their offices or cooking their food in the company's cafeteria. That wouldn't strike them as strange. It is the natural order of things. I would have to be the kind of Republican who found that thinking odd, at least a little bit—this taken-for-granted assumption that whites would always be on top (or the only folks worthy of anything important) if some minorities weren't given unfair advantages. Isn't that very logic what got America in racial trouble to start with?

So, I don't want to hear anything else from my fellow Republicans about Obama being the worst president in American history. We may want changes to his policies, but we can't pretend that something more brain-stemmy isn't a factor when Republicans talk about the president in such wildly histrionic terms.

And let's cut the talk about him being a closeted Muslim (what would it say about us that he would have to keep it closeted?) or that he is secretly in cahoots with Al-Qaeda. I think I saw that on a FOX News lower-third crawl the other day. Or that he was the ghostwriter for Jeremiah Wright's sermons. Or that Obamacare is any different from classic Republican attempts to force citizens to pay for their own health care instead of burdening the entire society with uncollected emergency room costs. Between all of that, and the concerted attempt to demonize Michelle Obama for wanting schoolchildren to eat a little healthier (if she'd come out with "Just Say No" instead of Nancy Reagan, who doubts that we'd see Tea Party signs declaring "Just Say No to Just Say No's Communist Overreaching"), I would have to insist that my fellow Republicans stop acting like the sky must be red if Obama is saying it's blue.

And no more Antichrist accusations from the peanut gallery, even if it is still a little saner than the birth stuff. I know it seems like the weirdest and most fringe version of the anti-Obama contingent, but I think that we sometimes learn a lot from careful consideration of how the fringe helps to contain and constitute the social center. Plus, I grew up Seventh-Day Adventist, remember? I came of age talking about antichrists.

One of the most recent pop-cultural renditions of the Antichrist was the amazingly successful Left Behind book series written by Tim F. LaHaye and Jerry B. Jenkins. In that saga, Nicolae Carpathia is a politician and humanitarian who transcends race, politics, and religion to unite the planet, triumphantly ushering in world peace. He is a much-beloved celebrity—warm, charming, intelligent, handsome. He's good in front of a camera and more than capable as a tactician behind the scenes. He is a seductive and charismatic leader, and it is just such seductiveness and charisma that allows him to plot against the world without most people being the wiser.

By the time a few Christian renegades put all the pieces together about Nicolae, he has already lulled much of the planet into a daze, made everyone renounce the name of Jesus Christ, deemed the Bible hate speech, unleashed biological weapons as a pestilence to decimate his rivals, and sparked Armageddon.

Given Obama's celebrity appeal, charisma, and so far sex-scandal-less background, it is easy to see why some people might want to describe him as a sly and seductive serpent, our real-world Carpathia.

I first remember folks talking about Barack Obama as the Anti-christ way back in 2004, right after that year's Democratic National Convention. I was switching back and forth between CNN and FOX News, which I always do (maybe I've always been a Republi-can-in-training), and I found myself totally impressed by how con-sistently the FOX commentators had negative things to say about the performances of the Democrats who took the stage. It got so comical that at one point I remember thinking that even if God's very voice had been bellowing out of a burning bush positioned in front of the podium that night, the FOX commentators would have found a way to spin it.

"Oh, Jehovah doesn't have nearly the focus and self-confidence he seemed to display during Moses's day."

"There are some who say that these many centuries have taken a toll on the Almighty, his burning branches are less magical than they used to be, his commandments out of touch with modern life, his son more a political liability than anything else."

"When you listen to him, it just doesn't really seem like he wants to be the ruler of the universe anymore. It is like he is just going through the motions. And I know the American people can see that."

"We are still waiting on God's birth certificate. We aren't going to let him off the hook on that one, even if the liberal media won't follow this story. Where did He come from? The country has a right to know."

Then Obama came on, and everything changed. FOX isn't sup-posed to like Democrats, and their positive accolades about Obama seemed to delegitimize him a bit in some people's eyes, to cast a faint shadow on his luster that night. If he were really that much of a political threat, the argument goes, Republican-friendly FOX would hardly fawn over him so unabashedly. And I still wonder why they did it. Was it a miscalculation about his viability as a presidential candidate?

Of course, that has all changed by now. And if they could have foreseen him taking the nomination from Hillary, they might have treated him like all the other Democrats they criticized that night. Of course, he is worse than all of the others combined. The worst president ever! The worst Democrat ever! Not even a Democrat! He's a socialist!

It is like someone is trying to gaslight us. Make us all think we are crazy. Our lives simulations that others can re-program at their whim. And I can't help but think that shows like *America's Got Talent* and *American Idol*, where viewers call in and vote on winners, are massive experiments in collective mind control. You listen to the judges give their opinions and *then* you vote? There is some testable data there, no? Maybe that's me being paranoid. Or just stupid.

Speaking of which, if I join the Republican Party for a few years, they have to cut out the anti-intellectual thing. They can be against particular intellectuals and their ideas, even ideas they used to champion. I know that Obama's scholarly disposition is part of what rubs some "hardworking" Americans the wrong way. So, sure, be anti-intellectual. But don't be anti-intelligence. Science and reason aren't enemies that have betrayed us when they don't rubberstamp every single one of your cockamamie claims.

Maybe, if I become a Republican and embrace the positions I thought were so crazy all these years, I'd be more American. Sometimes, I feel so out of touch with my fellow citizens. I just watched an episode of *America's Got Talent* with several semifinalists from its most recent season. Levitation and synchronized swimming? Really? Maybe we should all be a little embarrassed. Not about those contestants, but about our elected ones. Perhaps being a Republican nowadays, embracing my inner Republicanness, means short-circuiting the embarrassment gene. It might demand having no shame, which can be, as I'm slowly learning, quite empowering.

CORA

It's time to rethink the American Dream.

"Until recently, I thought that there would never again be an opportunity to be involved with an industry as socially destructive and morally bankrupt as the subprime mortgage industry—I was wrong. The For-Profit Education Industry has proven equal to the task."[3]

—STEVE EISMAN, RENOWNED HEDGE FUND INVESTOR
INFAMOUS FOR MAKING BILLIONS BY PREDICTING THE
HOUSING CRISIS, DURING HIS TESTIMONY BEFORE THE
SENATE ON THE FOR-PROFIT EDUCATION SECTOR

It was Todd Bridges who got me thinking that we may need a new American Dream. The former child star of *Diff'rent Strokes* and former drug addict in life and the forever poster boy for how Hollywood can screw people up was talking to me from my television set. I am a product of the 1980s, so a Todd Bridges sighting will always be a moment to pause. And so I did, curious about the reason for his brief return to TV. He was talking about college.

Like an addict myself, it took all my willpower not to twist up my face and spit out at the screen, "What you talkin' 'bout, Willis?"—no matter how appropriate it was now.

Bridges was begging viewers to apply to ICDC College. For those uninitiated with daytime TV when ICDC's ads run rampant, ICDC is a for-profit institution that offers associate degrees online in a handful of programs that read like fieldwork for a prime-time lineup including Alcohol & Drug Counseling (the degree Bridges was peddling), Forensic Scientist, and even, of all things, Homeland Security. Now you too can get instruction in securing our borders and airports; responding to terrorist assaults; analyzing intelligence; and utilizing the latest security technology—all online. (Do we really want our "Homeland Security professionals" recruited with a "Log in and learn!" slogan?)

Is it just me, or is this not what college was supposed to be. I'm not picking on this school specifically—honestly, it could have been most schools. Instead, I'm talking about our attitude toward education. Those thirty seconds—a school's recruitment via TV, the two-year-degrees, the uber-specific subjects of study, the online campus, the promises of a fast, fast, fast degree—were like the perfect storm for all that needs fixing with our relationship to college these days. And as much as I love a good '80s pop culture sighting (thank you, ICDC), it is the morphing of what education has become in today's world that really gave me pause that day seeing Willis back on TV. Let's scratch that: forget pause. It sent shivers—the kind that can make my kinky hair stand straight—shooting up my body.

Here's what most people don't want to admit: not everyone should go to college. More important, not everyone *deserves* to go to college. And the get-educated-quick mentality that is taking hold (Log in and learn!) is just one sign that we have forgotten that college is not a right but a privilege. There's my thirty seconds.

To be fair, I am not the first to question the value of college. Interestingly, now that more Americans are finally going to college (as much as 60 percent,[4] according to some sources), more people are bashing college.* Of course, these college bashers have all gone to college themselves, myself included. Wouldn't it be nice if talking heads had to disclose their degrees and schools before mouthing off that college is not worth it? (I'll start. Yale BA, Columbia MS.)

The current wave of bashing is often coming from economists and

---

*Please note this stat is for US students enrolling in college, not graduating college.

the financial community, who see college as a bad investment. The argument is compelling. Forgive me as I hit you with a couple pages of numbers. In 2013, for the first time in history, student loan debt outpaced credit card debt, and by the end of 2014 it is expected to top $1 trillion.[5] The numbers guys argue that the amount of college debt that students are taking on—graduating with an average of $24,000[6]—cripples opportunity. Meaning, the average student will never make enough money to sustain the amount of debt it now takes to earn a degree.

Mark Kantrowitz, the publisher of FinAid.org and Fastweb.com who compiled the estimates most often used for student debt, gave the *New York Times* this sobering forecast: "In the coming years, a lot of people will still be paying off their student loans when it's time for their kids to go to college."[7] Scared yet? (By the way, Kantrowitz has two bachelor's degrees from MIT and a master's degree from Carnegie Mellon, in addition to having done graduate work toward a PhD at Carnegie Mellon.)

Even more sobering is that nationwide about half of all students who start four-year colleges do not graduate.[8] At community colleges, which now account for 2 out of every 5 undergrads[9], the graduation rate is even lower, at 22 percent.[10]

For college to make economic sense, financial planners have long advised that students should look at the debt they will incur to go to school like taking out a mortgage. Even though college debt (like a mortgage) is generally considered good debt, we all learned the hard way from the mortgage crisis that there is indeed such a thing as too much good debt. Therefore, financial planners preach that students should consider the careers they hope to go into when taking on debt. (John, an anthropology professor, is in a field that has recently been named as the worst college major, financialwise, on the planet. Graduates with a BA in anthropology are the lowest-paid new workers coming out of college and face higher unemployment rates.[11]) When most of us think about career earnings, we tend to focus on where we could end up salarywise, but when it comes to college loans we really need to be paying more attention to where we will be starting out. That's when you will be paying the bulk of your debt and thus be most at financial risk. Later on you may indeed be making much more money in your career, providing you don't lose your job when the economy tanks again (these things are cyclical, you know), but you will also probably have greater financial responsibilities—including family, house, health—when those salary jumps occur, which means the amount of college debt you can realistically handle does not change that much over time. The argument is nothing new—financial planning 101—but in the wake of the Great Recession the numbers guys are finally being heard.

So what does crippled opportunity look like? We are living in an age when there are more than 317,000 waiters and waitresses who have college degrees (including 8,000 who also have doctoral or professional degrees). There are also more than 107,000 janitors and more than 18,000 parking attendants all of whom have graduated from college, too.[12] In fact, there is a total of 17 million Americans with college degrees who are doing jobs that the federal Bureau of Labor Statistics says don't require college-degree-level skills, like waiting tables, cleaning toilets, and parking cars.[13]

We can thank the Center for College Affordability and Productivity (CCAP), an independent, nonprofit, DC-based education research center, for crunching the federal data to produce the wealth of underemployed data available. CCAP's college-is-too-expensive research is prolific, including a popular blog, making it the go-to source for the bad investment camp. It should be noted that despite the focus of the bulk of its research, the center bleeds university blood, being led by Richard K. Vedder (PhD, University of Illinois), a professor of economics at Ohio University, and the research staff is dominated by his Ohio University students.

Overall, employment rates for new college graduates have fallen sharply in the last two years. Starting salaries for those recent college grads who can find work has also dropped, dipping to $27,000 last year from $30,000 two years ago.[14] That is a decline of 10 percent, even before taking inflation into account.[15] And, yes, only half the jobs landed by new college graduates even require a college degree.[16]

No one grows up and wants to be underemployed. Those who start out at lower-paying jobs, even within their field, tend to never really make up the difference in terms of earnings, according to career experts. Not only are their career tracks delayed but, because of their traumatic introduction to the workforce, as workers they often take less risk, which further depresses earnings. (The easiest way to increase your salary is to take the risk of getting a new job.) But graduating from college and then having to work as a janitor is not only bad news for that guy but for all of us. In the long run, that aversion to risk or festering fear can hamper innovation and creativity for the entire generation. (Think Japan.*) More immediately, when college graduates are mopping floors it displaces less-educated workers who would normally take those jobs. Being educated and underemployed sucks, being uneducated and unemployed sucks more.

It would be easy for me to just end things there. But, as compelling as the numbers may be that college has become a waste of time for many, I'm not making a financial argument. Or rather *just* a numbers argument. For instance, you will never hear me argue that college should be reserved for only those that can afford it. Nothing is that simple. Instead, life has layers.

———

My husband and I both come from family histories that won't let us take college for granted. My husband is the first person in his family or extended family to earn a college degree (Yale BA, Columbia MD). Unfortunately he remains the only one. Neither his cousins, who were like the siblings he never had growing up, nor the children of his cousins or the children of his cousins' children (since baby making has replaced degree getting, we are already at that ring of family) have gone to college.

On my side, my first experience with college was going to classes

---

*Economists have had a field day studying the Great Deflation in Japan. A generation of deflation has created a culture of pessimism, fatalism, and reduced expectations. For more details read the *New York Times* series "The Great Deflation."

with my mother. She had dropped out of college after her freshman year because of financial reasons. A small-town Virginia gal, she then moved to New York City and started driving a taxicab when she met my father, also a cabdriver, and before she realized it, college quickly became another lifetime ago. Two kids and more than a decade later, she decided to go back to school while juggling work and family. During one summer semester at City College, when I was eight and my brother five, we sat at the back of the lecture hall during my mom's Intro to Cultural Anthropology class and her Black Lit class. My mom earned her BA that summer at the age of thirty-one. (For her final paper in that Anthro course we shared, she studied the culture of NYC cabdrivers.)

When my parents would argue (we were a financially struggling family, in cramped conditions, crowded with unfulfilled dreams, so yes, arguments were inevitable), it was her school notebooks that would get thrown. That is how powerful a degree can be. Still, despite the friction that my mom's school caused back in the day, my dad eventually tried to follow in her footsteps by returning to school in his sixties. Again, that is how powerful a degree can be. When my dad died suddenly at age sixty-seven, he was one of the newly enrolled students at Hunter College. My mom made sure that his college student status was mentioned in his eulogy.

With such family histories, college was never negotiable for me or my husband. It was always seen as the means—the only means—to a happy ending. For our families, like many, the opportunity to go to college is the definition of the American Dream. Part of being a parent, no matter what rung on the ladder you hail from, is hoping for more for your children. And for our parents the biggest "more" they could hope for was a college education. To be honest, I think that reality most shaped the type of people my husband and I each became. So to have evolved to this point, where I stand with fist-up pride to shout that not everyone deserves to go to college—it is like family treason. Even un-American. Black folks fought off dogs and hoses in the name of civil rights so I could go to any school. The opportunity of education is what still brings immigrants from far-off lands knocking on America's borders. This is what the Dream is made of. Everyone doesn't deserve to go to college? I say it because it's the truth.

What the money guys tend to miss in their college-is-too-expensive-to-be-worth-it number crunching is they are seeing college as just a means to a job and not a means of education. Likewise, what educators miss in their education-has-intangible-merits rebuttal is that such idealism is a rich man's argument. Only someone who has never had to worry about making a living could honestly dismiss the desire to support oneself from our relationship with college.

Instead, closer to the truth is, yes, the goal of college is to educate society *because* a better educated society will be more employable. And that is where reality sets in. College today is not educating our students on the basic level—challenging them to think. (Sorry, John, who has devoted his life to being a college professor.) Concerns that quality and standards—both of the institutions themselves and of the students—have gotten so bad within academia that a recent survey of college presidents found that just 19 percent believed the US system of higher education is currently the best in the world and only 7 percent believed it would be the best in the world ten years from now.[17] And it is because of that spiral of decline that employability disappears.

Honestly.

Therefore the debt that the financial guys are concerned about is not creating the problems, it is a repercussion of the problems. They like to say that the debt cripples graduates from becoming financially independent. But it is really the lack of a true education that cripples graduates from becoming financially independent, thus resulting in debt. There's a difference. The second option allows for people like me, someone who graduated with crazy debt. But because the institution that awarded my degree did its job and provided an education in the truest sense of the word, I always had the tools needed to secure jobs and manage my school loans. That is the very reason why college debt is often referred to as good debt because an assumption is made that it is an investment: the debt you will go into now will pay off financially later.

But what if it doesn't pay? What if it never pays? The mistake is to say that the investment in college was the bad investment. In essence that is what the money guys are saying. I am not ready to admit that truth. Instead, the bad investment was in the specific school or degree program—in other words, the type of education. Click and save! This does not mean everyone has to get an Ivy League education for the investment to be worth it. Nor should we, as a society, stop encouraging everyone to go to college. Dream, America. Dream. But promising poor families that *any* degree will help them climb up is just not true. And that is what the proliferation of for-profit schools, uber-specific degree programs, online degrees, and even two-year degrees are, in essence, doing. There is a fine line between encouragement and applauding everything. Just because there is a school that accepts you does not mean it is a good choice. So, yes, we are graduating more people than ever before, but the value of those degrees is becoming increasingly worthless.

And that is what makes it a lousy investment.

Now those who argue that, given such challenging current economic times, a degree, even a worthless degree, is better than no degree, do make a compelling point. All you have to do is roam through the streets of my struggling neighborhood of Bed-Stuy, Brooklyn, where only 14 percent of residents have a college degree,[18] and see how little a high school education will get you. But I'd argue that that thinking is also shortsighted. Consider the case of grade inflation, something that has been rampant on college campuses for more than a decade.[19] Such inflating of grades may help individual students get the GPA they need to move on to the immediate next step, succeeding in the course, but it does not help the entire class of students achieve meaningful success—big-time graduate degrees, big-time jobs, or even big-time learning—if everyone has the same worthlessly inflated college grades. Those who can stand out, after all, have a better chance of succeeding. Thus short-term gains don't matter without long-term success. The struggle we are seeing now is a societal one (the entire class). It is American society that is now having trouble succeeding. That is what worthless gets you.

———

"I wanted to do it but do it quick," says Charmaine in Boston.

"College?" I asked meekly. I wanted to make sure by "doing it" Charmaine and I were still talking about the same thing. Charmaine is a rapid-fire conversationalist, so topics and lingo had gone flying during our phone conversation, from daughters (we both have them), to too much work (ditto), to juggling, to starting her business, to not wasting time, to lack of sleep. (The latter a favorite topic for all mothers with young children.)

"I knew the four-year route was not for me," she shot back.

I interviewed Charmaine about a year ago for a magazine story that I was writing about working women who were also launching their own businesses in their free time. The magazine affectionately called these budding businesses "side hustles." I called these budding entrepreneurs, survivors. Charmaine didn't make the cut for the story, but our conversation stuck with me longer than many of those that I did write about. She was a young single mom, working full-time and trying to earn a college degree. Her side hustle was helping other unconventional students like herself speed through college.

"They call me the CLEP queen."

Not knowing exactly what CLEP was, I was again not sure how to respond, so I let the silence on the phone dangle. Before a panicked Google search for a definition could help, I had almost convinced myself that CLEP was slang for some disease out there that my old, married bones couldn't remember anymore, like crabs, the clap, or even cooties. CLEP queen? It turns out CLEP stands for College-Level Examination Program. It is a way to earn college credit by taking a test. Pitched by the College Board, which administers the exams, as a way to save time and money, CLEP allows you to test out of required coursework. This type of exam option (also including DANTES and ACT-PEP) was originally intended to help the most nontraditional students, like those returning to school after being in the workforce or military, by giving them credit for what they already knew. Instead, Charmaine, like today's new breed of students, was using CLEP more strategically.

"When I sign up for classes I also look for classes that I can test out of," she tells me. "Testing out is part of my game plan." Charmaine has CLEPed out of 14 credits, potentially cutting the time it would take her to get a degree in half. Now she was taking her CLEP success and turning it into a business. The business major's budding business coaches others on how to navigate the CLEP system, including strategic advice on what tests to take, scheduling exams, and tutoring—sharing her old testing books with anyone willing to study. She had created a highly organized flash card system for studying and basically taught herself how to beat the CLEP tests, discovering patterns in questions and scope. Her school was so proud of Charmaine's hustle it profiled her CLEP business as one of its success stories.

"I wanted the opportunity to provide for my daughter," Charmaine explained. "I wanted to do it but do it quick, get my degree and start earning money."

Hearing Charmaine's story, I was a bit conflicted. Her intentions were good, the best. For any parent, time is important. My own mother would not have been able to graduate in a reasonable time without getting credit for "life experience." But Charmaine, I think, has gone beyond the scope of intention of these credit tests, which is to get credit for what you already know. She was not getting rewarded for her life experience; she was getting rewarded for test experience. Instead of devoting time to studying coursework, she admittedly would rather devote that time to studying for the CLEP test so she did not have to do the coursework. That is how she was designing her course load and college experience.

Now a zealot of the test, she often proselytizes to the unconverted. One day in line at the grocery store, a cashier fed up with her dead-end job started crying. Charmaine admits she responded not with the typical encouragement to go back to school but instead to take CLEP tests so she could go back to school as little as possible. The cashier is now one of Charmaine's clients. Next, Charmaine plans to take her CLEP business into high schools. She thinks it is important that struggling high school students know that college can be as short as they want it to be.

"Most people think college is about getting an education; it is really about time management," she spouted out. "Why take four years if you can do it in two?"

I did not have a response for Charmaine. How could I find fault with a single mom going to school to try to create a better life for her daughter? Still, my heart felt there was something missing in her logic, even though my brain couldn't figure out what. Maybe CLEP *was* a disease—speed learning. Doing four years of school in two may not be the American Dream but it does seem to be inherently American.

My pet peeve when it comes to college is actually the two-year associate's degree. Community college, which now makes up the majority of the public higher education system,[20] is sold as the best way for unconventional students—those who are working, raising families, struggling financially, or even weighted down with weak academic backgrounds—to go to school. Ideally these students would be able to rack up credits more affordably and then transfer those credits to a four-year program. It is supposed to be the gateway degree to higher education, and it is why community colleges have been a focus of President Obama's higher education initiatives. John's own sister took advantage of a job perk where her employer even paid for her to go to community college. Instead, the two-year degree is the gateway to debt and false dreams. Rarely do these vulnerable students finish this degree in the promised two years, if they finish at all. (In John's sister's case her employer ran out of money before she could graduate.) In fact, 64 percent of enrolled students attend community colleges part-time, making it impossible for them to finish the degree on time.[21] A recent report from the College Board found that few graduates successfully go on to four-year programs because the credits are often incompatible and ineligible to transfer.[22] Instead, they are stuck with a degree, the associate's degree, which guarantees that they will remain at the bottom of the workplace pool. It means that a lot of time, effort, and money is wasted on a degree that won't help that much. Now this is the definition of a bad investment.

A recent report by the Century Foundation, a progressive think tank that does a lot of research on economic inequality, found that while more and more Americans go off to college, a tiered system of higher education has developed.[23] The elite or top-tiered colleges have become whiter and richer, while colleges at the bottom of selectivity, including the two-year community college system, have become dominated almost exclusively by poor black and Latino students, says the foundation.[24] On the elite campuses you are twenty-five times more likely to run into a rich kid than a poor kid.[25] A Georgetown University study of the class of 2010 echoes this reality, finding that at the country's 193 most selective colleges only 15 percent of entering freshmen came from the bottom half of the income distribution, while 67 percent came from the highest-earning fourth of the distribution.

The Dream is that college will increase your opportunities. The reality is opportunity is directly tied to the education tier that you end up in. The rates of those going to college are rising because parents are hoping that at the least their children won't lose ground and at the most are betting that status will be raised by getting a college degree. That is no longer true. Getting the college degree from the *right school* is what will raise your status. So those graduating from the top tier go on to much-higher-earning professional jobs, and those poor black and brown kids graduating from the bottom tier are being groomed for more narrow technical positions and a life of lower earnings. Or rather poor and black and brown kids are *still* being groomed for a life of lower earnings. The only difference now is that with the addition of associate's degrees, rather than just stopping with a high school diploma, these students are going into debt to stay on the bottom. (That is something community colleges never put in their brochures.)

Although the two-year degree option is often billed as the more affordable choice, now with the proliferation of associate degrees offered by for-profit schools (in the past ten years, the for-profit education industry has grown 5 to 10 times the historical rate of traditional postsecondary education[26]) *affordable* should be taken out of the discussion. "The for-profit model seeks to recruit those with the greatest financial need and put them in high-cost institutions," testified hedge fund manager Steve Eisman (his words open this essay) during a senate committee hearing.[27] Eisman is infamous for making billions by predicting the housing crisis and now argues that subprime has gone to college.

Students who borrow to attend for-profit colleges are especially likely to default. They make up about 12 percent of those enrolled in higher education, but almost half of those defaulting on student loans. According to the U.S. Department of Education, about a quarter of students at for-profit institutions defaulted on their student loans within three years of starting to repay them.[28]

Because of this the National Consumer Law Center (NCLC), a nonprofit advocacy organization that fights for economic stability of low-income people, has zeroed in on student loan debt and for-profit colleges. Reading the newspaper one morning, I was stopped in my tracks by the words of one of the organization's attorneys who counsels the poor: "About two-thirds of the people I see attended for-profits; most did not complete their program; and *no one* [the emphasis is mine] I have worked with has ever gotten a job in the field they were supposedly trained for," Deanne Loonin told the *New York Times*.[29] "For them, the negative mark on their credit report is the number one barrier to moving ahead in their lives. It doesn't just delay their ability to buy a house, it gets in the way of their employment prospects, their finding an apartment, almost anything they try to do." Loonin (Harvard BA, UC–Berkeley JD) is director of NCLC's Student Loan Borrower Assistance Project and has been spouting out bold truths about student loan debt for years, recently authoring the NCLC study *Piling It On: The Growth of Proprietary School Loans and the Consequences for Students*, which slams for-profit schools for their predatory lending to students.

It should also be noted that the "Is college worth it?" discussion often makes the mistake of never mixing for-profits and traditional educational institutions in the same sentence. There is this unspoken understanding that these are two distinct worlds, like calling the fry cook at McDonald's and the executive chef at a Zagat's starred restaurant both cooks. Intellectually it does make sense to separate the discussions of for-profit schools and traditional colleges because the purpose of one type of school is to make money while the other is to educate, making them by definition different entities. But they are still all called schools, and drawing a line between these institutions makes little sense since that is not how the public sees them. The ICDCs of the world are targeting the same student population as the local public community colleges. Often those students are not making a distinction that one is a for-profit entity and the other a public college. They are comparing more practical concerns, like what serves their needs best in terms of price, degrees, or time. In fact, the nation's largest university is not an Arizona State or a University of Texas or another respected extra big public institution. Instead, the school with the most students in the country is now the University of Phoenix, a for-profit online two-year institution à la ICDC that boasted almost 600,000 students at its height in 2010[30] and a graduation rate of just 9 percent.[31]

Therefore, dismissing an entire genre of schools from the discussion because we don't respect what they do makes the discussion impractical. Leave that for the academics.

Besides, the world of traditional higher education is not doing much better these days. Looking at the stats for income distribution at selective and nonselective colleges including public community colleges, economist Anthony Carnevale, one of the authors of the Century Foundation's Strivers study and director of the Georgetown University Center on Education and the Workforce, calls the current dual-college situation a "polarized" system. That is academic speak for a caste system. Rich white kids are being groomed for increasingly better jobs and poor black and brown kids will never get off the bottom rung because it has become almost impossible to jump tiers.

Add to that the rising student loan debt that the economists love to talk about and going to college in the bottom tier is indeed a sucker's bet—house always wins.

"We have built a dual system in America," Carnevale (Colby College BA, Syracuse University PhD) preached to the choir at the launch of the Strivers study before explaining about the professional higher-earning track and the rank-and-file track.[32] Much of Carnevale's research focuses on class, so the mere existence of classes doesn't concern him. Instead what does concern him about these two tracks is the *power* that comes with them. After years of studying class Carnevale, the economist, cannot see it in just economic terms anymore. People in professional jobs are not only higher earners but more empowered in their lives, he argues, having more power over their own selves on the job and over others. Meanwhile the rank-and-file jobs are stuck with middle-range income and little autonomy. "Everyone gets a vote in America but most of us get our power from the jobs that we do," says Carnevale. "It is a systemic issue now. Most Americans go on to postsecondary education. All the data we have says the way postsecondary education and training distributes is the way employment and occupations and earnings distribute, and therefore empowerment in society. And through education it can be passed on through one generation to another."[33]

Hear the American Dream crumbling? If this were one of Charles Schulz's comic strips, Lucy's therapist booth would be so profitable she would have hired someone else to spike the football for her. Rushing to join the celebration, Snoopy, Woodstock, and the rest of the Peanuts gang wouldn't even bother lifting their feet as they run over poor Charlie Brown, who, of course, would never be able to get off the ground. It is the lack of the ability to climb, which the Strivers report highlights, that makes today's America a caste-system state, no different than traditional India. Good grief.

For those of us who exist far from ivory towers, academic talk can be almost comical. There is a lack of emotion to the conversation that can make even the most devastating news—like America's caste system—seem unstartling. There was a little of that going on during the chitchat after Carnevale's lecture. There was no shock and awe. Still, even for this room full of academics the news came down to one simple question: "Who is allowed to enjoy the American Dream?"

I must give credit to Richard D. Kahlenberg (Harvard BA, Harvard JD), Senior Fellow at the Century Foundation, because he was the one who asked the question out loud that morning. As a journalist my job is to ask questions. Typically I am annoyed by the lack of questions asked in life. Rarely are there questions that I wished I had asked first. This was one of those exceptions. I had been complaining for years about how community colleges are a waste of time. Years ago at a panel discussion I took part in at New York University about black business issues I made the mistake of calling community colleges a scam, and the education circles I was mingling with that day acted as if I'd just dropped the F-bomb onstage. Or, given my bourgie audience, maybe the N-word.* More recently, to balance my emotional argument I decided to delve into the research, which is how I found the Strivers report. But admittedly I had not gotten to the crux of why the issue bothered me so much until that day I heard Kahlenberg's question. And that is when I finally woke up. (Shout-out to *School Daze*.)

Digest this truth: The reason that not everyone deserves to go to college is because dreams take work, otherwise they are just fantasies. Fantasies are fun, but by definition are the impossible. Dreams supposedly can happen. In this country, hard work is what we have always been taught is how to make dreams come true. So instead of routinely pushing some students into useless programs like the two-year degree, we need to raise our expectations and encourage all our students to strive for a true college education and nothing less. That also means being honest and accepting that not every student will get there. If we, as a society, start playing fairy godmother and grant dreams blindly—that is, creating enough spots that every student is accepted somewhere, regardless of merit—then the dreams themselves lose all their value. That is what is happening with the college degree—its value is becoming a fantasy. As a result, strivers—the American ability to climb higher with each generation—become impossible. For it is only an empowered education that has the potential

---

*Nigger, please! Have you not been reading? Community colleges are a scam, sucking cash out of desperate people for a useless degree that never takes the promised two years to get. House always wins, remember.

to beat down society's structural issues, including the entrapments of racial and economic segregation, as well as the embedded inequalities that such issues bring.

The thing is the American Dream is not truly about college or the house with the white picket fence. The American Dream is the ability *to dream*. That's what comes from living in a society with possibilities. And it's fading away.

That's what I'm talking 'bout, Willis.

JOHN

Obama makes whites whiter.

The election of Barack Obama in 2008 and his reelection in 2012 represent very real threats to a traditional version of American political life. Before him, it would have been absurd to imagine such a thing. A black president? Of what? Now, with the browning of America and those various shades of brown increasingly willing to come out to the polls (and seemingly all the more emboldened and determined by attempts to keep them away), the era of all-white—and, relatedly, all-male—national tickets is probably over. Romney tried but got thumped. One of the problems is that the contemporary Republican party, the one I would test-join, is also increasingly the party of entrenched and nostalgic white exclusivity, which is why they should imagine that they need people like me. But that doesn't seem to be the dominant assumption. Instead, the browner America becomes, the whiter the Republican party seems to get. Of course, one thing drives the other. It is the fear of losing a nostalgic "apple pie" notion of Americana to an increasingly unrecognizable and multicultural horde (with weird religions, clothes, skin tones, and accents) that has created the populist backlash against a special-interest government that is dismissed as nothing more than a welfare state for the undeserving (and disproportionately dark?) 47 percent.

It is naïve to think that Obama doesn't represent the beginning of the end to a certain unremarked-upon version of white privilege, but premature to assume that this newly imaginable end is already here.

We haven't yet created a fully meritocratic multiracial democracy that is fair for all. The past is the present's stepladder, and it would take a long time to climb down from that crooked and compromised pedestal as we attempt to counteract the institutional and psychological effects of long-term white supremacy. Take South Africa. The country's political apparatus has been wrenched from the hands of the Afrikaners, the erstwhile leaders of that nation. With the end of apartheid in the last decade of the last century, free elections brought about a massive change in the racial makeup of elected officials. The government is now almost completely controlled by blacks. When the Nationalist party took office in 1948, formalizing the law of apartheid, they took their political power very seriously, using it to create wealth for white South Africans at the expense of everyone else. Although that nation's political machinery has changed hands, real economic power still separates whites from blacks over there. Unless black South Africans pull a Robert Mugabe and try to physically seize white wealth by force and political fiat (which was unthinkable with Mandela alive, and probably still even after his death), Afrikaners will continue to hold on to a form of power—linked to wealth—that blacks cannot access. And that makes the nation's boasts about having peacefully and quickly achieved a fair and just multiracial democracy less than wholly satisfying.

In America, white people are still the majority for a little while longer, but they know what is coming. They've heard the projections. Latinos will outnumber them after a few more Olympics, and that shift has already taken place in states like California. People often want to talk about the election of Obama as a form of racial transcendence. As a demonstration of how much America has changed. America has, but many Americans haven't.

If it were up to whites, we would have gotten McCain and Palin in 2008, not the first black president. Obama won just about every single demographic, except whites. That is deep. It was the O. J. Simpson verdict of our political system. The Rodney King trial. When blacks and whites are calling sociopolitical balls and strikes, they seem to have mutually exclusive strike zones. And for some whites, there is not a single pitch any black could throw that would ever be a strike under any circumstances, no matter where it flew over the plate.

But many whites see the demographic writing on the wall. And that has emboldened some of them to invest in their whiteness more unapologetically. Of course, since the 1960s we've gotten very good at invoking race without explicitly saying anything racial. At being racist without many of its traditional accoutrements: white-sheeted, public pronouncements about black animality and inferiority; separate, color-coded toilets. And reactionary whites have become the heirs apparent of Martin Luther King's color-blind rhetoric. Blacks see race. Whites ostensibly don't, or at least not in mixed company. One paradox of race in America today is that racists have had to learn a way to be racist without providing open-and-shut evidence. And even when it is open and shut, they deny and wriggle out, instead of just holding their ground. A football player calls someone a nigger (in a rage) at a concert and claims that he never uses the N-word and isn't a racist person. He wasn't raised that way. His parents taught him better than that. And his first order of business is to apologize to his black teammates, many of whom say that they don't think he's a racist, and then he goes to therapy.

But that's now. Back in the day, the N-word was like saying "good morning" or "rise and shine." And not too long ago.

I want to make a prediction. Even if we imagine racism transcended in another generation or two, eliminated in the coming years, we will still have more racist conflicts, not less. Darkest before the possibility of dawn?

The argument for less racism is fair enough. The younger generation doesn't have the baggage of the pre–civil rights era to contend with. Hell, they don't even know what happened in the 1990s. At least not firsthand. Let alone the exotic, seemingly foreign racisms of Bull Connor and Jesse Helms. Sure, we have neo-Nazi skinheads, and the angst and anger of their rock music is like a Pied Piper's serenade for some young people. But that isn't mainstream America. That isn't a sitting governor demanding that blacks not go to school with his state's white children over and against the protection and orders of the president and the National Guard. And it's still backwoods stuff. Not on the steps of the Capitol. Or in its main office. Not without denials and defensiveness. But people don't want to talk about whites feeling defensive or under siege. They want to talk about "white guilt."

Some scholars argue that Obama got the nod because of white guilt. That the Obama era is all about the power of white guilt. Again, the majority of whites didn't feel guilty enough to vote Obama into office in 2008 or 2012 (black and brown Americans did), but many critics invoke white guilt as a major driving force anyway. But is "white guilt" really real?

Slavoj Žižek thinks so. The Slovenian political philosopher (once dubbed "the most dangerous philosopher in the West" by the *New Republic* and "the Elvis of cultural theory" by *The Chronicle of Higher Education*) has written a communist manifesto, *First As Tragedy, Then As Farce,* challenging contemporary interpretations of 9/11 and of the 2008 global financial meltdown that still has everyone reeling—and so many people out of work.[34] I won't try to capture all the nuances of his ambitious and disturbing work, but I will give you my version of its punch line: that only what Žižek calls "a dictatorship of the proletariat" can make up for the limitations and exclusions that define capitalism (and liberalism and socialism) in all of their various guises. In other words, he is an unabashed communist, which probably also means (in the minds of some) that he must have some personal tie to President Obama.

Far from being a threat to capitalism's undeniable ubiquity and unchallenged global hegemony (as some Leftists attempt to interpret things), Žižek sees the current global recession as potentially clearing the way for even more ramped-up and utopian capitalist commitments. He also frames it as the context/pretext for intensified tensions between "democracy" (as a political system) and "capitalism" (as an economic formation). What if "capitalism with Asian values" (i.e., the invisible hand of the free market tightly clasped by an iron fist of totalitarianism) proves to be a more efficient and effective way to capitalize on the fundamental logic of capitalism? What if China can have its antidemocracy and impressive economic growth at the same time? What if it can exploit its complicated and competitive interdependency with the United States to outpace its "cool war" adversary in Africa and all around the world?[35] This is another version of the end of white power, some might say, just on a global scale instead of just a national one.

French historian Pierre Rosanvallon claims that Scottish Enlightenment thinker Adam Smith was, in effect, arguing for "the withering away of politics," theorizing the emergence of a free market system that could potentially govern all of social life (rationally and fairly) without recourse to merely political concerns and considerations.[36] It's the economy, stupid! Anything else is just smoke and mirrors. That is still considered the most powerful explanation for how the world turns, which is why Obama has all those economic advisors.

As part of his argument against capitalism's intrinsic excesses, Žižek rails against the pathetic hubris of "white guilt," which he labels "an inverted form of clinging to one's superiority." White guilt is real, he says, but it is also a bit disingenuous. Quoting from a section of activist psychoanalyst Frantz Fanon's *Black Skin, White Masks*, a classic in anticolonial literature, Žižek talks about Fanon's supposed "refusal to capitalize on the guilt of the colonizers." And Žižek demands that Americans follow suit, that we inoculate ourselves from the seductive sickness of "identity politics" in all its forms (race, gender, sexuality, religion, and so on).

To be fair, this discussion about white guilt is little more than a memorable aside for Žižek, a drive-by theoretical shooting along a tiny stretch of the much longer highway that eventually leads him home to the communist ideal, the idea that communist principles are not dead and buried, despite what everyone might say. It is the same claim that the Occupy Movement tried to make—and demonstrate—in its leaderless outdoor protests all around the world. But I do find it fascinating (and maybe a little gratuitous) that he would seem to go way out of his rhetorical way to lament white guilt as a particularly heinous (and self-evident) form of identity politics today.

Any real discussion of "white guilt," however, would have to talk about Shelby Steele, the poster child for reasoned and longstanding black criticism of affirmative action.[37] For Steele, white guilt isn't an aside in a larger argument about the continued value of communist thought in an increasingly vulnerable economic world. Steele positions white guilt as one of America's central dilemmas. His book on the subject, *White Guilt: How Blacks and Whites Together Destroyed the Promise of the Civil Rights Era*, argues that "white guilt is quite literally the same thing as black power," the reduction of moral authority to a zero-sum game between blacks and whites, wherein what was once the stigma of race becomes the new stigma of racism. The more guilty whites feel about race/racism, the more empowered blacks are to use accusations of racism (and invocations of America's racist history) as a disciplining rod, a whipping stick. Steele cautions against the lure of white guilt: for blacks, as a form of political capital; for whites, as a performance of social penance.

To hear Steele describe it, white guilt sounds like a social reality that overdetermines contemporary American life (and maybe not just the parts that have anything to do with racial issues). White guilt gets cast as the overarching organizing principle for race relations, but is that true? Does white guilt explain the central dynamics of contemporary interracial exchanges?

In Steele's version of things, "playing the race card" is political slang for attempting to exploit forms of white guilt. Every minor slight is met with righteous indignation and some contorted logic for how it pivots on the same pulley as antebellum slavery. The boss chides me for coming in late to work. Well, I'll show him.

"Excuse me, I just want to let you know that I was late because I take public transportation from the other side of the city, and someone had gotten shot on the bus, right across from me, and the police held us there while the ambulance carted off the body. So, I am sorry I was late, but I don't own a car like some people in the office. Though I will say that at least I can ride at the front of that bus now. My mother wasn't so lucky."

Maybe that's a little over the top, or not, but basically Steele says that blacks have developed the habit of much more subtly doing a version of just this. Not only will the boss be made to feel bad and apologize. He might even spring for a company car. Or at least sub-sidize monthly bus passes.

In Steele's formulation, affirmative action mostly gets dismissed as a policy predicated on misguided efforts to manage and minimize white guilt. If we let some blacks into the school who aren't really that qualified in terms of test scores or overall academic training, we can show how magnanimously nonracist we are.

But is "white guilt" really such an incredible driving force in American society? I mean, any more so than, say, what we might call middle-class guilt (vis-à-vis poor people)? Or heterosexual guilt (vis-à-vis homosexuals)? Or even, say, Christian guilt (vis-à-vis Muslims)? What manner of "guilt" is this? And does it make sense to offer it up as the central explanatory framework for our contemporary moment?

The Tea Party might demonstrate something very different from what Steele and Žižek highlight. White guilt doesn't seem to define the ethos behind the Tea Party's push. So many critics characterize them as reactionary and racist—as anti-Obama because they are an-tiblack. And relatively unapologetic about it, even if they continue to hide behind euphemistic proxies for the word "nigger." At least most of the time. Self-professed Tea Partiers take offense at being called racist, and they also seem to display a decided lack of interest, one way or the other, let alone guilt, about America's racial history. Kha-dijah White, a communication studies scholar at Rutgers University, argues that the Tea Party is actually very good at trying to make other people feel guilty for calling them racist.

But we don't have to make this just about the Tea Party. They are more like canaries in the coal mine, potential indications of where America might be headed.

Even though most white Americans aren't self-professed Tea Party types, and many are thoughtful about America's racial history and their gains from it, the browning of America may have the effect of actually making white people much more comfortable with the idea that they are simply one more interest group among many. The old model where whites were unmarked, uncolored, and universal, and where everyone else was a marked and specific interest group, may lose ground to a version that says we can talk about defending our identity and interests (which just happen to be white) just like every-body else. The logic behind the legal push to challenge the constitu-tionality of affirmative action (by having white students sue schools that don't admit them, schools using race as some kind of substantive criterion in the selection process) is basically that argument. The rhetoric is subtler, of course. It is about color-blindness and the ille-gitimacy of racial quotas. But as the country browns and as whites lose more and more exclusive control of entrance into America's most powerful institutions, it will start to feel like more of their children are losing out on what they have long taken for granted. And they'd be right. If you've traditionally had your fill of almost the entire apple pie, and someone is saying we have to cut the pieces in a more equi-table fashion, it means that you are going to get less pie, no matter how you slice it. Now, maybe you didn't need all that pie to begin with, but why should someone be allowed to take it away from you? And depending on how small your piece gets, maybe there won't be enough. Who knows? Fear mounts.

Personally, I don't think that white guilt is the most important thing to look out for in America's current racial landscape. Maybe a powerful film or book can provoke a pang of sadness, humanizing the past in ways that are poignant and real. And I wouldn't argue that white Americans never, ever reflect on how or why underrepresented minorities are so underrepresented in elite spheres. But is it really accurate to claim that "white guilt" haunts the American psyche in some central and fundamental way? In fact, people are increasingly willing to invoke bad genes or the "culture of poverty" or almost any-thing else (over and against America's sordid racial history) to explain contemporary racial disparities in education and employment. That seems like a powerful antiguilt move.

When he first got elected, some pundits predicted that many of Obama's detractors would be extra careful about deploying their political rhetoric so that they wouldn't find themselves described as racist, bowing to some of the mandates of a politically corrected public sphere. They got that one wrong. Critics have no qualms at all about attacking America's first black president with everything they have. Some are even actively trying to foment revolution. Sitting governors in the South are giving lip service to the idea of secession. And none of them seem to feel particularly guilty about that, either.

Of course, Steele and Žižek were talking more about liberals than conservatives. But no matter how you frame it, I doubt that "white guilt" is as big a problem as these cultural critics make it out to be. If anything, the election of President Obama might be ushering in an era of "white rage" that will only increase as white privilege's symbolic power (more quickly than its actual power) shrinks. It is easy to be liberal and generous when the slicing of the pie still works in your favor, when it isn't much thinner than it used to be. But the demand for pie from many quarters will only increase throughout the twenty-first century, and control over its distribution could get harder and harder to monopolize.

Obama is a harbinger of thinner pie pieces to come for white America. And his reelection, even with a faltering economy, indicates just how steady the march has become.

One way to guide this transition from a white to a browner America is to try to find all the ways we possibly can to make sure that our citizens are connected to one another in some kind of organic way. Sociologist Émile Durkheim once made the distinction between what he called organic and mechanical forms of solidarity. Societies with mechanical solidarity aren't as intricately integrated.[38] The metaphor of the organism is supposed to highlight the fact that "advanced" societies, like organs in a body, are carved up into subgroups that have specific functions. Each organ has its role to play—and all of those roles are necessary if the organism intends to stay alive. When the heart stops, it doesn't matter how efficiently the kidneys could keep working; the subject is dead. Organic solidarity is about that kind of mutually dependent relationship. Mechanical solidarity, however, isn't that interdependent. It is as though every component of the social group is fully self-sustaining. Collaborating is a luxury, maybe even a distraction, but not a necessity.

American slavery made relationships between blacks and whites organic, but on terms that were much more beneficial to one group than the other. All contemporary societies are organic by Durkheim's standards. We are all fundamentally interconnected. Increasingly, the globe is becoming more organically interconnected, as the recent global recession helped to demonstrate so dramatically. As whites lose more of their traditional share of say in America's future, what kind of organism will the nation become? If the idea is to think that blacks and Latinos represent foreign tissue, viruses in the American body politic that need to be eradicated, we are in big trouble.

What kinds of whites will white Americans become in a browner nation? There are many options. Anthropologist John Hartigan's work in Detroit is all about the specifics of whiteness and white people. There are different shades of white, he argues, and Obama's election has helped to catalyze the process of rethinking what white people are in America—and how they see their links to everyone else.[39] Now, this doesn't mean whites are relegated to simulating black and brown culture. But it does demand, as others have argued, a divestment in the safety of white privilege.[40] They can do that with gentle dignity, as some will. Or kicking and screaming. (Obama's election has elicited a lot of the latter from some quarters.)

After the initial shock has worn off, if white Americans are able to see their relative disempowerment, slow and steady as it may be, as something other than the end of the world, maybe we are talking about an America the better for its whiter white citizenry. The beginning of the end of white power and privilege is an invitation. And I would welcome a whiteness that can speak its own name without hateful yelling or the gnashing of teeth.

CORA

I don't care about first black presidents.

Let's start off by saying I don't like writing about politics. Part of me finds something pointless about it, because it is hard to make people think when it comes to politics, and you certainly don't change opinions, especially not these days. That is because while we try to act like politics is a cerebral or logical exercise—logical enough to have round table discussions, news analysis, talking heads—politics is really all about emotion. Politics is like the middle-aged white guys' version of teenage girl talk. Or at least what Hollywood envisions teenage girls are talking about when they create plots of asinine swooning about love and lust as if there was nothing else the female sex had to talk about. (If only they knew how much more we talk about.) Matters of the heart are accepted as emotional territory. Since they are not expected to make sense, things like "he's the one" and "at first sight" are not seen as punch lines but as aspirations. What makes love talk so unbearable to me is that there is nothing really to talk about. In the end emotion is going to be the deciding factor. Politics is the same way. Even the talking heads who try to make politics sound as logical as possible and steep their chitchat in data and historical analysis to prove how smart they are will also admit that emotion comes into play when people vote. Likability can decide elections, and there is nothing logical about that. The most heated arguments that I have with my mother all have to do with politics. And we actually sit on the same side of the political aisle. That doesn't stop us every election

147

(local, state, or national) from bickering over candidates and policy like schoolgirls. So politics is not my favorite topic to write about because I don't like that charade that goes on where people act like it is thoughtful, serious talk when we are really engaged in "he's the one" emotion. It has been why I have been reluctant to write an "Obama essay" for this collection. Therefore this "Obama essay" is not about politics. It's about good sense.

I never expected to see a black president in my lifetime. Some might argue that says more about me than it does about anything else, because in the scheme of the nation's racial story my New Yorker/fortyish/post–civil-rights/hip-hop-generation bones have not had it that bad for me to be so racially cynical. I must admit that occasionally I am a bit embarrassed by my racial cynicism considering how far we have come. It almost feels disrespectful to the shoulders I stand on and the benefits I am allowed because of those who came before. Still, sometimes when President Obama is giving a big, televised speech I have caught myself, for a moment, pinching myself in total disbelief that I am living through that moment. Then I catch my husband and he is pinching himself too, for a moment. So now I don't think it has anything to do with me. Instead, our can't-believe-it momentary rush speaks to just how screwed up our national race story still is, that despite all the progress we have benefited from we still cannot envision the reality we live today. That's when I stop being embarrassed. Instead of being in awe all the time of how far we have overcome we need to be more outraged by how far there is still left to go.

Now that President Obama rounds out his second (pinch! pinch!) term, there has been a lot of political blathering as to whether our first black president was good for Black America, considering that the economic gap between blacks and whites has grown during his presidency and that black unemployment, poverty, and foreclosure rates reached their highest levels in a decade. When NAACP president Ben Jealous waded into this ongoing discussion, his criticism went viral. Well, sort of. What Jealous said was this: "The country's back to pretty much where it was when this president started," Jealous told host David Gregory on *Meet the Press* in January 2013.

"White people in this country are doing a bit better. Black people are doing a *full point* worse."[41] Thanks to the shoddy journalism of the (conservative-leaning) *Washington Times*, which published a brief, 330-word story about Jealous's comments but didn't manage to quote the comments correctly, most people thought he said at the end of his statement: "Black people are doing *far* worse."[42] The misquoted "far worse" went viral, spinning over and over again in the political blogosphere from black psssst-let-me-tell-you-somethin' chatter to conservative yelling and everyone in between. I'm reminded of high school girl talk again: "She said what?" "Who said what?" "She said." "She said." "She said."

Call me cynical, but I find myself thinking more and more that the question is not whether Barack Obama was good or not good for Black America but whether electing our first black president might have been the worst thing for black folks, period. One of the side effects of opening the door is people start to relax. It is natural to think the hard part is over and thus become complacent. It is bad enough to be *far worse* off or rather a "full point worse." But what is even worse than that is that too many of us are not outraged by it. Sometimes there is nothing wrong with being the angry black man or woman.

One of the best of the blatherers, Gary Younge, a black British journalist who covers American politics, astutely wrote in *The Nation:* "Obama should do more for black people—not because he is black but because black people are the citizens suffering most. Black people have every right to make demands on Obama—not because he's black but because they gave him a greater percentage of their votes than any other group, and he owes his presidency to them. *Like any president, he should be constantly pressured to put the issue of racial injustice front and center.*"[43] (The italics are mine.)

Younge is really talking about the lack of outrage. I miss our outrage. Even the reality of a first black president does not erase the hurdles and inequalities that still need to be overcome. That's why this essay is not about politics. It is about life. It is about equality in all our moments.

Martin Luther King Jr. actually warned us about complacency—

both black and white—in his *Letter from a Birmingham Jail,* written in 1963.

Complacency in white:

> I must confess that over the past few years I have been gravely disappointed with the white moderate. I have almost reached the regrettable conclusion that the Negro's great stumbling block in his stride toward freedom is not the White Citizen's Counciler or the Ku Klux Klanner, but the white moderate, who is more devoted to "order" than to justice; who prefers a negative peace which is the absence of tension to a positive peace which is the presence of justice. . . . Shallow understanding from people of good will is more frustrating than absolute misunderstanding from people of ill will. Lukewarm acceptance is much more bewildering than outright rejection.

Complacency in black:

> I stand in the middle of two opposing forces in the Negro community. One is a force of complacency, made up in part of Negroes who, as a result of long years of oppression, are so drained of self-respect and a sense of "somebodiness" that they have adjusted to segregation; and in part of a few middle-class Negroes who, because of a degree of academic and economic security and because in some ways they profit by segregation, have become insensitive to the problems of the masses. The other force is one of bitterness and hatred, and it comes perilously close to advocating violence.

King's world was black and white so that is the complacency he talked about on the surface. But the fact that he talked about complacency in white and black, his entire world, is a lesson that each of us, no matter what box we check off, should learn from. Complacency is perhaps the one thing in our nation that is indeed color-blind.

In King's view the "do-nothingness," as he called it, of the complacent was just as dangerous as violent revolt. I actually think complacency is the worst road one can take. Revolution is often violent, from the revolt of the Seven Kingdoms in ancient China to the famed American Revolution to the Haitian Revolution (the most successful slave rebellion in history, establishing Haiti as the first free black republic in 1804), the Bolshevik Revolution, and the Arab Spring, just to name a (very) few. The challenge is making sure violence isn't led by emotion nor purely reactionary, but instead are means that are absolutely necessary.

The danger of what complacency gets you was illustrated loud and clear in the spring of 2013 when the Supreme Court effectively struck down the heart of the Voting Rights Act of 1965, thus allowing states to change their election laws without advance federal approval. The decision cleared the way for voter ID laws that were waiting in the wings and redistricting maps that would no longer need federal approval. At the center of the debate between the justices was whether people of color continue to face barriers to voting especially in states and areas, like the South, with a history of discrimination.

"Our country has changed," Chief Justice John G. Roberts Jr. wrote for the majority. "While any racial discrimination in voting is too much, Congress must ensure that the legislation it passes to remedy that problem speaks to current conditions." In case Roberts wasn't clear, the court's passing on the future of the law to the most divided Congress in recent history, in effect, means the death sentence for the provision.

I pinched myself this time to make sure the nightmare was real. I pinched again refusing to believe.

To be honest, there was *some* outrage. Afterward. I could showcase great quotes immediately following the ruling from big-name civil rights leaders and attorneys, black groups, Latino groups, LGBT groups, and social justice groups, as well as practically every politician of color blasting the decision. A taste: "I don't know what America those five Supreme Court justices are living in to be able to pretend that deliberate and blatant attempts to disenfranchise people of color at the ballot box do not exist," said Rodney Ellis, a Texas state senator from Houston. Of course, about two hours after the Supreme Court

ruling Texas announced plans to implement a redistricting measure that lower courts had ruled discriminatory, as well as the most
stringent voter ID law in the country, thus in effect disenfranchising
thousands of Texans.

It was not hard to find black and brown faces who were "disappointed" with the Supreme Court ruling, including President
Obama, who was even "deeply disappointed." But the fact that a challenge to the landmark Voting Rights Act had reached the Supreme
Court should have sounded warning bells and wide-scale outrage
long *before* the decision came down. That's what happens when you
get complacent—it becomes even easier to get stepped on. Whatever
outrage there may have been before was not loud enough. Furthermore, great quotes from big-name "leaders" don't matter much if
the rest of us don't hear the outrage. Folks on the South Side of Chicago, the Hill District in Pittsburgh, Liberty City in Miami, Prince
Georges County in Maryland, Jackson Ward in Richmond, South
Phoenix in Arizona, Compton and East LA in California, and my
beloved Bed-Stuy. For me the day of the ruling was a sad day because
in Bed-Stuy (and the rest) there was no indication that anything so
detrimental had happened. What good is the outrage from up top
if it doesn't prompt the complacency in all of us to end? Leaders are
responsible to inspire. The masses are responsible for revolution.

The best of the outrage actually came from the court itself in
Justice Ruth Bader Ginsburg's emotional dissenting opinion to the
ruling: "The sad irony of today's decision lies in its utter failure to
grasp why the VRA has proven effective. The Court appears to believe
that the VRA's success in eliminating the specific devices extant in
1965 means that preclearance is no longer needed. With that belief,
and the argument derived from it, history repeats itself." In case those
missed the legal speak of her dissent, she went a step further and, in a
highly unusual move for a Supreme Court justice, talked to the press
to explain her outrage, citing the words of the Rev. Dr. Martin Luther
King Jr. and said his legacy and the nation's commitment to justice
had been "disserved by today's decision." While Roberts and the court
saw the progress as a sign that the VRA was successful and no longer

needed, Ginsburg explained that the focus of the Voting Rights Act had properly changed from "first-generation barriers to ballot access" to "second-generation barriers" like racial gerrymandering and laws requiring at-large voting in places with a sizable black minority, and that the law was needed to *continue* to effectively thwart such efforts. Indeed today's legacy of the Voting Rights Act is widespread. It was used to block more than 1,000 proposed changes to voting laws between 1982 and 2006, according to the Brennan Center for Justice, a public policy institute at New York University.

It was just about a month after the VRA was gutted by the nation's top court that the verdict came in on the race-tinged Florida trial of George Zimmerman for the murder of Trayvon Martin. Zimmerman, an overeager member of his neighborhood watch, gunned down Trayvon, an unarmed teenager who, while coming back from a snack run for Skittles, made the mistake of Walking While Black in Zimmerman's gated community in Sanford, Florida, where the seventeen-year-old was visiting relatives. Prompted by nothing more than the sight of a black man in a "hoodie," Zimmerman followed Trayvon by car and by foot, dismissing instructions to stand down and not pursue from local police whom he had called during the chase. That February night another black family in America lost their son. A year and a half later when a jury of six women believed Zimmerman's claims of self-defense and acquitted him on all counts, our nation lost some of its morality.

In the days after the verdict folks across the nation, including New York, Oakland, Atlanta, Chicago, and DC (but not Sanford, Florida) took to the streets in protest. For the most part the wide-scale protests, many of which developed organically as people felt the need to gather, stood out for their peacefulness. In New York impromptu protests shut down Times Square, and in Oakland demonstrators blocked traffic along Interstate 880 during the afternoon rush hour. By Monday morning, two days after the verdict, I was struck to hear the morning host on Hot 97, the hip-hop radio station in New York City, tear up on air. Instead of talking about the travesty of the verdict like every other media outlet, Hot 97, which caters to a younger crowd—teenagers who could be peers of Trayvon—dedicated the day to a "discussion in rap," spinning old-school conscious faves like KRS-One, Public Enemy, Brand Nubian, Dead Prez, and Black Star, and I was enjoying finally having good stuff on the radio again to bop my head to.

I cannot say that there was no outrage this time. Folks were certainly not doing nothing. For the most part, though, people's outrage was focused on the racism. "Trayvon Martin will forever remain in the annals of history next to Medgar Evers and Emmett Till as symbols for the fight for equal justice for all," said Benjamin Crump, the Martin family attorney, in a press conference after the verdict. Like politics, racism is an emotional argument. You are never, ever going to convince someone that racism exists if they don't want to see it. That is how jurors in the case and others watching could believe that race had nothing to do with Zimmerman's hot pursuit of a black teen that then led to the shooting. Even the judge in the case banned the use of the phrase "racial profiling," insisting that attorneys use simply "profiling" instead. So such protests about racism are cathartic, but I'm not convinced that they will change things that much. What got much less discussion in the outrage of the masses was the law that enabled the jury to acquit a gun-toting vigilante like Zimmerman.

Zimmerman was protected by Florida's infamous Stand Your Ground provision in its Self-Defense Law. Under that law, which was passed by the Florida legislature in 2005 and since then versions of which are now on the books in more than thirty states, a person may use deadly force if he or she "reasonably believes" it is necessary to protect themselves. It basically empowers people to stand and shoot rather than run to safety, thus dismissing the advice that law enforcement has been giving us since grade school. In Stand Your Ground states, even if your attacker is running away you are still permitted to shoot without fear of legal repercussion. Thus in the Zimmerman trial all the defense had to prove to a jury was that Zimmerman "reasonably believed" he was in danger, a ridiculously low bar considering that for much of America a black man is the definition of danger. When you combine Stand Your Ground laws with lax conceal-and-carry legislation, it is in effect deputizing every racist in the state. I don't know about you, but getting shot by the Zimmermans out there or getting lynched by them is all the same to me. I'd rather see mass outrage and protest to stop legislation like that since it can empower people's racism. That would actually be doing something.

Three days after the verdict, the peaceful demonstrations had pretty much stopped and press reports started trickling in that "protests" in Los Angeles turned violent . . . again. The fact that it was LA, home to more than six nights of deadly rioting in 1992 after the acquittal of police officers in the beating of Rodney King, served as a glaring reminder of how history repeats itself. Back home for me in Brooklyn, Hot 97 was pumping nonsense again, and my head stopped bopping. In fact, life had returned to the post–gutted VRA world, where it will be that much harder to elect politicians who would vote against racist Stand Your Ground laws.

Even though my examples may have been political, the point is that our "do-nothingness" tendencies, no matter where they show up in life, have big repercussions.

Make no mistake: I don't wish the door to the White House wasn't open. On Election Day 2008, I took both my children into the voting booth with me. My daughter was almost three and my son was barely a month old, sleeping in a baby carrier strapped to my chest, so both were too young to really grasp what was happening. But I insisted on bringing them anyway, because I wanted my black children to always know that they were there in the voting booth the day the nation elected its first black president. Now the first president they ever learned the name of was Barack Obama, and I love that. My pinch-me self can't even begin to imagine what that does to their sense of possibilities and their worldview. I would not want to change that moment of reality for anything. But despite the joy I get from seeing the moment the doors open, I honestly don't care that much about the first black anything. More important is the second, third, and fourth. That is because the bigger fight for any community trying to climb is not about opening the door, but keeping it open.

And that's what complacency puts at risk.

CORA

It actually *is* Mama's fault.

"Nothing so dates a man as to decry the younger generation."

—ADLAI E. STEVENSON, TWO-TIME DEMOCRATIC
PRESIDENTIAL NOMINEE, DURING A SPEECH AT
THE UNIVERSITY OF WISCONSIN, OCT. 8, 1952[44]

I never understood the bad-mouthing that the old do about the young until I became old enough to do it, too. It was a revelation. I know I am now past old, because I am at the point where it takes all my strength not to bad-mouth. Who knew so many things could get under your skin? Things like: "nigga," "my nigga," "yo nigga," "you niggers"; HBO's *Girls*; txt spelling and :) as emotional commentary; or "I want, I want, I want rather than I work, I work, I work." But it all does, and more. Thankfully, I hold back from bad-mouthing's partner: romanticizing the good ol' days—my knowledge of history won't let me. I once got chastised by an elementary school principal at a school assembly in Atlanta for snapping at a fourth grader because of my refusal to romanticize.

"If you could go back in time, what era of history would you like to visit?" the child asked innocently from the audience.

"Why would I ever want to go back in history?" I snapped back from the stage. "Life doesn't get too good for black women when you start to go back in time."

I wasn't invited to speak at any more elementary school assemblies.

Frankly, I'm waiting for a time when instead of talk of the good ol' days we could collectively bounce our heads and relish that "today was a good day" (shout out to Ice Cube, and shout out to the Isley Brothers, old-school references are always deliberate). But I've discovered that despite my resistance to the good-ol'-days amnesia, I am not as immune to the young-are-dumb bad-mouthing. I blame motherhood.

My first Mother's Day as a mother I had to go to a wedding. The wedding date was deliberate, the bride's mother had passed away, and the ceremony was as much a tribute to a daughter's love for her mother as it was for the soul mate she was vowing her love to. In between the ceremony and the reception, I had to run home and nurse my newborn daughter, who was being watched by my own mother. Taking advantage of the rare moment during those new motherhood days that I was all dressed up, my husband sneaked a photo of the three of us—my mother, my baby daughter, and myself—each of our curly heads lined up in a row. When I emailed the shot to my mom, who then did the proper thing and got a print (which I now have framed), I titled the jpeg "Curly Heads." Whenever I see the photo, that day comes flooding back: I can see the bride lighting a candle for her mother at the altar, and I still get misty. It was that day that I recognized that my motherhood had shaped my identity.

Those who know me will probably be stunned to read that statement. It is no secret that I am a much better journalist than I am a mother. My husband is the one the kids run to when they want dinner, fun, guidance, and everything to be better. I tend to keep my family life and professional life so rigidly separate that the two sides often do not know the other exists. Just recently an editor I work with off and on, armed with "news" of my son, ended an email congratulating me on the second baby. I felt a tinge of bad-mother-guilt because the "second baby" was four and a half years old. To make up for it I tiptoed into my son's room when he was sleeping and tried to snap some photos of him with my phone; taking kid shots is something I so rarely do that I couldn't figure out how to zoom the camera so that you could actually see his face. To get him into frame I had to stand so far back that he indeed does look like a baby, which perhaps makes up for the fact that I don't have any baby pictures on my phone. I imagine great mommies don't have such issues. Still, the day of the Mother's Day wedding it sank in that regardless of all the things I am, may be, or want to be, I will always be a mother. And when you embrace the importance of that identity it is hard not to let the nonsense of the world piss you off.

This brings me to the Millennials, or Generation Y. There is a lot of Gen Y bashing going on in the media of late. Magazine cover stories blather proclamations that this generation of the first digitally connected is the most disconnected from any characteristic that is desirable: hard work, empathy, innovation. A *Time* magazine cover story went so far as to declare the Millennials as the most narcissistic generation of young people ever to be unleashed on the rest of us. Online the generational warfare gets even worse, with each side bad-mouthing among themselves and upping the viciousness. It makes one long for the Archie Bunker and Meathead–style bickering that managed to make this somewhat entertaining.

Such scapegoating of the next generation is nothing new. In all the coverage of the Millennials I was struck by how familiar the negativity was to when my own Gen X generation were young and dumb and the focus of magazine blather. In the wake of *Time* magazine's Me Me Me Generation cover, *The Atlantic* responded with a brilliant photo-essay highlighting similar cover stories disparaging the youth of the day dating back to an *Atlantic Monthly* story in 1907.

It is very easy to get annoyed and bitter and bad-mouth. I find myself bad-mouthing several times a day when a young'un just doesn't seem to understand it is not his world but our world. After I became a mother, I noticed my groans became louder and louder as I would rant: If *our* world falls apart because of some entitled, shallow, selfish young folks, then what world will be left for *my* kids? Of course, I was shallowly overlooking my own selfishness and entitlement.

But becoming a mother has also helped me see that we are also the ones to blame. If we don't like how the younger generation is turning out, then that is our fault because we are the ones who raised them.

The thing is while we have been bad-mouthing the younger

generation as "me, me, me," we have also become the "me, me, me" parents. Our focus has become so narrow that it now extends just to the family living in our household. The nuclear unit has been so idolized that it exclusively drives our focus to obsessive levels. Good parenting is not just loving your child anymore; it is only loving your child at the expense of anyone else's child. Our home is indeed our castle, and like a selfish king we do not care what happens beyond the gates, or, simply, outside our door. That is why it is so easy for us not to care what is happening in urban public schools in places like Chicago and Philadelphia, where they can't even pay for office staff or school nurses. What do their problems matter as long as we can find a good (suburban) public or private school for our kids?

That was never the tradition of this country, though. One of the earliest initiatives after the Revolutionary War was to set up a foundation of free public education. Forgive the jump into history. My daughter is obsessed with an old TV show she found on Netflix called *Liberty's Kids* that turns the American Revolution into a cartoon. Benjamin Franklin is voiced by Walter Cronkite and the kids are reporters for Franklin's newspaper the *Pennsylvania Gazette,* covering the fight for independence starting with the Boston Tea Party and ending with the drafting of the Constitution. It means she is constantly slipping names like Phyllis Wheatley, Benedict Arnold, John Adams, and Thomas Jefferson into the conversation, so my mind has been stuck on our nation's beginnings. It has helped put things in perspective though. Most associate a free public education system with Thomas Jefferson, who gets credit in our historical memories for championing the rights of the common man. But the concept of a public education system was even embraced by founding fathers on the other side of the political aisle from Jefferson as well, such as John Adams, our second president and a member of the Federalist Party, which had the reputation of a more elitist view of government compared to Jefferson's Republicanism. Still, in 1785 Adams, the "elitist," cared enough about the common man to say this:

"The whole people must take upon themselves the education of the whole people and be willing to bear the expenses of it. There should not be a district of one mile square, without a school in it, not founded by a charitable individual, but maintained at the public expense of the people themselves."[45]

(Of course, "whole people" gets a little sticky when the view at the time of whole was really just white boys. To his credit Adams, not Jefferson, has the distinction of being one of only two US presidents of our first twelve who did not own slaves. The other was his son, sixth president John Quincy Adams. John Adams's personal views against slavery never translated into policy, though, nor did it convince him of the need for gender equality. During the drafting of the Constitution Adams ignored letters from his wife, Abigail, pleading for language that would guarantee rights to women.* Whether it is slavery or women, Adams is an example of how much our inaction matters.)

But even if my black-girl self wouldn't have been allowed in any of the one-room schoolhouses of early America (life doesn't get too good going back in time), I do take comfort that the discussion of the founding fathers was always about a collective. That collective was not limited to education, but ran deeper. What happened beyond our door was at the heart of how we were defining what it meant to be American. And that is the point of this simplified history lesson.

I think with all our more recent hyperattention to self, we have forgotten our responsibilities as parents that we owe our communities. It doesn't matter what the makeup of our individual household is; as grown folks we are all parents to the larger community. Or should be. We serve as examples of behavior, role models, and voices of reason. It is our obligation to set high standards and constantly raise our expectations. These are the things that good parents do. Generations don't just evolve because of what is happening inside each of our households, but also what we as the collective allow to happen outside of our households, too.

---

*In March of 1776 Abigail famously wrote to her husband: "Remember all men would be tyrants if they could. If particular care and attention is not paid to the ladies we are determined to foment a rebellion, and will not hold ourselves bound by any laws in which we have no voice or representation." Always nice to hear talk of rebellions, isn't it?

I found out in the spring of 2013 that "collective" has become a dirty word. Trying to hammer out my thoughts for this essay, I was doing some research and came across the online brouhaha over, of all things, a thirty-second MSNBC promo featuring host Melissa Harris-Perry.

"We have never invested as much in public education as we should have. We haven't had a very collective notion of 'these are our children.' We have to break through our private idea that children belong to their parents, or children belong to their families, and recognize that children belong to whole communities. Once it's everybody's responsibility and not just the household's, we start making better investments."

That's it. That is the entire transcript of what she said. That is what caused the bombardment of conservative criticism. Glenn Beck called the promo "terrifying" specifically for its promotion of "collective." Sarah Palin tweeted, "Apparently MSNBC doesn't think your children belong to you. Unflippingbelievable." Rush Limbaugh ranted, calling the notion communist. And the list goes on. FOX News dedicated so much coverage to the "controversy" that MSNBC ad folks were "giddy" over the attention the blabber was bringing to Harris-Perry's weekend morning talk show. We had been through this before. In 1996 First Lady Hillary Clinton got trounced by the Right when she came out with her book *It Takes a Village to Raise a Child*—adopting the African proverb to argue what children's advocates have always promoted: for our communities to take collective responsibility for our children. In Bob Dole's acceptance speech at the Republican National Convention that year, he barked, "With all due respect, I am here to tell you, it does not take a village to raise a child. It takes a family to raise a child."

Seventeen years later we are having the same argument.

I have to admit, the uproar over MHP left me a bit speechless. It was one of those moments where I felt so disconnected from our reality, it was as if I were actually not part of the world where everyone could be shouting about this but watching that world unravel on a big screen somewhere. Since we are talking about parenting, I then checked in with my mother to ask her about her memories of the uproar over Clinton's collective parenting words, and she said virtually the same thing. "I remember I was really stunned," she said, not knowing her reporter daughter would record her words forever. "I just couldn't believe that she could be criticized for saying such a thing." For my mom it is always a Right-Left issue. In fact, the next thing she said was: "They really hated her!" They being the big bad right wing conspiracy.

But it is not only the Glenn Becks that have trouble with the idea of collective parenting. Most of us may not be yelling and screaming about the issue, but our actions do the screaming for us. Again, John Adams's personal views against slavery didn't matter as much as his inaction as president on the issue did. Likewise, no matter what we think or say we support, we are all *acting* the same: like selfish kings, blind to what is going on outside our castles. As a result our communities are hurting for some parenting. The founding fathers would think that was unflippingbelievable.

———

I often feel like I am the only bad cop on the playground. I discipline my own kids, a lot, but I have also—*gasp!*—disciplined other people's kids, too. I've tapped kids on the shoulder who were not listening in my son's capoeira class and told them to stop being disrespectful. I've stepped in at the schoolyard when kids start pushing or generally acting rude. I've told teenagers on the subway to watch their language. To be honest, sometimes I've been yelled at by other mothers for my discipline dishing. To be honest, I don't care—when I see behavior that is unacceptable, my responsibility, as a parent, is to speak up. That's part of what it means to be parents on a societal level—once you are grown you have to speak up.

Perhaps it makes sense that we are not living up to our obligation as parents in our communities, because to a certain extent I think we often wipe our hands of parental responsibility for our own children's bad behavior in our households. This is especially clear when our kids are toddlers and teenagers. There is something about those two periods where we convince ourselves that it is part of the age to misbehave, so no matter what we do as parents it is still not our fault. Hence the crying mothers on the evening news with their "he was a good kid" defense to whatever misbehavior got their kid into trouble. On some level most nod in agreement as if teenagehood is like Las Vegas, or even the Amish Rumspringa, where what happens during those years stays there, not staining the "good families" whom we claim young people are always raised by. The exception to society's forgiving nature would be when young people turn out to be monsters—those who take or destroy life. Then everyone is quick to finger point at the bad mamas who must have raised them. (Our shaming of *only* mothers—think Susan Klebold [Columbine] or Nancy Lanza [Newtown]—further shows how uneven we are at dishing out blame in general.) I say all this because I've done it, too—the nodding and the pointing. My four-year-old son, who parenting books would call "spirited," sizes people up very quickly and then deliberately chooses whom he will cooperate with or not. If he decides you are on his misbehave list you are in trouble. This year his antics brought his Pre-K teacher close to tears. The mommy literature tells me it is not my fault. I still spend a lot of my time apologizing, though.

I apologize for his behavior because I am a big believer in personal responsibility. Because of this, my mom, the good-old-school New York Jewish liberal, likes to criticize me for sometimes being too conservative. I tend to think her Left/Right view of the world is too simple. It has led us to many a political catfight, even if we often are not arguing over party affiliation but rather a specific candidate or issue. But without embracing the role of personal responsibility, then, in essence, you are handing over the outcome of life. We have no part in shaping our own destiny without taking personal responsibility. That does not mean you dismiss the world and its ills, but the one thing you can always control is your role in that world. Despite what my mom thinks, I don't believe that makes me conservative: it makes me a realist.

The problem with bringing up the issue of personal responsibility these days is that it's become code for giving black folks a spanking. That is why President Obama, who loves to argue that he is not the president of just black people, does not see anything wrong with giving a commencement speech at Morehouse, chastising our best and brightest about personal responsibility. It is a discussion black audiences have heard before from others. More important, it is a discussion that black audiences have heard before from him. It doesn't make the message a bad one. It just weakens the message if only one set of the nation's ears are the ones always hearing it. Part of my mother's conservative finger pointing at me is she thinks my view of the world is too narrow, that I look through only a black lens. She's wrong. I actually look through only a black woman's lens. That is who I am, no apologies. Although I see the world through a lens that some may argue is narrow—I'd say specific—I'd argue that the ideas that sprout from that viewpoint are never limited to just that lens. Because, as Obama says, "just black people" is not reality (even if it can feel that way sometimes in our hypersegregated lives). So, yes, I am a big believer in personal responsibility but personal responsibility for *everyone*.

That said, what is overlooked in our discussions of the role of personal responsibility is that there can be a collective use of that responsibility. For me that is what is at the heart of societal parenting, the collective, the Village. The problem with folks like MHP and Hillary is they don't go far enough. For them, the center of the collective is still the State rather than a collective of individual responsibility. There will always be a personal responsibility element to parenting. How could there not? But part of that personal responsibility is what we do as parents beyond our household. Liberals will always point fingers at society when things go wrong; the conservatives like to point at the individual. If we want to stop having that same argument, then I propose pointing to the society of individuals—each of us is to blame. In short: it is indeed Mama's fault. But dads are to blame, too. And so are we. What happens on a community level is always all our fault. We are all parents.

———

There are many parents who will say that they don't want the village to help raise their children. MHP's comments not only caused a stir in conservative circles but in the parent blogosphere as well, where some parents were frightened by the thought that they alone were not the deciders in their children's lives. That kind of thinking is a bit naïve, though. The village is helping to raise our children whether we like it or not. As much as Americans try to raise their children within protective bubbles (and Americans seem to "bubble" more than other cultures), those children are still part of a community that is larger than their home. The social scientists call it the "neighborhood effect." In the last twenty years there has been a flurry of research from sociologists, economists, and public policy academics, trying to document and quantify just how much neighborhood affects the outcome of our lives. In other words how much does the community contribute to the citizens our children become? Not surprisingly, the consensus among the neighborhood effects team of research is well, "neighborhoods profoundly matter" according to Lawrence F. Katz, a Harvard economist who spent more than fifteen years conducting a national study of neighborhood dynamics that involved giving vouchers to poor families so they could move to better neighborhoods. As an economist Katz's focus is on dollars and cents. He argues that "the difference between living in a very poor neighborhood and a moderately middle-class neighborhood is as large as doubling your income in terms of happiness and well-being."[46] While much of the focus of the "neighborhood effect" research is on class, the implication for real life is really much broader. To some extent it helps document what our common sense as parents already told us: that it is impossible to block out the community. The community helps mold our views and behavior and thus our children's views and behaviors. Most of us may hope we have an impact on the world, but whether we do or not, the world definitely has an impact on us. Most important, by not engaging in how the community is shaped, we are handing over our personal responsibility when it comes to our kids. I can't think of anything more frightening than that.

Part of relishing the good ol' days that we do is to reminisce about how as kids we were surrounded by caring, loving neighbors who looked out for us. This memory, especially in urban settings, typically includes a curfew tied to when the streetlights came on, and if you weren't home Mrs. Williams or Mrs. Johnson or Mrs. Jones would do some scary finger wagging to make sure that you didn't do it again. Growing up in Manhattan, there were never any Mrs. Johnsons around my way who cared enough to finger wag. I was from an era of New York City when Etan Patz, the boy on the milk cartons, was a peer and trick-or-treating was banned for fear of razor blades popping up in the candy. I always thought I was missing out, that everywhere else there were these wonderful neighborhoods where grown folks felt it was their obligation to watch over the community's children. But when I got to college and met people from across the country, I discovered that no one really grew up in such communities. Not in cities like Pittsburgh or Boston or Chicago. Not out west in Dallas or Oklahoma. Not down south in Richmond or Atlanta. Not out in California—northern or southern. Not in the 'burbs or the cities or the countryside. (I once mentioned to my freshman roommate, who grew up on a farm in Iowa, making the two of us aliens from different planets to each other, how it must be nice knowing all her neighbors by name back in Iowa. She responded puzzled: what neighbors?) At first I attributed my failure to find signs of these idyllic communities to life from a different era—those good ol' days before my childhood must have been the time these neighborhoods existed, where we watched out for each other's kids. But now that the good ol' days romanticizing is setting in amid my own generation I am starting to hear these idyllic stories about "back in the day" from peers. How could that be? It seemed to me that we were all suffering from historic amnesia. I reached out to John, the professor, to get to the bottom of things. As an urban anthropologist he should know when and where these idyllic neighborhoods, with the many eyes to answer to, that we all cling to, existed. But he didn't. Professor Jackson assured me that there are many social scientists and historians who debunk what's called "the myth of the ghetto's golden age." The idea that there were once—before integration—healthy neighborhoods where the black poor and black middle class lived together in perfect harmony is a myth. That doesn't mean that some of us may not have been lucky enough to have a Mrs. Johnson in our lives who did take it upon herself to watch over all of us. But she was the exception of the neighborhood, not the norm. There were not as many watchful eyes as we think. I admit I liked it better when it was just me missing out.

Still, to me what is more important than that the myth existed is what the myth was. As a nation we mourn the loss of a time where we parented beyond our household. It doesn't matter that such a time never really existed; what matters is that we wish it still did exist now.

Once in a while there are glimmers that give me hope that we are moving in that direction. In the sorrow after the Boston Marathon bombing, I was comforted by a glimmer. It was two months after the bombing and the city of Cambridge, where the Tsarnaev brothers were raised, was trying to understand how these terrorists could have come from a community known for its diversity and tolerance. Some even protested the city's decision not to allow older brother Tamerlan to be buried in the city he called home, saying it did not represent the values of Cambridge. Of the brothers themselves, questions of "how could this happen?" were on everyone's lips. A series of gatherings started popping up, where residents grieved together by trying to talk through these issues. Many residents were focused on the younger brother, Dzhokhar, who had immigrated to Cambridge when he was eight and went on to graduate from its big public high school, Cambridge Rindge and Latin, which also claims Ben Affleck, Patrick Ewing, and New York City's new mayor, Bill de Blasio, as alums. How could a kid who two years ago had been sporting Cambridge wrestling team T-shirts now be sitting in a federal jail cell, facing charges for the use of a weapon of mass destruction in a bombing across the river in Boston that killed 3 and injured 264 of us? And that's when the glimmer happened for me: the conversation across Cambridge turned inward. Some began to wonder what was Cambridge's contribution to the men whom the brothers had become? "We have to take responsibility that he was one of ours," Peter Payack, Dzhokhar's high school wrestling coach, told the *New York Times*.[47] I read those words while riding the subway in Brooklyn. I read them over and over and over as if to make sure I had read them correctly. If Cambridge could do that—claim responsibility for raising, of all things, a domestic terrorist—the rest of us should be ashamed of how little blame we take for things much less horrendous that go on in our neighborhoods every day. I put down my paper and felt shame. And then I felt hope. It was happening. We were acting like parents.

If we truly want that myth to be a reality, then we have to start to take parenting seriously. When I was pregnant a friend of mine who, with his wife, had adopted their two children, used to joke all the time that adoptive parents were more prepared to be parents compared to birthers like myself. That is because the adoption process requires a tremendous amount of work to be approved as parentworthy. Prospective parents go through an examination of values, personal lives, and finances. Depending on where you live, this process can sometimes take years. When my husband and I briefly considered adoption after our daughter was born, I had not seen a process for something that extensive—questionnaires, essays, interviews—since I had applied to college. My friend was joking, of course, but his point was that adoptive parents have to work for the privilege. When you are not automatically given the title of parent because of DNA, the result is you are forced to take responsibility for your parenting. He has a point. Just thumbing through the adoption applications made me think about parenting concretely in ways that I had not done before, even though I was already a mother. It occurred to me that adoption is the closest thing we have to requiring a license to becoming a parent. Sometimes (when I'm bad-mouthing) I have to admit, that doesn't sound like such a bad thing.

When it comes to preparation, we are in an age where we think we can take a class for everything. Some have called it the education bubble. A bubble in economic terms is when too many people keep expecting the value of something to rise. Like the tech bubble or the housing bubble, higher education is now seen as the best investment for success. It is one of the factors driving the nation's record-breaking amount of student loan debt. The trickle-down effects of the race toward higher education is that you now can take a class, get a certificate, or even a degree in just about anything these days. At my children's elementary school it has become impossible to schedule a birthday party because of all the enrichment classes that kids are scheduled for throughout the week. Piano or ballet? Oh, that is so last generation. Now we are talking about piano and ballet and a variety of martial arts from across the globe and swimming and soccer (not soccer teams but soccer classes in addition to teams) and gymnastics and circus (yes!) and Chinese and cooking and robotics and chess and gardening class (which is different from forest class, a mommy-and-me class that helps get toddlers comfortable with trees) and science and, of course, test prep. Admittedly, this is just a very thin, not-random sample of classes that I actually personally know kids (some mine) are taking in the hyper corner of Brooklyn where my children go to school. But the key word in that list was "and," since kids are taking all of it. When my daughter was in the first grade one girl in her class on a single day after school would have a piano lesson, then French lesson, and then tae kwon do class. The point is nowadays we seem to think you can be taught everything—if you look you can find a class (live or online) in about anything you want to take. Middle-class parents can now outsource any lesson they could think of passing on to their children. And they do. That is part of the effects of a bubble. What I find interesting is of all the things we now teach, we don't see more teaching of parenting.

Although I believe the absence is telling, I actually am not advocating that we teach parenting. The problem is when we think we teach parenting we end up just lecturing poor people on how to parent. The assumption is that a dysfunction of being poor is that you don't know the best way to raise children. The best way is, of course, always the way of the mainstream middle-class value system. So you will see parenting classes in prisons. And for a few years there may be a parenting class in underperforming high schools until the budget runs out. You will see a scattering of free parenting classes in economically struggling neighborhoods. Sometimes even a single lesson will be dished out in the maternity ward at the public hospital. In the weeks after my first child was born, I kept getting calls from the NYC Department of Health, which wanted to do a home visit to impart some parenting wisdom. I was so overwhelmed with everything that comes with a newborn, I kept missing the calls. That didn't stop them from calling, though, usually at the worst possible times—as I was changing a diaper or after finally getting my daughter to nap. The bombardment of voice mail messages felt like I was being stalked by the City of New York. I couldn't believe that the city was so dedicated to visiting every new mother. The sheer size alone of the city made it seem impossible to me. It was. The details of my visit years ago are admittedly hazy now because of time, but what I do remember was that it was immediately clear that not every new mother in the city was getting a house call. I was getting one because I was a black mother living in (struggling) Bed-Stuy, Brooklyn, which for the City of New York was code for "bad parent." Three years later when my son was born, I didn't get a visit. Not sure if funds had run dry, or if it was because Bed-Stuy was gentrifying, thus knocking it off some master-plan list, or perhaps second children were not considered in need of parents indoctrinated with the city's one-visit words of wisdom. But the calls did not come. The point is this kind of half-hearted commitment is what we usually do when we "teach" parenting. We don't need more of that. But there is a difference between just teaching and truly learning. Learning is active; it requires that you think to figure things out. It also requires that you study. Instead of teaching parenting I'd like to see us study parenting. Of all the things we are trying to study nowadays, why don't we study how to raise a generation?

Ideally, studying how to be a parent would entail researching and observing practices of a variety of households and cultures and evaluating theories and data from a variety of different disciplines. Sounds like a lot of academic mumbo jumbo and not the real-world talk I typically cling to. But studying is scholarship, so there will always be a bit of idealistic theory. It would also require a lot of thinking about issues facing parents and, hopefully, discussion. It all sounds like eat-your-vegetables type of stuff—the merits are difficult to object to. But truly studying how to be a parent would also mean that on some personal level we are each creating standards for parenting for ourselves. That would be the only way one could evaluate the information being exposed to and decide what is worth adopting. I can't think of any better real-world payoff for this studying than the development of such personal standards. Standards are, in essence, what the paperwork for adoption was demanding applicants think about by asking questions like: "What makes a good parent?"

You have to be careful when you start throwing around phrases like "parenting standards." The problem is, standards cannot be dictated (that is why government parenting programs can't work). I also don't buy that standards just happen organically. So unless you are thinking about these things, you can't assume that you have them or are sticking to them. Instead, standards should be set deliberately. That doesn't mean that our standards can't change; that is part of development. The answers to what makes a good parent should transform over time rather than stagnate. But the point is we should constantly be asking ourselves the question "What makes a good parent?"

Some have suggested that we are already obsessing over that question. That part of the stress of today's parents is the impossible goal of perfection. According to Ann Hulbert, the author of *Raising America: Experts, Parents and a Century of Advice About Children*, we have, in fact, become more neurotic as parents with each generation. But just because we are in a moment where some of us are obsessing over that question doesn't mean we are actually doing any in-depth thinking about the answer. It also needs to be said that the am-I-a-good-parent? obsession the media likes to blabber about is only part of the parenting story—the educated upper-middle-class part. It feels very far away back home in my (struggling) Bed-Stuy, where parents are obsessed about more John Adams basics like good schools for their children. The media, always the last to recognize its own privilege, tend to be in the first group (hence the blabber), while most of the rest of us are in the second group.

Despite what the Tiger Moms think, our children are not robots we can program to perfection, no matter how many enrichment classes you sign them up for. Instead, children are a work in progress that we must constantly mold and shape. That takes thought, that takes ideas, and that takes respect for the work of parenting itself. That's how we begin to sincerely answer the "What makes a good parent?" question.

There is a difference between physically creating life and raising life. While those of us who contribute the DNA are automatically anointed the title of parent, it is the raising part that is the real work and should be given the respect of the title. Of course, these are often the same people, but not always or not exclusively. And I am not just talking about cases of adoption where the distinction is obvious. Part of thinking about parenting more deeply is broadening our definition of parenting to include those people who already help us raise our children—teachers, caregivers, and relatives, among others, and yes, the community. While this collective village may not ever be a primary parent to our child—a mother or a father—they are still contributing parent*ing* to our children. Molding and shaping. And that is something that we need to acknowledge on all sides. Moms and dads need to recognize that, like it or not, the village already has a parenting influence. If you don't like it, then work to change the village: parent beyond your household. Likewise, the village needs to take that parenting obligation more seriously by adopting our communities—parent regardless of if you are a parent in your own household. My friend, the father who adopted, got it wrong. What matters is not which of us is more prepared. What matters is that too many of us are not preparing.

The thing is, every generation is the "worst generation" at some point. (Remember *The Atlantic*'s collection of "damn youth" magazine covers dating back to 1907?) How we stop this constant cycle of blame is to take responsibility for what we do, and not do, for the next generation. Because every time we bash the younger generation, we are really bashing our failure as parents. All of us.

RACE

JOHN

We're all haters.

I'm sitting in the passenger seat of a tow truck in South Philadelphia and having a casual conversation with the driver, a complete stranger, about "those damned Mexicans."

To be honest, I hardly did much talking. My contributions to the discussion boiled down to a very active brand of listening, only occasionally punctuated by a gentle attempt at playing devil's advocate, very gentle, without any hint of definitiveness or indignation:

"Mexicans can be as hardworking as anyone else, no?"

And even those blunted gestures were carefully tempered by toothy smiles and enabling head nods, all served up in hopes of collecting more xenophobic pronouncements, and decidedly *not* as a direct challenge to ostensibly hostile and racist remarks.

Many would blast me for even taking part in any conversation that includes references to "those damned Mexicans," and that's justifiable, but I should also say, in my own defense, however feeble the defense might seem, that I have a PhD in cultural anthropology, which gives me informal license to let folks say all manner of craziness in my presence without calling them on it. If anything, the profession requires me to drag more and more of such talk out of people. The nuttier, the better. Anthropologists "suffer fools gladly," as the biblical saying goes, even if we also love to stumble upon everyday forms of bona fide (and usually underappreciated) genius, which is ultimately much more fun to find anyway. And I've been fortunate enough to discover my share of those, too.

Part of my willingness to participate in a conversation that includes talk of "those damned Mexicans" can be chalked up to the fact that many anthropologists reserve their most scathing critiques for the printed page, just like I'm doing right now, saving seemingly righteous rebukes for published books or journal articles. They might be disgusted by something they see or hear, but they can sometimes keep a poker face in the moment (for the sake of social science!), to witness more of what repulses them, a feat that some would rightly characterize as cowardly or conniving or both.

But that wasn't the only reason for my open-faced smiles, for those rhetorical softballs I tossed back at anti-immigrant rants. There is also anthropology's long-standing commitment to "cultural relativism," one of its golden rules, and something that detractors use to pummel it every chance they get.

You are being a cultural relativist when you try to take other people's practices and beliefs very seriously, especially when those practices and beliefs diverge most radically (and seemingly irreconcilably) from your own, a stance meant to offset the combination of hubris and small-mindedness that comes with being a part of *any* social group. It is a mind-set that attempts to dampen some of the intrinsic boastfulness that usually accompanies calling a particular "culture," any culture, your own. Cultural relativism argues that we should respect different worldviews, take other cultures on their own terms, avoid knee-jerk hostilities and snap judgments about alien ideas, especially since the dismissiveness bred from that would be a consequence of unfairly and self-servingly measuring another group against your own culture's yardstick.

But some critics lampoon the cultural relativist position as a cop-out, a kind of political wimpiness, an excuse for tolerating all kinds of cultural cruelties and nonsense in the name of a false sense of social respectfulness. If Ugandan women are complaining about being subjected to painful forms of female genital mutilation because of cultural traditions (and without any urgent medical reasons to justify them), which is one of the textbook examples of cultural relativism's ethical and political implications, would non-Ugandans be morally justified if they ignored those cries for help out of some deference to a foreign culture's internal coherence and distinct moral standards?

Or maybe very few members of a particular cultural group are even complaining about some practice that looks cruel or dangerous or humiliating or evil to the outside world. They just accept it. Their community has been doing things this way for as long as anyone can remember. This is how their parents, grandparents and great-grandparents lived. They can't even imagine an alternative. It is just how things are—how they have always been. In that scenario, what would it mean for an outsider to convince members of the community to think about their age-old cultural practices as inherently oppressive and in need of reform, especially when it tends to be the same cultures (read: Western) condescendingly pouncing on the same *other* cultures (read: Third World/Global South) in the name of universal rights and wrongs?

Cultural relativism troubles claims to universalism, with all of their assumed self-evidence. Western culture can't boast an objective and universal position on things in supposed contradistinction to everyone else's particular and partial ones. It is just as particular and partial, even if—like just about every other culture known to man—it has far more grandiose aspirations and self-conceptions.

I don't mean to sound like an "introduction to anthropology" textbook, but if I am going to invoke terms like "Western culture" and "cultural relativism," I should also probably take a second to explain what "culture" actually is, especially since it has such an integral part to play in what makes human beings human and fosters every single one of our social anxieties and hatreds, including race-based ones.

Defining culture isn't easy. We often don't know where "culture" ends and its ostensible opposite, "nature," takes over. We used to highlight the same debate all the time: nature versus nurture, which is more powerful in determining human behaviors and life's outcomes? It is one of the most seductive questions in science and social policy, and we continue to look for more nuanced ways of answering it.

The debate usually wends its way around the same basic formula. Someone picks a practice, any practice, and then asks, is it hard-wired? Is it something we are born with? Like ten fingers and toes. If we are born with it or with a propensity for it (think, the gene for androgenic alopecia, i.e., male pattern baldness), we call it "natural," the assumption being that it is, therefore, extremely difficult (if not impossible) to change. The jury is in and one's fate is sealed. If what we are talking about being born with is a tendency to do something, to act in a particular way (say, walking upright instead of on all fours), doing anything other than that practice would be considered unnatural by definition.

But if we are talking about a social practice or belief that has to be learned and nurtured, something that had to be taught to (and modeled for) us by our parents and teachers and ministers and elected officials and friends and enemies or anyone else, then we are squarely in the realm of culture.

Compared to nature, culture is supposed to be flimsy and fungible. If we don't like an aspect of our cultural world, we can teach ourselves to do something else; we can learn a new culture, which wouldn't necessarily be labeled unnatural, even if some people might consider it weird or unwise.

After finding out that the soul food cooking you grew up on isn't particularly healthy for you, even though your grandmother might have prepared it with every last drop of her love, you could decide to give up meat and become a vegetarian. You might even join a network of similarly health-conscious plant eaters who also regularly attend Bikram yoga classes, purchase provisions from community-owned gardens (or Whole Foods), and annoy meat-eating family members to no end with consistent criticisms about their dietary choices. And you could call all of those new practices legitimate parts of your newfangled cultural repertoire. Vegetarianism might take discipline and self-control, but it is doable. And it would transform many other aspects of your social life.

If someone wanted to, he could reject portions of his cultural inheritance one item at a time: first diet, then dress code, then speaking style, then religious beliefs, and on and on. The nature versus nurture distinction pivots on this central premise: that we would have a much better chance of reworking the merely cultural stuff of life than we would trying to fool with Mother Nature.

It might seem quaint to invoke nature/nurture concerns these days, but we continue to have that quintessential debate—in the popular media and in the sciences. And all the time.

New parents can be especially obsessed when it comes to questions about raising their little ones. People want to know how much the local environment and family upbringing counts over and against genetic and biological predeterminations of social outcomes. Many classic "twin studies" were designed to get at this very question, trying to figure out if identical twins (with the same genetic composition) raised apart (with different mothers and fathers and social environments) developed similar personality traits. But parenting concerns don't corner the market on the nature/nurture theme.

We are constantly battling over how much of our social actions are based on cultural rules we have had to learn versus biological mandates we passively inherited. There have long been arguments about whether or not people might be biologically prone to, say, criminality, with scientists trying to figure out if criminal tendencies might be predicted simply by looking at the shape of people's heads and faces. Maybe their striding gaits or skin colors.

Intelligence is also situated at the crossroad between nature and nurture. What do we mean by "intelligence," and how do we test for it? When we do administer those tests, do they capture some kind of inherent genetic capacity for cognitive achievement or only the test taker's access to learned information that he or she might (or might not) share with the test's designers? People still fight over this question, with admission to the elitist schools and access to tens of millions of dollars in tuition money hanging in the balance.

And it isn't just criminality and intelligence that provoke nature/ nurture knife fights. There are those ongoing debates about sexual orientation, disputes about whether people are born homosexual or can be made straight through religious therapies. This is still a quintessential part of the nature/nurture discussion, even as its front lines have moved to the question of marriage itself—many people, including defenders of the Defense of Marriage Act, talking about certain marriage arrangements as more or less natural than others.

According to some social critics, and not just right-wing economists, the capitalist market is the most "natural" way of organizing social exchange. To tamper with the free market of goods, services, and labor, they argue, isn't just a slippery slope to communism; it more fundamentally means putting artificial and unnatural barriers on the human spirit—all to society's ultimate detriment.

Forget about "the race card"—the nature card is the highest trump in the deck.

But debates about race can be very informative when it comes to this nature/nurture stuff, especially since race often crosscuts those distinctions in peculiarly instructive ways.

Are racial groupings natural? How about identifying races in the first place? Is that something we do because of some biological imperative? How early do young people start seeing racial differences? How much of that is simply an extension of our more general human capacity for categorization? Does being hardwired to categorize necessarily explain our commitments to traditional racial categories themselves? Those kinds of questions are favorites in many social scientific and psychological circles. And you'd probably hear versions at many proverbial water coolers if you loitered long enough.

A lot of the work in human genetics and genomics today is just a more sophisticated way of trying to find the Holy Grail of nature's full design, of redrawing the line between social learning and DNA coding. Early versions of the project of predicting criminality, some of which have long been debunked (such as physiognomy) are now being reinvigorated and reimagined as fMRIs attempt to examine the shape of the brain's architecture with a similar goal in mind: determining whether criminals are born and with what kinds of biological markers/defects.[1]

Neuroscientists examine the brain's circuitry to make claims about all kinds of behaviors and traits. Evolutionary psychologists seek evidence for contemporary cultural practices in excavated evidence from (or conjecture about) prehistorical human societies. Primatologists compare human actions to our closest animal relatives for clues about how nature might have preprogrammed our approaches to sexuality, social bonding, child rearing, alliance building, mourning, and just about anything else we do. Much of this work operates from the premise that culture might be little more than a lapdog to nature's surreptitious suggestions and straightforward demands—that we are giving culture, nurture, and social learning more credit than they deserve.[2]

But culture is more stubborn than some people think, much more than certain versions of the nature/nurture divide imply, and it isn't necessarily a foregone conclusion that the nurture side of things is easier to manipulate. Mapping the human genome is ambitious, and it potentially opens human nature up to active modification and prediction. The coding of a DNA sequence could be about trying to figure out how we might engineer hardier human beings in the future. Or we can use it to determine if someone has an extremely high chance of coming down with something like Alzheimer's disease or breast cancer, well before any actual symptoms are ever observable. Science has long been about demystifying or taming nature, understanding its inner workings, and in many ways such taming might look far more definitive than any prognostications that might be made about culture's more inconsistent and probabilistic machinations.

Culture is a powerful thing, and maybe even more so in its distance from what we might call practical reasoning, from simple and supposedly objective cost-benefit analysis.[3] In fact, cultures can seem quite unreasonable by certain economic or utilitarian standards, which is where cultural relativism comes in—to remind us that their logics are easiest to spy when taken on their own terms. Anthropologist Marshall Sahlins provided one of the classic cases against any understanding of culture as simply a puppet for more powerful natural, economic, or material forces.

Part of culture's power stems from the fact that it can feel utterly natural. We learn it so fully and completely that it seems instinctual. It can even try to cover up its nonnatural moorings. That's the reason why we call it "second nature." It passes itself off as natural, which is how we experience many parts of our cultural world—like the air we breathe. We couldn't imagine doing things another way, believing in something else. At least not for the things we treat most preciously. In fact, we naturalize most of the stuff that we take for granted or cherish. We naturalize culture by fooling ourselves into thinking its directives are biological or otherwise more than just culture.

One good example of this is religion. What feels more natural to believers than their religious beliefs? Sure, people convert to new religions every day, but most believers on this planet will die a member of the same religion they were born into. And a good proportion of them will spend a lot of time trying to convince other people who believe something else to change religious affiliations. As we know, real hard-liners are even willing to kill nonbelievers—and feel fully justified to murder based on their interpretations of religious tenets.

For an anthropologist, the "truth" of any particular religion can be separated from the fact that its adherents have to learn it. They might be serving the supreme God, but they still have to be taught how to do so—and why. They didn't come out of the womb knowing the doctrine and effortlessly conforming to it. Some neuroscientists have made the argument that religious belief itself is "natural" (just like having ten fingers and toes)—much more so than believing in science (which might be more like adding a handy but prosthetic eleventh digit to your hands). Someone like Robert McCauley contends that our brains are built for religious adherence.[4] He argues that religion has been around for thousands of years and exists in almost every social community precisely because it makes more folk sense than the analytical moves of scientific research.

But even if we concede that religion seems to be an almost universal human institution, every religion is different, and any particular religious belief system still has to be taught, making it the stuff of culture. And once learned (especially if the teaching began at a very young age), it can be hard to unlearn, to give up. A person's entire sense of the world and her place in it might be saturated by that belief, and messing with that notion in even small ways could wreak havoc on a person's sense of self. The meaning of life might even vanish completely—and with it, conceivably, the very desire to live. Being a Catholic or a Buddhist or a Muslim or a Baptist can cut to the very core of who someone thinks she is, and if we are only talking about a lukewarm believer, then other social categories serve that existential role instead.

In the United States, racial identities work in a similar way, and for everybody, whether we are talking about people who are committed to color blindness or to unabashed racial chauvinism. Many social scientists and geneticists have argued for a long time that "race is a social construction," which simply means that it shouldn't be on the nature side of the nature/nurture fold, even if one of the things our culture tells us to do is place it there. We look at people and slot them into prefabricated racial boxes in an instant: black, white, Asian, Indian. But just because we agree on how to assign people to racial groups based on how they look doesn't make those racial groups natural. It isn't the same thing as having five differently shaped solid blocks and five corresponding holes they can fit into (square, triangle, rectangle, oval, and circle) and simply trying to match them up. You can't put a square peg through a round hole, as the aphorism goes, and we badly want to treat race just like that, like self-evidently matching pegs and holes. It is more like having squares that might look like squares to the naked eye but can just as easily—at just the right angle—slide through triangular or circular slots. Genes, blood, skin color, hair texture. These are all things that have been used to draw out the shapes of race, and they always fail to give us the definitive and absolute boundaries that we crave. Even still, when we talk about blacks or whites, we know what we mean. Just like we know the difference between circles and squares, right? Everything else is merely academic, in the dismissive sense, no?

Remember, culture tries to pass itself off as nature, as objectively and universally true, something that wasn't simply taught to us but

written into us by nature—or even better, bequeathed to us by a supernatural entity. We have to learn the difference between circles and
squares, but once we do, the difference is hard and fast. It is physical,
natural. So, too, for race, right? We have to learn it, but that is only
part of the story. Isn't it true that races are as physically different from
one another as squares are from circles? Yes, except when they aren't.

The first couple of years I knew Cora, for instance, I didn't know
what she was. Black? White? Latina? What was her racial identity?
As a high school student with many more bizarre antics to perform,
I didn't necessarily obsess about it, but I remember being curious. I
knew she had to be something; nobody escaped the racial order completely. There was no outside. But what? Without acting like I was
looking, I would scour her physical features for some kind of smoking gun, some definitive proof of her racial background, an indication
of where she belonged.

We tend to call people who look like Cora *multiracial*, but even
that doesn't quite work. Very few African Americans are monoracial
in any genetic or biological sense; the history of transatlantic slavery's
forced intimacies helps to explain that. But still, we want to find
natural dividing lines, and to call something—like race—cultural almost seems paltry and feeble compared to the eternal and everlasting
boundaries that we want racial lines to represent.

But what does any of this have to do with me and "those damned
Mexicans" evoked in a truck with notably bad shock absorbers cruis-
ing through South Philadelphia?

Well, one of the first things that culture teaches us to do is separate *us* from *them*. And we use a lot of different criteria for that
distinction. Religion and race are two of our most common, but they
stand alongside a number of other ways of parsing people. We have
categories for all kinds of social groupings. To start with, we distinguish, say, parents from other relatives. Relatives from nonrelatives.
In the United States, we can be caught distinguishing Northerners
from Southerners. Native New Yorkers from Bridge-and-Tunnelers.
Country bumpkins from city slickers. These are all categories with
social referents. That is, we aren't making these distinctions up out of

thin air. We're extrapolating on differences we see in the world itself.

And the very things that make us similar to one another and different from every other species on the planet (our physical bodies, our capacity for language, our cultural elaborateness, and more) are the same things we use to carve ourselves up into smaller and smaller social units: West versus East, primitive versus modern, American versus Canadian, believer versus infidel. The line between *Homo sapiens* and chimpanzee seems pretty clear (though scientists, before and after Jane Goodall, have been remapping it like crazy), which is part of why we don't think it is far-fetched to imagine that the line between, say, blacks and whites, or even Southerners and Northerners, might be similarly and incontrovertibly real.

And can there be differences without tension, fear, competition, and conflict? Without hate? Historians have demonstrated that one of the first things you have to do to convince people to wage war is prove to them that the folks they would be fighting are a *them*, usually a demonized and dehumanized *them*. The classic example of this, of course, would be German propaganda films that literally show Jews as hordes of disgusting rats. They, Jews, are not us, Aryan Germans, and every other potentially genocidal impulse is perched atop that single presupposition. Differences worth noting are often enough to merit attacking.

We have a tendency to read all kinds of differences as physical, material, and even existential threats. But anthropology, the study of what makes human beings human, demands, somewhat ironically, a rather inhuman capacity to look at other people's beliefs as something other than just potential danger, to see our differences as a virtue, and to appreciate the elasticity of humanity. We are the same and different, so how do we hold on to the productive tensions of that opposition without making a fetish or a war drum out of either? That's a question for nations, civilizations, and even just two Philadelphians chatting as they drive across town.

The tow truck driver and I were doing a similar solidarity dance in his truck. Our dance was to the rhythm of race and ethnicity, as well as class and gender.

A working-class white tow truck driver had been dispatched to rescue me and my sidelined Saturn, which he did with efficiency and professionalism. Once my lifeless car was chained down to his truck's flatbed, he invited me into its front cab, and we took off.

The radio was on, playing '80s rock and roll, but not so loud as to drown out—or foreclose—conversation. And the anthropologist in me is always ready to ask a question. So I did. I can't even recall what excuse I used to chat him up, but as soon as we got started, he immediately proved himself to be quite the talker—articulate, thoughtful, and clearly full of beliefs about how the world is and how it should be.

Pretty early on, we got to the question of how long I'd been in Philadelphia. He was born and raised less than half a mile from where he picked me up. A native Philadelphian, he relayed with pride, he knew the area like the back of his hand, especially downtown, near his old stomping grounds, but about seven years earlier he'd decided to move to the suburbs.

I told him that I was born in New York, but that my wife and I had spent a few years in Durham, North Carolina, before relocating to Philly, a city she and I knew almost nothing about before we arrived. New Yorkers can sometimes seem so provincial and insular.

"How you like it?" he asked.

"We love it," I beamed, though at this point I knew not to add "because it reminds us so much of Brooklyn."

"Different as hell now, though," he added, "changed from when I was growing up."

"How so?" I asked.

The Philadelphian's answer included several markers of transformation, from how dangerous Philadelphia's streets had become to how gentrified, two seemingly opposite directions of change. But he spent a lot of time talking about the Latino influx, glossed as "those damned Mexicans," a group that wasn't necessarily a major part of either of those two kinds of changes he specifically highlighted.

There used to be a much-publicized sign in a South Philly cheesesteak shop, a famous eatery with lines of customers often snaking around the block and up the street, that declared: "This is America. When ordering, speak English." When the Philadelphia Commission on Human Relations filed a discrimination complaint, the establishment's owner defended the sign, though he also pointed out that he had never actually refused service to anyone who couldn't speak English. Even still, part of the point of English-only discourse is the fact that language is a factor that distinguishes us from them. Speaking English may not be enough to forge lifelong relationships all by itself, but not knowing the language is often an early disqualifier, especially for Spanish-speaking Latinos seen as overrunning otherwise English-only cities and towns. Language is a difference that can feel most terrifying of all, the literal production of incomprehension.

My tow truck driver tried to stay polite at first, but when he started talking about why his hometown had changed beyond acceptability, "those damned [Spanish-speaking] Mexicans" were flagged as culprits, and as part of the reason why he eventually moved out of the city.

"I said forget it. This isn't even South Philly anymore like it used to be, not with those damned Mexicans taking everything over. I couldn't take it no more. Just wasn't for me."

Most of the time people aren't nearly so straightforward about ethnic frustrations, at least not with strangers or in mixed company. They don't just start ranting about "those damned Mexicans." First of all, we know that it isn't polite, and public discourse tends to place a premium on decorum and respectfulness. We don't spend a lot of our day telling complete strangers our deepest, darkest thoughts—or even just our pet peeves. And certainly not our xenophobic anxieties. We have to be driven to do that. Or specifically asked about it, and even then we tend to be circumspect so as not to court unnecessary trouble.

Most people wouldn't ask colleagues or even friends who are "mixed race" like Cora, individuals who might be a little harder to fit into prefabbed racial boxes based on physical features, "Hey, what are you, anyway?" Even as a teenager, I knew it wasn't necessarily polite. I knew better than to ask. It is what people used to call "home training," which meant understanding what was appropriate to say when you weren't at home. It was always better to check, Columbo-style, for clues. Or to ask indirectly: "Where did you grow up? Where are your parents from?" Hoping to triangulate around an answer to "the race question." People knew what you were really asking about, but at least you tried to be discrete. That might get you a few points for effort.

But my tow truck driver started talking about why he left the city, and quickly jumped to "those damned Mexicans" as the biggest reason he moved to the suburbs. He framed his emigration in cultural terms. Language, a part of culture, was one of the first points of difference. He didn't understand these foreigners, and a lot of them likewise didn't understand him when he spoke. He relayed a story about almost getting killed on a construction site because "one of those Mexicans" was operating high-powered electric equipment and didn't understand what any of his non-Latino coworkers were saying to him.

"I said, you know what? 'I quit.' It ain't worth it, getting killed."

"Those damned Mexicans," he explained, also ate different kinds of food and opened up restaurants all over his old neighborhood. Even the much-famed "Italian Market," a major tourist site in South Philadelphia, was awash in Latino and Asian stores of every conceivable variety. These new residents had other strange cultural practices, too. Even the Catholicism they practiced included different rituals and everyday behaviors than the ones he had known all his life. Even among Catholics, there could be religious *thems*, not just an all-encompassing and Pope-following *us*.

For all I knew, he could have been doing the same dance to "those damned niggers" when he towed someone else, but he wanted to bond a bit over the fact that as native-born Americans, he and I could create (even just for the few minutes of our short drive) a multiracial *us* from which the Latino *them* could be barred.

I never saw that driver again, but I remember thinking about how easy it was for us to entertain an anti-Latino narrative that fused him and me together across the long and brutal racial tracks that constitute American history.

We do versions of this us-and-them dance, this sameness-difference shell game, every day. As the father of two young children, I see this all the time with my little ones' kindergarten and second-grade playmates' parents. Kids play across the color line with ease, especially when they haven't been taught to see physical differences as proxies for social worth. And most of the parents of the children my children know don't seem particularly invested—to their credit—in explicitly teaching their offspring to obsess about racial or ethnic or religious differences. The children, of course, take that mandate and run with it, oblivious to the hatreds that racial animus breeds. They might get preoccupied with gradations of skin color (and clearly they learn early on about the premium placed on gender difference), but they don't commit themselves to seeing us vs. them on the playground in absolutely color-coded terms unless and until someone models that kind of parsing for them. "Why are all the black kids sitting together at the lunch table?"[5] Because they are older schoolchildren, and in a few years they will start to internalize America's culture of racial fetishization. But when they are still learning simple arithmetic and basic spelling at the start of elementary school, lunch tables tend to be mixed (provided there is diversity in the school to begin with, a related but distinct issue).

The parents are in a slightly different boat. By the time we are adults, we have all been socialized into racialized camps, and racial categories help to determine how we interact with the entire world, including the parents of our children's classmates. So, for instance, some of the white parents, the ones I see every morning, will smile and say "good morning" to me pretty consistently, but they seem to be quite content with the fact that these before-school pleasantries are the extent of our relationship. "Content" might be the wrong word; a better one might be "comfortable." And it is all about comfort levels—who people feel comfortable interacting with. Us/them fault lines often feel too loaded to walk across without fear and trepidation.

My book *Racial Paranoia* argued that the problem of race in America starts with the fact that most people's most intimate relationships are racially homogenous, almost entirely filled with members of their own race, starting with family and extending to close friends. One reviewer took that to mean I was implying American racism would vanish if white people just had more black friends. That wasn't even close to the point. Really, it was about challenging people to simply monitor their closest social networks, to see how easily we reproduce racial segregation without even trying. (Check your own most intimate networks on that score. How do you do?)

America has a huge and historic us/them divide—a very intimate one—that runs along the fault line of race and reproduces itself effortlessly in the friendships we forge and the families we procreate.

On that elementary school playground, lining up with other parents as our little ones wait for their teachers to take them in, there are a series of mostly race (and class!) homogenous conversations going on between small clusters of parents. And the crazy thing is that this is mostly small talk, which should be a relatively low-cost way to experiment with contact across racial lines. Commenting on the weather, or last night's big game, or (in Philadelphia) the government's disavowal of public education. These exchanges need not blossom into real relationships, but you tend to hope that adults can pull off five minutes of talk about nothing. Kids try to force the issue, with playdates and birthday parties, and while they are still young, parents have to be involved every step of the way. And each one of these events demonstrates that for the vast majority of Americans just a few minutes of idle talk (with no strings attached) can be tough, maybe out of fear that such talk might send the wrong signal: "No, I don't want to be invited to your house or your neighborhood or your birthday party. I actually want as little substantive contact with you as two parents of an interracial kindergarten friendship can manage."

I used to do this thing where I would try to go out of my way to make white people feel comfortable, especially white people I didn't know. The burden was on me to meet them on their side of the color line. Even in that tow truck, we only had our conversation because I had clearly signaled my willingness to hear his take on the world. I made a point of not performing the cool-posing "Angry Black Man." It takes work for most people to talk to strangers at all—and the anxiety is even more complicated when the stranger lives across the tracks.

We think of culture as fairly innocuous. The food we eat. The clothes we wear. The music we listen to. But even those things can be considered dangerous. Anthropologist Oscar Lewis helped popularize the term "Culture of Poverty," which is based on a theory that tries to explain why the seemingly innocuous stuff of every culture can have a pernicious impact on people's ability to succeed and thrive.[6] It argued that poor people of color have a pathological culture, one they pass on to their children, and that is the immediate cause of their social problems. They have a different culture from mainstream America, and that difference means they are the ones most directly responsible for their own misery and misfortune. They need to fix their own problems by first fixing their culture.

Why is it so easy for us to relegate other racial groups to *them* status? It is hard to empathize with folks we don't think about as *us*. They, and their problems, aren't our concern. Economist Glenn Loury once made the argument that the only reason why America allows black people to suffer the disproportionate degree of violence and poverty that they endure is because white Americans can accept blacks as a *them*.[7] All of the issues that overwhelmingly impact poor blacks and Latinos are a "them" problem. If blacks were deemed *us*, a truly American *us* (as opposed to a *them* that lives among *us*), it would be a different kind of crisis, an all-hands-on-deck response to a dilemma that has to be fixed right now. It would be the top story on the nightly news every evening. If it were white youth dying at those rates, it would be a stop-the-presses emergency. But when it is a "stigmatized" them, Loury claims, we might still show alarm and concern, but it isn't *us*, so we look upon it from a constructed distance.

But we can be very fickle about things. We can turn any part of us into them in a heartbeat. It is all terribly context-specific. So, even if culture provides a way to naturalize our attempts to privilege some parts of the social world over others, with all kinds of implications, including finding us people to hate and despise, we can also jerry-rig things, even just temporarily, if the situation demands.

South Philadelphia's most recent school clashes have been between blacks and Asians, especially since many whites have abandoned public schools altogether for relatively nondiverse private schools. There were always working-class blacks across the tracks in South Philly, but now there has been an influx of Latinos and Asians that has sparked many new conflicts. And those conflicts get narrated through cultural difference. "Those damned Mexicans" don't want to work, aren't clean, and don't watch their children. Of course, the irony is that those same Mexicans can also be considered very hardworking (attacked as illegal immigrants stealing jobs from Americans), clean (at least enough to professionally clean other people's homes), and extremely committed to family, depending on who's making the case. They can represent circles and noncircles or squares and nonsquares at the same time.

In that truck, the driver was telling me how much things have changed—for the worse. Things used to be safer. Cleaner. There was a real neighborhood. And he laid much of the blame on "those damned Mexicans"—though, again, it isn't unimaginable that in a different conversation with a different demographic of stranded driver he might have laid more of the blame on another group. But on that day, he wanted to argue that it was all about illegal emigration from Latin America, and I was at least an ostensibly legal American.

He continued to talk about missing city life, and he told me more about the things he did for a living (besides driving a tow truck), and it was an important moment, because given the freighted history of blacks and whites, "those damned Mexicans" was supposed to be an olive branch. A gesture of alliance against a foreign threat. And it is an easy move to make. Classic, even. We all do it, not just that fifty-something urban cum suburban Philadelphian.

For that tow truck operator and me, we pretended as if any anxiety there might have been (between relative strangers forced on a vehicular escapade together for a short while) could be dissipated by displacing it onto a third party, "those damned Mexicans." But the thing is, racial truces built on the backs of absent scapegoats don't last very long. And they are always treaties poisoned from the very start.

CORA

One box rules.

Psssst . . . I have a confession. I have been dreading writing this essay. Despite its location in this book it was the last essay that I wrote. And it was because of that dread—the kind that weighs down in your heart, mind, and soul. My dread of this essay goes beyond this book but dates back to my entire history as a writer. With very few exceptions, for the most part I have avoided writing about my own biracial genes my entire career. Even when I could have been paid to do so I've often turned those assignments down—sacrilege for a working writer who hopes to pay bills. Honestly, I just never saw the point. Where others might have envisioned stories of who-am-I journeys, mixed musings, biracial or multicultural—or whatever the next buzzword is—chronicles, for me there was only one thing to say: I'm black. End of essay.

So why write this essay now? Well, there's the practical reason, John outed me in his Haters piece with his high school memories of trying to figure out my racial makeup—to not speak up after that would be like not finishing a thought or conversation. A more important reason, however, is as a journalist I couldn't ignore the chatter around the issue now, since we are in an era where increasingly (other) people are choosing to identify with all their racial parts. In the last census 9 million people checked off, more than one box for race, an increase of one-third from a decade before.[8] Demographers say these numbers are poised to dramatically increase due to not only the rising rate of interracial relationships but more important, the shifting racial views of younger generations who see not being forced to choose just one race as an act of defiance. That surge of multi-identifiers is often (mistakenly) hailed as a sign of progress. And last, I couldn't avoid writing this essay now because what conversation could be any more impolite than one that begins with, "What are you?"

A couple of years ago Halle Berry caused a TMZ storm when she declared her daughter Nahla was black. The actress was in the midst of a bitter custody battle with her daughter's father, white Canadian model Gabriel Aubry, which turned ugly when tabloids exposed, among other things, that Aubry was fond of calling Berry a nigger. According to the tabloids, Aubry also likes to insist that Nahla is white and gets incensed when the press says otherwise about his child. In the midst of all that, Berry sat down with *Ebony* magazine and did something that folks in the public eye rarely do—she spoke honestly about race. "I feel like she's black," the actress, whose own mother, as we all know, is white, said about Nahla in the March 2011 *Ebony* cover story. Speaking how you would with your girlfriends and not the public, she continued, "I'm black and I'm her mother and I believe in the one-drop theory." The comments went viral instantly. The media was abuzz about Berry's "racial scandal" as if she was the one who was now somehow the racist. Headlines everywhere shouted: "Actress believes in the one-drop rule!"

Well, duh, of course she does. Most of us do, even if we don't admit it. Despite what my blood may be, I don't see society's move to claiming multiple races—including on official forms like the U.S. Census—as a good thing. Instead, I long for the day when we all embrace our One-Drop support, without shame, apologies, and, yes, defiantly the way those multibox checkers do.

The One-Drop rule was one of the social traditions born during slavery, and further emboldened under Jim Crow, of classifying people as black if they had any African ancestry. As early as 1662 states tried to legally define people's racial status (and thus freedom) based on the one-drop social rules.[9] But these definitions didn't officially become law until the early twentieth century when states, most notably Virginia, with its Racial Integrity Act of 1924, started enacting more explicit legislation to "protect" whiteness. Trying to distance themselves from the violent tactics of the KKK, elite Virginians wanted "scientific" standards for their racism and so wrote the one drop of blood standard into law.[10] Other states, including Texas and Louisiana, tried to define blackness based on 1/16th or 1/32nd, but Virginia's notion that *any* African blood—or one drop—is what stuck.[11] (Think such fractioning is antiquated? Consider that during the uproar over Nahla, what was common among the chatter online was talk that the child was "only 1/4 black"). It was not until 1967 that Virginia's Racial Integrity Act was struck down when the Supreme Court outlawed the state's ban on interracial marriage in *Loving v. Virginia.* Still, the legal notion of the one-drop rule persists, according to Harvard researchers, who argue it has been upheld as recently as 1985 when a Louisiana court ruled that a woman with a black great-great-great-great-grandmother could not identify herself as "white" on her passport.[12]

Something that is often overlooked in multibox discussions is that the one-drop rule applied to no other group but American blacks, according to one-drop expert F. James Davis, a retired professor of sociology at Illinois State University and author of *Who Is Black? One Nation's Definition.* The concept was specifically about defining blackness. It is also worth noting that this one-drop definition of blackness did not carry over across the world, which is why every region and culture seems to have its own (screwed-up) definitions of race.

Even before I formally knew of the historical existence of the one-drop rule I still knew the importance of my dad's blood. Although I always knew who I was, my background has often been an issue for others, prompting a lifetime of their "What are you?" questions. (Despite the discretion that John thought back in high school that people would show, most definitely do ask.) Those who ask such questions are typically not satisfied with my answer of "black" because what they are really interested in is the fractions. That is how we determine if you are one of us or one of them, which is the purpose of race, after all. The fact that I never indulge in the fractioning even when asked repeatedly often frustrates people, as if I am the one who is being impolite. Every once in a while I do give the fuller response of "I'm a black woman with a white mother." That blunt honesty usually shuts folks up instantly.

When people don't immediately know what box to put you in it throws them off balance slightly because, unconsciously or not, we use race to determine how we relate with each other. Race, gender, and age are all part of the immediate visual clues we use to interact. It helps shape our expectations and in some cases comfort level. Because our reactions are typically not overt, we often don't realize we are doing it, but we are still doing it. The biggest proof that we are doing it is in the cases when you don't know. When your mind can't immediately interpret what it is seeing it is forced to think about it, even for a moment. Then in some cases our mouths start the asking.

My favorite what-are-you moment was the time when I was a teenager sitting with both my parents in a restaurant in Chinatown in Manhattan. As we gobbled down our pork-fried rice and beef lo mein, the waiter hovered before turning to me and started on the what-are-you kick. He was convinced that I was "part Chinese." My mom starting laughing so hard, she was cackling, literally. It was a first for me. The only part of the what-are-you game that I have enjoyed over the years is that everyone has wanted to claim me as one of their own. Honestly, I don't look exotic at all. But for some reason everyone thinks I am mixed with their homeland. (A few years later my brother would have a story that trumped my Chinatown one for exotic adopted homelands, when a man actually chased him down the street just to ask him if he was Yemeni. Still school-aged at the time, my brother didn't even know what or where Yemen was, so the conversation quickly turned comical in a "Who's on first?" kind of way.) The case in the Chinese restaurant was interesting not only because I had never been mistaken for Asian before (check that box off), but because it was perhaps the only time in my life that I had gotten the what-are-you question when the two people responsible for what I am were sitting right there with me. Even with the parental answer key in front of him, the waiter insisted that I must be "part Chinese."

Through the years, all this questioning did was teach me how important my race (our race) matters. Even if you subscribe to the theory that it doesn't or shouldn't, the reality is that our race, those drops, matter to others.

———

Recently folks were abuzz about the racism on, of all things, CBS's *Big Brother* reality TV show. Bloggers, glued to the continuous live feed of the show that aired online, uncovered an unprecedented barrage of racist, sexist, and homophobic remarks casually doled out by contestants in the house during the season. One of the worst offenders, twenty-two-year-old college student Aaryn Gries, was nicknamed Klan Barbie on Twitter. The slurs were originally showed only online, and some began to campaign for the network to air the house's dirty laundry on TV, as well, in order to shame the hatemongers. The national media eventually picked up on the controversy in the house and soon tried to use *Big Brother* as a national teaching moment to showcase that, yes, indeedy, racism still exists. Just three days after George Zimmerman was acquitted in Florida for shooting Trayvon Martin, a headline in the *New York Times* called *Big Brother* the "Lab Experiment in Overt Racism." (Apparently someone being acquitted for killing an unarmed black teenager wasn't overt enough.) Despite the *Times*'s lack of irony, I did appreciate that the paper at least called the behavior in the house overt racism in contrast to other media outlets, which often called it casual racism. Not that you need either descriptor. Racism is like pregnancy (or blackness): there is no halfway. You either are or you're not. Saying something is casual racism is like saying she's kinda pregnant.

I must admit that when the news broke I was miffed that I had never watched a single moment of the show before. Although I enjoy some reality TV show muck like anyone else, *Big Brother* was never one of my guilty pleasures. (I'm more a *Real Housewives* or even *Mob Wives* kinda gal.) So when racist words got out, I didn't even know the premise of the show (contestants compete for a $500,000 cash prize by avoiding eviction from the house), much less who any of these people were that I suddenly found myself being bombarded with news about. (Some lowlights? When Klan Barbie told an Asian contestant: "Shut up and go make some rice!" Or when another racist contestant, GinaMarie Zimmerman, was bad-mouthing a black housemate, referring to her not by name but as a token, Klan Barbie piped in: "Be careful what you say in the dark; might not be able to see that bitch.") What struck me about the whole thing was not the existence of racism—reality, not reality TV had already shown me that—but how unashamed all these young people were about it. Even knowing the existence of 24/7 surveillance cameras was not enough of a deterrent for these folks—they didn't even find it necessary to at least go and put on their white hoods. Wasn't it the Millennial generation, with their multiracial dating patterns and multibox pride, who were supposed to be the ones who are leading us into a color-blind future? I am feeling dated now because I still remember a time when the worst thing you could call someone was a racist. I don't think the social stigma helped to curb the amount of racial hatred among us, but at the very least people knew better than to put it out in public for all to see. Our hatred of others was our dirty secret. Nowadays we have returned to the point where folks no longer feel shame. Not only is racism often something that is not recognized, but when it is there is no stigma. (In another one of the *Big Brother* low points contestant David Girton casually complained to housemates that some bed sheets smelled because "black Candice" had been on them, and then quickly added, laughing, "that was totally racist.") The bloggers misjudged the situation. Airing such "overt racism" on television couldn't have done much when there are plenty of folks out there, like David, who see it all as a joke. So, I don't think we are any more racist now than when I was growing up. The difference now when it comes to racism is that everyday folks don't care anymore. And no matter how many boxes we mark off in multiracial pride, nothing will change that.

What the multibox checkers overlook is that race(ism) is not scientific or logically sound. Racists don't see degrees. L'Oréal may look at Beyoncé and see "African American, French, and Native American" as it did in a TV ad for its True Match foundation, but the lynch party brigade just sees another black woman. Take *Big Brother*'s Candice Stewart, who received the brunt of much of the show's racist bullying. She is a graduate of the historically black Xavier University and a former beauty queen known for being the first African American woman to be crowned Miss Louisiana in 2005, which paved the way for her to compete in the Miss USA pageant. But "black Candice" was also adopted, and although she was raised by a black family, her birth mother, whom she reunited with as an adult, is white. (If you take a peek at her *Big Brother* audition interview she argues that her "biracialness" would be an advantage in the game because she thought it would allow more folks to identify with her.)

The L'Oréal ad was not the first time that Beyoncé's lack of blackness has caused a stir. Through the years folks have accused the magazine industry of lightening her skin on its covers (*Vanity Fair*'s 2005 issue being the most prominent). And granted, Bey's brand of entertainment will never be mistaken as an outlet for social and racial justice like that of, say, comedian Dick Gregory, whose activism has become the stuff of legend. (The other day I was in a bodega in Bed-Stuy, where I noticed a stack of flyers urging residents to protest the closing of a local hospital. The flyer contained a list of numbers to call that included local politicians and every major and minor news outlet. The very last name on the list of people to call for help was "comedian Dick Gregory." No other explanation was needed.) Still, when you put Beyoncé's blackness front and center as Larry King did in 2009 when he asked her: "Have you experienced racism?" The star doesn't fraction the answer: "Of course!" she said, straight out. Just like any other black woman.

Although, personally, I believe the racial fractioning of Beyoncé is as ridiculous as Senator Elizabeth Warren's claim to Native American heritage early in her career, it is still a sign of our times that such an ad can exist. Increasingly we think everything matters. That is where the L'Oréal thinking is coming from and speaking to. The fact that Madison Avenue is trying to tap into society's multibox leanings is an overt example of how mainstream and desirable those leanings have become. Despite our tendencies to identify every single one of our parts, studies of how people perceive multiracial individuals found, unequivocally, that the "one-drop rule" (or what academics call hypodescent) is still pervasive in society today. And what matters most.

Researchers at Harvard presented people with computer-generated images of black-white and Asian-white individuals, as well as family trees showing different biracial permutations. They also asked people to report directly whether they perceived biracials to be more minority or white. By using multiple approaches, including face morphing technology to alter whiteness from 5 to 95 percent, their work examined both conscious and unconscious perceptions of biracial individuals, presenting the most extensive empirical evidence to date on how they are perceived.[13] The researchers found, for example, that one-quarter-Asian individuals are consistently considered more white than one-quarter-black individuals. At the end of their 2011 study, the researchers concluded: "The findings presented here suggest that the American racial hierarchy is still intact." That hierarchy, the study says, assigns highest status to whites, followed by Asians, with Latinos and blacks at the bottom. The team found few differences in how whites and nonwhites perceive biracial individuals, with both assigning them with equal frequency to the lower-status groups of their heritage.[14] The Harvard study is significant because although the one-drop rule started as a way of defining blackness, the results show one-drop thinking now permeates our conception of race for everyone. No matter what the mixture, the "lower status" group dominates what (one) box people get put in.

"Our work challenges the interpretation of our first biracial president, and the growing number of mixed-race people in general, as signaling a color-blind America," says lead author of the study Arnold K. Ho, in an issue of *Harvard Gazette*, who at the time was a PhD student in psychology at Harvard and now is an assistant professor of psychology at Colgate.[15]

Although Ho makes a great point about our color blindness being a sham, I stumble every time I hear President Obama described as our "first biracial president." Because he is black like me it never ever occurred to me to identify him as anything but our first black president. The first time I heard the "first biracial" I was at a kids' birthday party in bohemian Brooklyn that was the epitome of the new multiracial mosaic that good liberals dream about. The hosts were an interracial couple, and the number of multibox subscribers on the guest list was enough to start a revolution. The hipster quotient was also in full effect, with the organic milk and wine a-flowin'. It wasn't really my thang, but when your kids are young enough that they still need chaperones you often find yourself in social situations that aren't your thang. In a boozy moment one of the white mothers of black children started praising our "first biracial president." I was shocked. I had, honestly, never heard such a thing. Sure I heard from black folks the argument that he wasn't "really black." But even then I still never heard someone go as far and talk about our "first biracial president." Hearing it that day sent me on a journey through the online world of interracial, multiracial, and biracial forums as well as parenting sites, and discovered that while the rest of us, including Obama himself, saw his blackness, the "multi" community saw his "biracialness" and were often excited that one of *their* own was in the White House. It is striking to me how a community that is all about racial choices doesn't respect the choice of those of us, like our first black president, that openly embraces the one-drop rule.

In fact, Obama is a constant reminder of how much we care about the boxes no matter how hard we fight it. Perhaps it is the writer in me, but this becomes most blatant for me after Obama gives a well-crafted speech. The media like to analyze the storytelling of his words, trying to follow the trail of his influences and references as if they were on a treasure hunt. If the road turns black, which it often does, the media often stumbles over itself. That's what happened after the 2013 State of the Union, when just as much attention was given to Obama's calls for a vote on gun control as the way he said it. The dramatic "deserves a vote" calls over and over again caused the pundits to fixate on what they dubbed his "call-and-response" cadence. "There was a little bit of church at the end of the otherwise policy-laden State of the Union,"[16] the *Washington Post* dryly concluded, analyzing the speech on its faith blog that night.

I often think the media loves to point out when they think Obama is borrowing a speaking style from black preachers, because they spend most of the time *thinking* they are ignoring that he is black, and failing. Who could forget the chitchat immediately after the 2010 State of the Union, when MSNBC's resident foot-in-mouth host, Chris Matthews, moronically gushed, "I forgot he was black tonight for an hour." For which he was Internet-whipped by the blogosphere. Jon Stewart quipped, "You know what else you might have forgotten: you're miked." Telling, the humor from Stewart's comeback lies not really in making fun of what Matthews said but more from his saying it for everyone to hear. Truths like that are not meant for mixed company. It was the *Daily Show*'s black correspondent, Wyatt Cenac, who actually mocked what Matthews said. In the skit, Cenac jokingly forgot he himself was black and admitted being distracted during the discussion that Stewart was Jewish, and then ultimately imagined out loud that Stewart was Asian when the host started talking numbers.[17] The point is, contrary to what liberal hearts tell themselves, ignoring or forgetting—that's not actually a good thing. We are who we are, race is part of that. "Color-blind" has become shorthand for an equal society, but treating people equally and with respect does not mean ignoring our identities. "Color-blind," instead, is a Band-Aid that doesn't necessarily have anything to do with helping the wound underneath heal. By saying Obama is *borrowing* from the black church is just another way to keep him verbally a step away from saying who he is: a black man, period. He doesn't have to borrow what is already him. The black church talk is the media stumbling over itself to figure out what to say when their cheap color-blindness glasses get shattered. Kind of like the awkward moments when parents get caught by their kids doing things they don't want their kids to catch them doing.

———

The only time that I wrote extensively about all my drops was about a decade ago in the introduction of my first book. With the book's title being *Black Power Inc.,* I thought starting off with my own what-are-you? experiences would be a bold move, and so I allowed myself to step into the waters I had long avoided. I told the story of an incident in my third-grade class when I was surrounded by a swarm of bowl haircuts and turtlenecks (it was 1979) in the cafeteria, all of them eager to know "what I was":

"Ooh! Ooh! Ooh! I know! I know!" Someone was bursting with an answer.

"She's mixed . . ."

Even at the time that phrase didn't make that much sense to me. "Mixed" is a generation removed from "mulatto" and a step before "biracial" and then "multicultural." All I knew was that I had never heard of any People's Republic of Mixed before . . . Besides, weren't all kids a mixture of their mother and father? Sure my mom was white and Jewish and from a tiny town in Virginia, and my dad was black and Methodist and from the big city of Chicago. But that didn't mean I was mixed (up). So, I corrected the crowd in the know-it-all tone of an eight-year-old and told everyone: "I am Black." It wasn't any big realization, political statement or power to the people affirmation. . . . This wasn't a discovery of my Blackness. I always knew and was comfortable with who I am. In my racial memory, there are also much more painful events, including the usual benchmarks of nigger calling and overt discrimination. But that moment at the cafeteria table, I realized that my Blackness mattered to *everyone else*.[18]

———

After the book came out I heard from one of the other black faces in my third-grade class. It was someone who I went to school with from the third through the eighth grades but had not spoken to since. He was also my first crush, and to hear from him after so many years immediately made me feel like I was still in the third grade. After reading the above details of my parents, he emailed me with a confession: "I had no idea your mom was white—I always just thought she was light-skinned." When I told my mom that back in the day she had been mistaken for black (for years), she cackled. The truth is, my parents, not my brother and I, are the exotic ones in the family. They are the ones who met as cabdrivers in New York City and in their very first conversation got into an argument in the cabbie garage over whether my dad's invite to get some coffee was restricted to coffee (which my mom did not drink) or could also include tea, soda, or even conversation. From that moment they went on to build a life together of arguing and love that lasted until my dad died thirty years later. Each of them is truly one of a kind. That is what the "multi" community misses. Being unique is not dependent on how many different drops you have. The "multi" community often argues that acknowledging the entirety of their racial makeup is honoring all of who they are. I can't agree with that, because we are more than our race. If we truly want to honor our parents and their parents and their parents' parents, then live each day showcasing the best values, ideals, and beliefs that our families had to teach us. (And by "showcasing" I don't mean we have to parrot every behavior or belief of those in our bloodline that came before; my guess is Klan Barbie probably picked up some of her world order view from family.) But being true to all who you are is simply being who you are. Be you.

So what about the boxes? Yaba Blay is a professor of Africana Studies at Drexel University in Philadelphia. She is the big-time brain behind the (1)ne Drop project, a multimedia exercise that seeks to challenge common perceptions of blackness. Blay argues that such perceptions of identity are too narrow, often overlooking the visual and physical variety and diversity of people of African descent. According to its website: "(1)ne Drop takes the very literal position that in order for us to see Blackness differently, we have to see Blackness differently."[19] Blay hopes that through a collection of stunning portraits and memorable testimonials she can help people see. (To out John now, his wife is featured in one of the website's portraits.)

As I was scrolling through the (1)ne Drop project's striking photos of blackness in all its variety and shades, I figured out just why I don't find the multibox times we are in as progress at all. It is because being black in this country is still one of the most difficult identities you can be. That's why instead of getting caught up with all the boxes (the fractions), embracing that one drop and being proud of it, is truly what it means to be defiant about who we are. End of essay.

CORA

Color Wars!

"[Marcus Garvey] is a little, fat, black man, ugly . . . with a big head."

—W. E. B. DUBOIS IN AN ARTICLE "BACK TO AFRICA," *CENTURY MAGAZINE*, FEBRUARY 1923[20]

"W. E. Burghardt DuBois As a Hater of Dark People."

—TITLE OF MARCUS GARVEY'S RESPONSE ARTICLE IN *NEGRO WORLD*, FEBRUARY 1923[21]

When my daughter was in kindergarten a few years back she was very fond of pointing out the peach people. Her class was doing a year-long self-portrait project where every month the kids would create a new crayon masterpiece of themselves. The idea was that with each drawing they would add more realistic details so that by the end they would finally have a self-portrait that looked more like a child's face instead of scribble. At the end of the year the teacher created nice little books of each child's monthly self-portraits that parents could ooh and ahh over. I am not much of an ooh-and-ahh type of parent, but it was interesting to see the growth of five-year-olds over a year in terms of their observation skills and their crayon-holding dexterity. Early on in the project the class must have been encouraged to notice skin color, because at some point, en masse, every face in the class got colored in. When I visited the class that month to see the portraits on the wall, there hung twenty-four peach faces and one dark brown—my daughter. Interestingly, however, my daughter was not the only "brown" kid in her class. In fact, although "peach" did dominate, there were at least four other kids whose skin was actually darker shades of brown than hers. (Yes, I counted, as does every black parent, even if they claim not to.) But for that first showing she was the only one who chose to color her brown face brown. By the end of the year, two other faces on the wall were also colored in brown, but never the full gang of five. (From the beginning she also gave herself curly brown hair and not straight, which made my black woman soul ooh and ahh with pride. It took a few more months before her glasses appeared in her portraits, though.) My husband and I raised a fist and patted ourselves on the back for our contribution to the Race.

The debut of the portraits is about when my daughter started describing people as either peach or brown, like the crayons. It became part of her regular description of people. When she would tell me about kids at school who had the same name, instead of relying on the age-old last initial tactic to clear up confusion, as in Jessica D. or Jessica L., she initially described them as "Jessica D., who is peach with yellow hair" or "Jessica L., who is peach with black hair." She dropped their "colors" once she was convinced I knew the difference between the two Jessicas. When she started teaching her brother, who was then two, the colors of our family I decided to step in. Not because my young children were talking about race, but because they weren't. In my five-year-old daughter's description she and her brother were brown, Daddy was dark brown, and Mommy was tan. Actually, the two argued a little bit over whether Mommy was really tan or peach. They were sure Grandma was peach, and Mommy, they reasoned, was lighter than them. I got the sense that in their minds we were all different because we would each require a different crayon. It was during the tan-peach debate that I stepped in to inform them we were all black.

"Even Grandma?"

"No, she's peach, I mean white."

"Okay."

"So, remember," the five-year-old turned to the two-year-old, as if she was going to impart life lessons, "we're black even though we're brown."

That is when I went into a long lecture about how black people come in a wide range of wonderful shades of brown. We do not live in a color-blind house, so it wasn't the first time I had talked to my kids directly about race. My children, at the lighter end of brown, would have passed any paper bag test. Proof of the power of recessive genes, their curly brown hair gets streaked with blond in the summer to the point that we are often stopped on the street in our black neighborhood by people who ooh and ahh. In fact, my son's curls have the nerve to be so loose (even looser than the peach side of my family) that a comb refuses to get caught, making me with my tender-headed tear memories wonder where this child came from. Because of my children's lightness, as a parent I have made an extra effort to openly talk to them about their blackness. When my husband and I bought our house, long before we had kids, most important to us was buying in a black neighborhood, even though our income could have afforded us otherwise, because we wanted our future children to know that is where home is. So it wasn't a light bulb oh-I'm-black moment for them when I stepped in. If they thought about it before they spoke, they always knew they were black. That's why my daughter did not hesitate to color her portrait brown. But before that moment I don't think they had thought about the shades of blackness before.

As a parent there are a few moments where you feel smart, and many more when you feel dumb. That is because children test you to explain things that you never realized would ever need explaining. I honestly can't remember the details of my "wonderful shades of brown" lecture, but I like to hope that it was one of my few smart moments.

In the years since, I've thought about that conversation a lot. Mainly because even though I felt compelled to step in to offer a dose of reality, I have come to think that my children's fixation that day on color over race was actually much closer to the real world.

When we talk about social issues there tend to be two camps—the race thinkers and the class thinkers. What about light skin versus dark skin? Color, like some bastard child, is often not invited into the conversation. But just how much race and class entrap you depends on color.

Don't take my word for it: There is a growing body of academic evidence that examines just how important your darkness or lightness is in effecting life's outcomes, from marriage to income. The academics call it the "preference for whiteness" or "preference for lightness" theory. In these studies, smart people at top universities break down the population not into racial categories like white and black but into color categories of white and light-skinned blacks, medium-skinned blacks, and dark-skinned blacks. I'm serious.

The research finds there is a direct correlation between better health, wealth, education, and status and how light-skinned you are. In academic speak: "Dark-skinned blacks in the United States have lower socioeconomic status, more punitive relationships with the criminal justice system, diminished prestige, and less likelihood of holding elective office compared with their lighter counterparts."[22]

When it comes to income, on average, darker-skinned black folks would experience a 6 percent wage gain if they were still black but with lighter skin. (The difference in income between whites and black people—any shade—of comparable background is about 15 percent.)[23] "Lightness is rewarded in the labor market," the academics concluded.[24] Although still a small sliver of discrimination suits, the number of lawsuits charging discrimination based on skin color instead of race has been steadily increasing. In 2003 the EEOC settled a landmark color harassment suit when it ordered Applebee's to pay $40,000 to a dark-skinned black employee who the EEOC found was discriminated against for his dark skin by his light-skinned black manager. The EEOC press release about the precedent-setting case noted that the commission was seeing an "increasing number of color discrimination charge filings at agency field offices across the country."[25] At the time, color bias filings had increased 200 percent since the mid-1990s, from 413 in 1994 to 1,382 in 2002.[26] By 2011, the most recent year data is available, that number had climbed to 2,832 color-bias filings.[27]

Findings have been similarly depressing in studies of skin color and marriage. Researchers found light-skinned black women have a 15 percent greater probability of marrying than darker-skinned black women.[28] Among black women, there is "a premium associated with light-skinned complexion,"[29] says Darrick Hamilton, professor of economics and public policy at the New School in New York, and coauthor of the study "Shedding 'Light' on Marriage," along with Arthur H. Goldsmith, a professor at Washington and Lee University, and William A. Darity Jr., a professor at Duke University. (The trio teamed up to do the wage study mentioned earlier.) Economists see life through numbers, so to make the marriage conclusion they actually came up with a formula:[30] $P_m=q(s,X^f)[1-F\{E_r(S,X^f)\}]$. Or in other words, dark-skinned black women are getting screwed.

When it comes to the criminal (in)justice system darker-skinned black defendants are also getting screwed. (I am not intentionally trying to link marriage to jail time, but wages, love, and incarceration tend to be the three general areas of research when it comes to color discrimination.) Black defendants with darker skin are twice as likely to receive the death penalty than lighter-skinned black defendants for crimes of equivalent seriousness involving white victims, according to research at Cornell Law School.[31] A recent study found that women with lighter skin receive more lenient sentences and serve less time than their darker-skinned counterparts.[32] Although there are many studies that look at race and sentencing and a few that have looked at skin color, this was the first to look at color and women.

Like everything, colorism has a history. In this country it is traced back to slavery. And I hate to write that. Once the roots of anything get traced to slavery Americans tune out—myself included. As a nation we typically don't like to concern ourselves with the happenings of the last news cycle, much less think that our history more than 150 years ago (when dark-skinned slaves were given the field work and lighter-skinned slaves assigned house work) matters today. Still, like herpes, biases based on skin color have been hard to shed.

Before there were rapper dis tracks there was the feud between W. E. B. DuBois and Marcus Garvey, who would duke it out in competing essays. It is understandable that the integrationist and the nationalist would not play nicely together, but there is evidence that underlying their animosity toward one another was some old-fashioned color bias, too. The DuBois quote that opens this essay is from a 1923 essay called "Back to Africa." It is the first time DuBois makes his attacks on Garvey personal, and it is significant that he does so by making a black and ugly reference long before Biggie made it pop. Garvey slung back in an essay that same year that he titled "W.E. Burghardt DuBois As a Hater of Dark People." Not that one needs to say any more than that, but the essay begins: "W.E. Burghardt DuBois, the Negro 'misleader' who is editor of the *Crisis,* the official organ of the National Association for the Advancement of 'certain' Colored People . . . this unfortunate mulatto who bewails every day of the drop of Negro blood in his veins . . ."[33] To which DuBois spat back: "Marcus Garvey is, without doubt, the most dangerous enemy of the Negro race in America and in the world. He is either a lunatic or a traitor."[34] DuBois went on to call for Garvey to be deported back to Jamaica, which he eventually was after being convicted of mail fraud. Ninety years later, the raw emotions still jump from the page. That's what happens when color comes into play.

And more recently, of course, were the infamous comments of Senate Democratic leader Harry Reid, who predicted that Barack Obama could become the nation's first black president because he was "light-skinned." I bring up all this history just to give context to how long colorism has been simmering.

Although that history is interesting, honestly, the roots of color bias don't concern me. The fact that the "preference for lightness" exists today is what concerns me.

———

"If you're white, you're all right.
If you're brown, stick around.
If you're yellow, you're mellow.
But if you're black stay back."

I was thirteen years old. That was the summer when my brother, who was ten, and I went to a free summer program called the Big Apple Games. It was a program run by the city at public schools in chosen neighborhoods in an effort to keep have-nots off the streets. The highlight for my brother and I was the long walk home. I'm not sure how the decision was made, but it was decided that it would be better to go to a Big Apple Games location closer to my mom's job than our apartment. It meant that everyday my brother and I were responsible for walking ourselves home across the entire stretch of the Lower East Side. It took us more than an hour to walk home every day, which we did to save on bus fare. By today's overparenting standards, such lack of supervision would never happen. But the freedom of that long walk—no cell phones, no person waiting for us when we got home—was empowering.

The highlight of the summer was at some point in the journey we got invited to a second lunch. Along our walk we passed a soup kitchen for senior citizens. One afternoon there was a volunteer standing out front who insisted we come in and get something to eat. The do-gooder was thinking that two kids walking the streets alone must be both poor and hungry. Although the Daniels household did know struggle (we were, after all, trying to save on bus fare after attending a free city program), we were not at the soup kitchen point yet in our lives. We were, however, too polite ever to turn down anything free, so we sat down, the only children in a room full of seniors, for our second lunch of the day (the Big Apple Games provided our first [free] lunch). The two lunches became part of our routine, and we visited the soup kitchen most afternoons to break up that long walk home. Of the Big Apple Games itself, I don't remember much except taking a bus trip one day to Bed-Stuy, Brooklyn, the city's biggest and baddest black neighborhood back then, to see the Big Apple Olympics, where the have-nots from across the city competed for medals. (This was at a time when every kid did not automatically get one.) During the opening ceremonies I squinted from the stands to see track star Carol Lewis (sister to the Olympian), who told us, in true '80s fashion, to say no to drugs. Never much of an athlete, I spent the afternoon trying to avoid as much physical activity as possible. It was then that I passed some girls jumping rope.

That's when I heard it: *"If you're white, you're all right. If you're brown, stick around. If you're yellow, you're mellow. But if you're black stay back."* Honestly, I didn't even blink. I was more concerned with the Double Dutch skills since it was something I was always too afraid to try, for fear that my uncoordinated body would prevail and the schoolyard bullies of blackness would take away some of my black girl points. (Interestingly, now at my daughter's elementary school Double Dutch is one of the afterschool offerings parents can pay to send their kids to. When I peeked in one day, to check out the skills, I noticed that the entire class, teacher included, was peach.) Hearing the anthem of colorism in a schoolyard at thirteen is not as dramatic as at, say, six. But consider that this was not some childhood memory of life in a quaint rural southern town circa pre–civil rights marchin' and singin'. Instead it was 1985 in New York City. How could the supposed capital of liberalism retain any side effects of slavery? How could it not?

The point is, color matters. Our blackness matters. It did yesterday, it probably will tomorrow, and it matters today.

The level of importance that I give color bias is probably why I cannot stand the catchphrase "people of color." I am honestly not sure what makes it supposedly more culturally sensitive than "minority," "nonwhite," "or colored people." When I'm chitchatting with my husband or select close friends I will jokingly replace the phrase "people of-color" with "colored people" to mock the PC police. I get great satisfaction in sarcastically slipping it in at times of great angst, and I can always depend on those closest to me not to indulge my lame attempts at humor but instead offer necessary "shut yo' mouth" glares. Keeping that balance is necessary. I once gave a speech at a local college in Northern California after being up all night traveling and up all day doing interviews. It wasn't the audience's fault, but by the time I appeared onstage that evening my mind was mush and I could barely focus my eyes to read the words of my speech. During my talk I slipped and accidentally said "colored people" instead of "people of color." I noticed my mistake instantly and waited for the tomatoes to be thrown. Instead there was no reaction. Silence! An entire auditorium of young people of color was too polite to stir when called "colored people." That is why that phrase is so wrong. Outraged by their politeness, for the rest of the speech I made a conscious effort to use "colored people" over and over again in a lame attempt to shake up their souls. It didn't work. At the end they applauded, bought books, and took photos. That night, still mad, I flew back home wondering what it takes to get the meek outraged these days.

———

Red bone, light skinned, high yellow, Creole, mulatto, chocolate, "Indian blood" claims, dark skinned, blue, black . . .

For me my color has always been intricately tied to my racial identity. I have always noticed differences in treatment not only based on race but also race and skin color. (It is a bias that often comes in pairs.) I think I noticed because for others my lightness has always been a much bigger deal than it has ever been for me. It has attracted attention both good and bad. The lighter shade of my brown skin allows me certain levels of access, especially in mainstream circles. Period. The areas where this privilege is easiest to recognize is in work and love, just as the academics predict. But privilege, no matter how slight, trickles down to every facet of life. Let me make clear that I am not condoning or embracing or encouraging these benefits. But to not admit that such privilege exists would be the same as condoning, embracing, and, most of all, encouraging it. Our silence on the privileges that we each enjoy is in effect an endorsement. So here's me not being silent. (Can I get a shout-out from all the upper-class white men?)

When I was pregnant with my first child, I was not prepared for the attention that pregnant women get. Everyone feels the need to talk to you when you are pregnant. It is as if pregnancy is supposed to make you this beacon of chitchat, a being who always smiles and is permanently friendly and who welcomes every word uttered from intrusive strangers. Since even in my best mood I don't want to chitchat, especially when I'm lugging thirty pounds of extra weight, making every ounce of my body uncomfortable, I never got used to the intrusions. What I wasn't expecting, though, was the pick-up lines. Maybe it is a Brooklyn thing, since we are the land of no respect, where men stand on corners and literally whistle catcalls at (any and every) woman walking by, but my pregnant belly seemed to attract Brooklyn brothas. And the lines would always include something about my lightness and how I will make beautiful babies because of it and their desire to take part in making those babies. Nothing like being hit (on) with some self-loathing ignorance to dampen that pregnancy glow.

Always more of an issue in white circles, my lightness has meant that some have tried to overlook my blackness. Upon returning to school after summer vacation, there would always be those kids, the same ones who were obsessed with asking "what are you?" questions, who would put their newly suntanned arms next to mine and claim that I wasn't really black because they were now darker than me. In elementary school, being a smart-ass was my defense of choice, so I would usually respond with something like "My great-great-grandparents were slaves—how about yours?" or "What plantation did your ancestors work on?" That would quickly end the game.

Kids who play stupid games grow up to be adults who say stupid things. I always felt the best part of being a business journalist was that I had the advantage of being close to corporate America without being part of it. The closest I came to being part of it was when I worked at a magazine owned by one of the world's biggest publishers. Its building was a mix of writers, artists, and admen from the biggest brands on the newsstand. It meant that the elevators were swimming with wannabe suits and the hallways with politics.

My running buddy in those days was the only other black girl on staff. We were young and still on the rise, and in that stage of our career where that is what matters most. Whenever we broke through doors we would count the (dwindling) black faces. She would also count the dark-skinned black faces. Many times hers was the only one in the room. In the office, the reaction to us was interesting, because people were typically much more careful talking about race

pretty enough by da brothas. And all shades of brown fingers start pointing at each other. The thing about infighting is the big picture ends up getting lost.

The preference for lightness is not just a black thang, it's a global thing. From India, Pakistan, the Dominican Republic, Mexico, Brazil and beyond, there are color caste systems embedded in cultures around the world. Brazil is infamous for its color identification and classification. As it gets set to host the World Cup in 2014 and the Olympics in 2016 its racial problems have fallen under the spotlight recently, with the bulldozing of poor black shanty towns to build stadiums and superhighways. The census in Brazil officially counts five official color categories, including Preta (Black) and Pardo (Brown). If you talk to folks on the street, though, most use between seven and ten categories to break down the different shades of brown even more. When a government survey conducted in 1976 asked Brazilians to identify their race, it got back 136 different answers, helping cement Brazil's rep for its hyper color consciousness. In 1998 when the government went back to do the survey again, in part in an effort to erase the chatter about the previous survey, they got back 143 different categories.[35] Currently there is a debate going on in Brazil on whether to import American-style affirmative action to help lift up the masses of darker-skined Brazilians at the bottom of the pecking order.[36] Amid the arguments against the move is that Brazil doesn't have "black people." This is a surprise to Brazilians of African descent leading the movement for the government to take action.

Not only are Latin American attitudes about race migrating to the United States, the evidence is growing that our own color biases are much more entrenched than we have given them credit for. "The treatment of race may be more similar in the U.S. and Latin America than previously thought,"[37] according to the study "From Dark to Light: Skin Color and Wages Among African Americans" that looked at the economic effects of skin color in the workplace.

A recent study out of Vanderbilt University Law School further challenged the American Dream by looking at how skin color affected the success of immigrants.[38] Guess what? How dark or light they were mattered. Even taking into consideration other factors that could affect wages, such as English-language proficiency, education, occupation, race, or country of origin, researchers still found that skin tone seemed to make a difference in earnings. That means that if two similar immigrants from Bangladesh, for example, came to the United States at the same time, with the same occupation and ability to speak English, the lighter-skinned Bangladeshi would make more money on average. In fact, the lighter-skinned earned 16 to 23 percent more than compared with darker skin.[39]

"I thought that once we controlled for race and nationality, I expected the difference to go away, but even with people from the same country, the same race—skin color really matters," said Joni Hersch, a law and economics professor at Vanderbilt University and author of the study.[40] Despite conventional thinking that in a new land, each year would have to get better, Hersch's paper soberly concluded: "Furthermore, the skin color penalty does not diminish over time."[41]

I am the type of journalist who loves data and research. My habit is to overreport stories, which means I typically have more information left over in my notebooks than what ends up being published. Academic journals are treasure troves of uber-specific research. They can be my own personal Candyland. For any point you want to make, there is probably a professor out there who has done some kind of research that can help you "prove" it. Despite my reporter geek side I have major issues with academics. The problem with all this generating of intellectualism is that the points that academics make, in practical purposes, often tend to be small. You may be surprised to hear me say that, considering I've willingly and happily teamed up with a respected member of said academy to write this book. And I respect the work that John does tremendously. Still, the point about academics in general missing the point is simply, well, the truth. So as a reporter, where, by definition, my job is to do research for an audience, which means putting that research into context and drawing conclusions for the public, it is frustrating to take a journey through academic journals and see research for research's sake. I think of it as the piles of lost sparks—sparks of ideas that never add up to the big idea. Too many academics never take the leap from their research to real life. They can spend years proving a tiny slice of an issue, which they will layer onto the ongoing conversation that is always already happening among other academics. Reading their papers can be hilarious, as every other word is referenced and attributed to previous papers, as if the reader should be up on all this internal banter. That's what it was like reading Hersch and the others. Economists love algorithms, so there was lots of number crunching and formulas and data. Reading these papers that were touching on issues of discrimination and colorism you get the sense that the researchers have forgotten that they are writing about a situation that is completely messed up, as the real world would say. Life is not just a bunch of numbers and formulas. It's people. And people are messy.

Hersch used her numbers to propose that maybe color matters more than race. Or as the last line of her paper mechanically puts it: "By comparing immigrants of different national origins, races, and ethnicities, the findings of this paper and of Hersch (2008a)* provide evidence consistent with the hypothesis that color matters more than nominal race, as the wage penalty to darker skin color exists across races and ethnicities rather than simply within races or ethnicities."[42] (Huh? Isn't that a big deal?! How can one make such a conclusion and not get outraged?)

Interestingly, the color-matters-more-than-race thesis is exactly the argument that I set out to say when I started this essay. I thought that in a world where you can mark off black *and* white, it will be the shade of brown you are that will matter more. But seeing it in black and white in Hersch's paper, I began to question my conviction. The difference between me and the academics is that I live in the real world. So I am not ready to throw out race just yet. But it is naïve to deny how significant color is in how much race will entrap us. And that is the difference.

By admitting this I am not dismissing race or class or gender, for

---

*Yes, she is referencing herself!

that matter, nor trying to replace the isms that go along with those identities with the ism of color. Our identities are intertwined. That is why race vs. gender arguments never make sense. I am never just black. I am always a black woman. Specifically, I am a light-skinned black woman who has managed to jump class from humble working-class roots to educated, professional elite. Still, although intellectually I will argue that you cannot isolate our identities; it is dangerous not to admit how much color is contributing to how we experience those identities. Therefore it is not good enough to just say that it is harder for black folks to climb, it is necessary to also say it is hardest for black folks with darker skin to climb at all. That matters. By not acknowledging the "preference for lightness" we are simplifying how race is lived. In my mind, to ignore colorism is just as big a crime as ignoring racism. They go hand in hand.

The other reality is that our world is no longer black and white even if our discussions about race still are. To think about race as black and white is a previous generation's debate. I was reminded of this when I took my kids to visit Washington, DC, for the first time and we went to the Smithsonian National Museum of American History. My kids were only three and six at the time, and people were constantly telling me they were too young for a week full of museum visits and monuments. We did it anyway, also throwing in the Library of Congress and the White House, as well as sitting on the steps of the Capitol to sing "I'm Just a Bill," and their youngness did not stop them from enjoying museums and monuments. When we visited the American History Museum we discovered that on the same floor as an original Jim Henson Kermit the Frog is the infamous Woolworth lunch counter from Greensboro, North Carolina. I stood there with my (young) kids and tried to explain the significance, retelling the story of four black students who changed the world. It was then that I realized just how foreign to them that world I was describing was, right down to the concept of a lunch counter at Woolworth. Their world is not black and white or rather just black and white. Instead, thanks to immigration trends, where Latinos are now the nation's largest minority group, and a growing multiracial population, the

America of tomorrow is going to be shades of brown. Before my kids turn forty the U.S. Census Bureau projects that the country will be a "majority minority" nation.[43] They already live in a "majority minority" city, New York. (The term "minority" is sounding sillier and sillier to use, isn't it?) In fact, nonwhites are now the majority in twenty-two of the nation's largest cities, including Los Angeles, San Diego, San Francisco, the entire DC metro area, Las Vegas, Houston, Miami, Memphis, and even Jackson, Mississippi.[44] The last census also revealed that for the first time the majority of the babies born in the United States are not white.[45] Officially, the nation may not ever be headed toward a complex Brazilian take on race, but there is no denying that this browning has to affect people's attitudes about race and identity. Unfortunately, attitudes also include biases, prejudices, hang-ups, issues, and hatred. If the lines of race are being blurred, then why wouldn't the lines of color substitute as an outlet?

I used to work with a woman who would use the term "brown people" instead of "minorities" or "people of color." "What up, brown people?" she would say jokingly, and always too chipper, to the few fellow nonwhite faces in the office. "As brown people we . . ." she would utter when speaking up for the Race. Ethnically her family was Caribbean, specifically Indian hailing from Guyana. Her social circles were almost exclusively black, but her insistence on using the term "brown people" was a constant reminder that she was not. At the time, I used to find her "brown people" utterances grating. Since she was young, I thought "brown people" was a holdover from her recent college days, and so I put it in the people-of-color bin of annoying PC terms that should never leave college campuses. Turns out "brown people" wasn't what the kids were saying, just this one annoying kid. Our office wasn't the poster child for diversity, so I think what bugged me most was that these "brown people" she was always "what upping" were all black folks. The term "black" for me is enough. There is no need to dress it up or dilute it; it is instead at its most powerful just by letting it be. But these days, given the browning of America, surprisingly, I don't find her word choice as annoying anymore. I once even caught myself uttering to an audience of "people of color," "As black and brown people we . . ." as I tried to uplift the Race, of course.

———

My father died white. I wasn't with my father when he died. None of his family was. He was at a late-night jam session playing music when he had a heart attack. He died, surrounded by friends and strangers, waiting for the ambulance. Dying in public meant that his body was delivered to the city morgue, where the search began to find us, his family. I had never thought about my dad's skin color growing up. He was black and my mom wasn't and that was enough. When we took a trip to Chicago to visit his relatives they called him Red, and that is when I noticed that although I only saw my dad's blackness (or mine), others saw his lightness. When my mother, brother, and I arrived at the morgue the next day after my dad's passing, there was lots of paperwork to fill out. Leave it to the government to make even death feel like a bureaucratic transaction. I refused to do the official identification, so I busied myself with the paperwork. That is where I noticed that the coroner had mistakenly marked off on one of the forms that my dad was white, despite the Frederick Douglass Afro that he sported. He was so light-skinned in life, that in death, with his little color drained from his cheeks, he was seen as white. He would have been outraged. My dad's life was not ruled by race, but he did not ignore it either. Politeness wasn't in his vocab (his normal speaking voice was more of a constant yell), so if you were racist he would tell you. And in his view many people were. His honesty about race and pride in self was instilled in me, and it is why, despite our multiracial household, I never thought I was anything but black or thought I could be anything but black. The "we are all black" comeback that I spouted to my kids that day was a lesson learned from him.

It has been a few years since my daughter was in kindergarten, so she doesn't do the brown people and peach people thing anymore. I still think her Crayola references were closer to the reality we live in than my black-white talk. But, maybe the coroner's mistake was trying to teach me something, too. Sure, color matters in life. (Those wage studies should never let us forget. That's why when we are talking big thoughts on how to make the world better we cannot afford to not invite that colored bastard into the conversation.) But no matter how much color matters in life, in death, it is all the same. And there is some hope in that.

JOHN

All my best friends are light-skinned women.

My wife and I pull out our wedding memorabilia every June for our anniversary, and we take a few minutes to reminisce about the cere- mony. Everything we've kept from the event fits into a shoebox-sized carton ornately decorated in colors from the wedding, including ex- cess cloth from the bridesmaids' dresses and unused stationery from our homemade invitations. The box protects keepsakes: place settings from the dinner, the RSVPs that people returned with funny notes scribbled on them, and a Kinkos-produced booklet we put together for folks to take home that included photos and short blurbs about everyone who attended.

The last thing we usually do, after we've rummaged through the box, is watch some of our wedding DVD, which includes everything from the start of the ceremony (when the entire wedding party, min- ister included, danced up the sanctuary's center aisle to a Nyabinghi drumbeat) to the reception's dance party with all of its *Soul Train*–like aspirations. We even have a few seconds with the last couple left on the dance floor after the party had long petered out.

One thing that always sticks out about the ceremony whenever we watch the video is our unconventional wedding party. We called it "a wedding posse," and it included four of my wife's closest friends, most from her time as an undergrad at Brown (even a Howard alum, like myself, has to respect how thick-like-thieves those Brown grads seem to be), along with my brother, sister, and three more of my friends: Cora, the only person from high school whom I still keep in touch with and my gracious coauthor for this book (I was also the "bride's gentleman" at her wedding); Larry, the first person I met in college (fighting over which of our cities was better, New York or Los Angeles); and my closest friend from graduate school, Martha (whom I just emailed because it has been far too long since we last spoke). Part of what made the "wedding posse" so interesting (and it is something that I was surely cognizant of at the time, even if I didn't really think about it too much) was the fact that Cora, Martha, and my wife, Deb, are all three of the lightest black women you'd ever meet. They could all pass the proverbial brown paper bag test. In fact, Martha and (maybe?) Deb could pass for Caucasian without much second-guessing, but Cora would probably have to settle for some kind of Latina or Middle Eastern.

Watching the video now, I realize that I surely must have looked like a textbook example of a "color struck" black man to all of our family members and friends that day. "Color struck": someone preoccupied with skin color and particularly infatuated with light-skinned black women. They must have been thinking that (if they didn't simply assume that those light-skinned women were white). For the folks who knew me and my half of our wedding posse/party, it must have been worthy of a comment or two, even just in passing, and even if only to write it off, generously. "He probably doesn't really have a skin-complexion thing, but what a coincidence, huh? I never noticed that before."

But do I have a problem? Back in the day, successful black men, especially dark ones, always had very light black women as their girlfriends and wives. I watch period movies set in the early twentieth century, so I know that's true. The doctors and lawyers would have very light-skinned women who would give them light-skinned children. As some sisters might say, these black men may not have been "average," but they were surely "typical." One rationale for the practice (other than the internalization of European beauty standards) was that their slightly lighter kids would be able to move up the pecking order of America's color-coded racial hierarchy a little more easily. Maybe just slightly, but every bit helps. The girls might even get "good hair." A tragedy of riches.

We don't nearly talk about color as much as we could. There is enough shame and discomfort around the topic that we usually just leave it alone. Maybe a quick joke among very close friends, as a demonstration of just how special the bond is: it can even withstand color talk. But anything else is rude. And nothing good could come of it.

The "talented tenth" that sociologist and historian W. E. B. DuBois wrote about more than a hundred years ago, a group that would be Black America's political, social, and cultural vanguard, its leaders and spokespeople, was definitely skewed in the direction of lighter-skinned blacks, just like DuBois, and for a number of different reasons, including more access to the economic or institutional support of white fathers or grandfathers, whether or not they were publicly acknowledged. And color continues to be correlated with social success for African Americans today, whether whites notice the subtler gradations of skin color or not. I can't tell you the last time I went up to Harlem and saw a very light-skinned black person homeless and panhandling on the street. I'm not saying they aren't there, but their numbers are relatively small compared to their darker-skinned race mates. Although maybe the lighter ones are passing for white and panhandling in nicer parts of the city. Even still, I'd wager that the darker you are as an African American, the more likely you are to end up homeless and on the street. (Maybe someone has already done the study on that. If not, there's a dissertation topic.) Lighter skin has long meant more perks within the black community—and for black people interacting with white folks, too.

Remember that old childhood rhyme about color? It was a little before my time, but I heard it chanted in many of those aforementioned period films (though Cora is right that black girls were probably still using it to narrate their jump-rope routines when we were kids):

If you're White, you're all right.
If you're Brown, stick around.
If you're Black, get back.

But we're not talking about brown or black. Or even white. We're talking about women described (in dated vernacular terminology) as "high yellow" or "high yella." A different color entirely. A derogatory term in the nineteenth and early twentieth centuries that has fallen just about completely out of favor, "high yellow" was also a reference to class, a term used for members of the colored elite, especially its female members. High-yellow families were the light-skinned leaders of the black community, and their high-yellow complexions were an indication of their more visible amounts of white ancestry.

The famous folk song that many confederate soldiers, especially the ones from Texas, sang during the Civil War, "The Yellow Rose of Texas," was specifically about a high-yellow girl who was meant to inspire at least one "darky" (a term later changed to "soldier") in his quest back home from the battlefield:

There's a yellow rose in Texas, that I am going to see,
No other darky knows her, no darky only me
She cried so when I left her, it like to broke my heart,
And if I ever find her, we nevermore will part.

She's the sweetest rose of color this darky ever knew,
Her eyes are bright as diamonds, they sparkle like the dew;
You may talk about your Dearest May, and sing of Rosa Lee,
But the Yellow Rose of Texas is the only girl for me.

Was I falling into the tradition of favoring light-skinned women? My own Yellow Roses of Brooklyn?

For the folks at the wedding who really knew me, they'd also be aware that my two previous relationships had been with (1) a white graduate student from Seattle, and (2) a very light-skinned Creole grad student born and raised in New Orleans. So the wedding party wasn't even the entire story. It was only the tip of a high-yellow iceberg.

When one of my grad school friends, a browner-skinned black woman, first found out I was starting to date Deb, she remarked on the fact that my new girlfriend was even lighter than the last one, the Louisianan Creole mentioned above. I can recall some of our conversation fairly well. I also remember that, inexplicably, I was taking a shower while talking to her on the phone. (Who talks on the phone in the shower?) The echoing sound of spraying water didn't seem to bother my interlocutor too much, though; she simply made a point of noting the color similarities between the two women and then waited for my response.

I don't have any proof of this, and I was certainly clueless at the time, but I have grown to believe, maybe incorrectly, that my friend's question might have been posed specifically because she was also potentially interested in me in some kind of romantic way. I'm not sure about this theory, and I definitely didn't think it at the time, but I was particularly dense back then when it came to such things, and she would have had to run me over with a Mack truck, or just about, for me to get the hint. And even then, those very intentions should have been plastered on the sides of that truck as well, just to make sure I didn't miss it.

But I wasn't thinking any of that at the time. I just joked to her about the fact that the light-skinned thing was something of a departure for me. All through high school and college, I had always dated very dark-skinned women. All of my girlfriends had been about my own skin color or darker, and I was rarely attracted to anything else. In fact, I even had a moment in college when I thought it was my political duty to only date dark-skinned women. This was also about the time when I decided—based on related political calculations—that I would never get caught dead applying for a Rhodes scholarship (like I would have gotten one anyway), because Cecil Rhodes was a racist and a colonialist, and I wouldn't think of insulting my enslaved ancestors like that. So, although dating dark women became, for a short time, a kind of political statement for me, I was also very attracted to them, and always had been, which made that political mandate very easy.

Meanwhile, I continued to lather up (in my shower) as I offered my friend some joke about already having "put in my time with dark-skinned black women as an undergraduate," and we went on to something else. Or maybe she just quickly got off the phone in disgust. That part I can't remember. I do know that we never spoke on the phone again, and I might have only seen her two or three more times after that. And this was a good friend of mine, a person who had spent nights at my home and was part of my eight-member graduate student clique in upper Manhattan.

I didn't take her question seriously at the time. I laughed it off, but I do think that it is an important one. What is my relatively recent investment in light-skinned women? Why are so many of my best and closest female friends light-skinned? Not all of them, but the wedding moment was striking. And antiquated. If anything, such a skin preference was supposed to be going out of style. The darker the berry and all that. So, it was like I was some kind of holdover from the Harlem Renaissance. I hadn't been trying, but it didn't matter. And I know that folks must have noticed.

At some level, many of us are all still preoccupied with the color issue, whether we know it or not. Not just the Eddie Murphys and Martin Lawrences of the world (whose girlfriends, at least the ones I see in the tabloids, seem to be getting lighter and lighter after each breakup).

I think I heard that someone did a study of skin color in "black movies" and found that the darker characters were usually more sinister and less redeeming than lighter-skinned ones. And not just in Tyler Perry's films. Of course, there has always been the "tragic mulatto" figure, doomed to heartbreak or death on account of her personification of racial impurity and her indifference to inter-racial taboos—a character famously updated, some argue, by Halle Berry's Oscar-winning performance in *Monster's Ball*, which included graphic interracial sex scenes the likes of which some black viewers had never seen before—and never wanted to see again.

Halle Berry strikes me as a very good actress and a strikingly beautiful woman, but I made much less of a big deal about her physical beauty than a lot of my friends did back then. Long after I had jettisoned my position on the political imperative of exclusively dating dark-skinned women, and many years after I graduated from Howard, I was still more into a Kelly Rowland than Beyoncé during Destiny's Child's early run. Like everyone else, I considered Lauryn Hill absolutely gorgeous, stunning, which is part of the reason why I even bought her second solo album. The crazy one, which I love, by the way. This isn't just a fetish of movie actors and celebrities, though. When we aren't talking about color out loud, we are still seeing it. And commenting on it to ourselves in our heads.

Throughout junior high and high school, I was preoccupied with my female classmates. I had many young crushes, but being a dark-skinned, average-looking black kid with a large nose and thick glasses didn't stand me in particularly good stead with many of them. Was my light-skinned thing, if I indeed had one, a response to some of that early rejection by those black female teens?

I remember one year, in junior high school, I intercepted a beauty chart that several of the black girls in my math class had written up, a chart that rated the attractiveness of me and several of my male friends on a scale from 1 to 10. Craig was probably about 6 feet tall (in junior high!) and bore an uncanny resemblance to Michael Jackson, especially when he put on sunglasses, seriously; his high marks were to be expected. But there were about five other boys' names on their list, and my 4s from the girls were the lowest of the bunch. I didn't internalize it, though, at least not too much. And I just decided they were really playing hard to get and didn't want me to know how much they were into me. But was my subconscious getting the memo and laying the foundation for future retaliation? "When I get a chance, I'll reject you, too. Just wait." Was I positioning myself to subsequently prove my worth and attractiveness by getting trophy girlfriends that embodied mainstream America's privileging of white skin?

Even with that early disappointment, I actually didn't really know and accept that I wasn't a young Denzel Washington in the making until my last year of college, when a light-skinned pretty boy who lived in my off-campus building (and might have been Puerto Rican) made fun of my nose during one of our games of the dozens. I had said something that really ticked him off, and he was going for the jugular:

"It's like you have two regular-sized noses in one." He laughed. "Save some oxygen for everyone else."

All throughout high school, I'd never gotten a single comment about my nose, at least not to my face. But maybe everyone was talking about it behind my back. I will say that I had a fairly strange high school career. Not so much in terms of my grades and scholarly productivity. I was a middling student who had long hit cruise control and settled into the B+ to A– range quite comfortably—and without having to do very much actual work. So, I had time to do other things, like obsess about my lackluster wardrobe (which was way slim, compared to those of my peers, on the number of pin-striped Lee jeans and Le Tigre shirts it contained) and about stopping acne breakouts on my face.

At some point, I even started using a skin-lightening cream. Ambi. I think the acne medication opened that dark (or should I say "light") door in my high school career. I had long been experimenting with all kinds of lotions, ointments, and acid-laced cleansing pads, and I don't know how I found the skin lightening stuff. Maybe cocoa butter was a kind of gateway cream.

And I honestly didn't believe it was going to lighten my skin, just even out the dark blemishes, or at least that's what I think I told myself. And what it said on the box. But my face, below my hairline, ended up several shades lighter than the rest of my body, including my neck. The difference between caramel and dark chocolate. My yearbook picture that term made me look like I had broken out with some kind of sympathetic vitiligo in honor of Michael Jackson. The lighter skin, I remember noticing, did seem to get the ladies a little more interested; again, at least that's what I told myself. It seemed to bring them out of the woodwork. Or maybe it just gave me more confidence to approach them, my skin not as blotchy as it used to be.

But even then, all of my love interests were dark-skinned, including my high school sweetheart, my first real girlfriend, who threw a huge party—with about a hundred of our friends from school—during that year, a party organized with the express purpose of providing cover for our first attempt at having sex in her upstairs bedroom. My first time ever. Like all but one of the girlfriends I'd had before then (the exception being a two-week romance with a brown-skinned girl at church), she was also dark-skinned, darker than me, even in my pre-Ambi days.

So, how do I explain the move? From dark-skinned girlfriends (almost exclusively) to light-skinned ones. Even my closest female friends who weren't girlfriends, people like Cora and Martha from that wedding posse, tended to be extremely light-skinned. I had other female friends in college, and many of them would be called light brown and hardly fit into either the dark or high-yellow categories. In fact, my two closest female friends from college fit squarely in the middle of Crayola browndom. So, none of this was hard and fast. But the wedding optics were striking. Maybe it was just the law of averages balancing the scales after all those darker-skinned girlfriends of yore. Or had I gotten a little postgraduate education in me and thought I was too good for dark-skinned girls anymore?

I will say that I had formerly been pretty successful courting darker women, at least in college. I found them attractive, and a few of them seemed to like me, too. Even a couple of the ones I found most breathtaking. My wet-palmed overtures were sometimes reciprocated. Or others even took the initiative. I remember thinking that my girlfriend at the end of high school was the prettiest and smartest young woman I had ever known.

My two long-term girlfriends in college were both dark-skinned, and they also struck me as mesmerizing. I had a "type," and dark-skinned was it. All of my long-term girlfriends from the second year of high school through college graduation fit that model.

That all ended abruptly in graduate school. For some reason, the only women who seemed remotely interested in me at that point were much lighter. I'd lost my dark-skin mojo. I was taken aback at first. I was rebuffed by every single dark woman I mustered enough courage to ask out. Fellow grad students. Newly minted lawyers. Fast-food cashiers. You name it. Shot right down. Some of it was downright brutal. I just wasn't their type. They weren't attracted to me. I even had folks try to hook me up with their friends, but nothing panned out, no matter how sweet and wonderful the women were. They wanted to be friends but nothing more. They weren't looking to take things slow, to try out friendship first. They were looking for someone else. And actively.

Other than that short stint as a romantic black nationalist, I never really thought all that much about the differential hues of my relationships. There was always some variety, even if none of them had been quite high yellow until I got to graduate school.

And then everything changed. All of a sudden, light-skinned women seemed much more interested in me than anybody else. It happened so fast that I started to get paranoid and suspicious. Maybe these lighter-skinned women just wanted to make sure they had children with less of the racial ambiguity and angst than some of them might have had to live with. No "what are you?" questions to deflect—or to answer unsatisfyingly. How did all of this change overnight? And where did all the dark-skinned sistahs go? Why were they starting to diss me?

Eventually, I just decided to fall in love with the love of my life. And to befriend the people who wanted to be friends with me. Get in where you fit in, that's what my friend Khari has always said about this kind of thing, with a matter-of-factness that didn't feel forced or fake. It was meant to be nonjudgmental, which is entirely different, by the way, from pretending to be color-blind.

CORA

F*ck the N-word—bring back the word "nigger."

Samuel L. Jackson is one of those annoying folks whom I find myself loving to hate. I hate the hat, I hate the buffoonery, I hate the yelling, I hate how this smart guy dumbs down in mixed circles, and I hate that he has given Quentin Tarantino a coveted black friend pass. One of the funniest moments in film I've ever seen is the scene in the B-movie *Deep Blue Sea* when Jackson is doing one of his trademark barking baritone monologues and the fakest great white shark to ever hit the screen jumps out of the water and swallows him whole—midsentence. It is a moment meant for rewinding. And every time I bust a gut laughing I know it is because Samuel L. Jackson just got swallowed by a motherf*cking shark.

Most of all, because of Jackson's superannoying package, I hate it when I find myself agreeing with his stupid ass.*

That is what happened when Jackson was doing press for the Tarantino slave western (enough said) *Django Unchained.* Jackson plays house slave Stephen, or as he proudly boasted to every reporter who would listen, "the most hated negro in cinematic history." Much of the discussion surrounding the movie came down to the movie's

---

*I am not one to curse regularly. My own mother has called me a prude because of the words that don't come out of my mouth. My aversion is simple: as a writer I think cursing is lazy. It is much harder to come up with the language to express great emotion or anger without curses than it is with. But how can you discuss Samuel L. Jackson and not let something slip?

use of the word "nigger," which, according to the entertainment press, was used 110 times.[46] For the 165-minute film, that translates to one "nigger" every 1.5 minutes. Filmmaker Spike Lee boycotted the film because of it, and comedian Katt Williams threatened to punch Tarantino because of it. Even Howard Stern weighed in making the point with the help of sidekick Robin Quivers that the movie is, after all, about slavery, so what did people expect to hear black folks called?

Interestingly, during all these conversations about the word, no one was actually uttering it. Instead it was the phrase "N-word" that got all the scolding. (During the Stern-Quivers debate, even the shock jock reframed instead. Instead, in rapid fire usage, the N-word phrase was uttered fifteen times in just under an eight-minute segment, not counting the additional usage in three interview clips he aired.)[47] In fact, when Katt Williams made his infamous televised threats to "punch Tarantino in the mouth," here are the exact words he used on *TMZ*:

"Quentin Tarantino thinks he can say the N-word. But I checked with all of Niggadom and nobody knows where he got his pass from."[48]

Then Jackson had his moment.

During an interview with a Houston television reporter, Jack Hamilton, who admittedly was dressed like a reservoir dog for the segment, Jackson took the boy to school by refusing to discuss the "N-word controversy" unless the journalist could actually utter the word he was asking about. It is better to hear the spanking for yourself:[49]

HAMILTON: There's been a lot of controversy surrounding the use of the N-word in this movie and—
JACKSON: No, nobody, none. The word would be . . . ?
HAMILTON: [sigh] Oh, I can't say it.
JACKSON: Why not?
HAMILTON: I don't like to say it.
JACKSON: Have you ever said it?
HAMILTON: No, sir.

JACKSON: Try it.

HAMILTON: I don't like to say it.

JACKSON: TRY IT!

HAMILTON: Really? Seriously?

JACKSON: We're not gonna have this conversation unless you say it.

[HAMILTON SAYS NOTHING]

JACKSON: You wanna move on to another question?

HAMILTON: OK. Awesome.

[JACKSON LAUGHS]

HAMILTON: I . . . I don't like to say it.

JACKSON: Oh come on!

HAMILTON: Will you say it?

JACKSON: No, f*ck no. That's not the same thing.

HAMILTON: Why do you want me . . . ?

JACKSON: They're gonna bleep it when you say it. On your show—

HAMILTON: I know, but . . .

JACKSON: SAY IT!

HAMILTON: I can't, I—If I say it, this portion won't make it to air.

JACKSON: Okay, forget it.

HAMILTON: Okay, I'll skip it. Sorry, guys. It was a good question.

JACKSON: No, it wasn't.

HAMILTON: It was a great question.

JACKSON: It wasn't a great question if you can't say the word.

And there I was, loving Samuel L. Jackson.

One of my biggest gripes in life is the use of the phrase "N-word." In my house my husband is a much better person than I, and so he is always teaching our kids not to use the word "hate." But I hate, hate, hate the N-word euphemism. I have to say I find it even more offensive than the word it replaces, because it is trying to make acceptable something that should never, ever be acceptable. I've written about this point briefly before in my book *Ghettonation*, in which I told a Dick Gregory N-word story that is worth repeating (and yes, I am aware that this is now the second time in our conversation that I am bringing up the aging comedian—clearly I need to get out more):

I heard Dick Gregory ranting once about one of my favorite ghetto pet peeves—the "N-word." I find the PC term even more offensive than the word it replaces because it devalues language. It is trying to make acceptable something that has no business being so. In that way, using the N-word is no different (and no less ghetto) than when the Hip-Hop generation uses Nigga. Apparently Gregory thinks so, too. "Can you imagine if Jews changed Concentration Camps to the C-word?" he asked a hotel ballroom of Black journalists during a recent convention in Atlanta. . . . "The word is Nigger!" he said, spitting out every last syllable with the full hatred that the word is supposed to be uttered. "Changing that to the N-word changes history!" Then proof that the comedian had never really disappeared, he couldn't resist and added: "I say Nigger every morning to keep my teeth white." The audience couldn't resist and laughed.[50]

This point about history and language is why I find Jackson's exchange with the reporter so brilliant. I have built my whole life on the premise that words matter. Regardless of what we may have been taught when we were young to brave the schoolyard, words do hurt. As a writer, words are my weapon. So I can't understand why we have allowed ourselves to believe that just because we take away some letters of a word we have taken away its meaning. If you heard a kindergartener in class utter: "Where the F-word are my crayons?" you wouldn't commend him for being polite. We don't send out holiday cards with "Merry Christmas MFers!" wrapped in red and green. Around the office coffee machine if there was a debate as to whether it is okay for men to call the new dragon boss lady the C-word or if it should just be reserved for girl gabfests in the ladies' room, using "C-word" wouldn't make the conversation any less inappropriate. (And, of course, by C-word I don't mean concentration camp but cunt.) We don't have those conversations. Yet we constantly say "N-word" in intellectual discourse—newsrooms, college classrooms, political debate, dinner parties—and no one even hesitates. Even if we are trying to make the point that the word "nigger" is so awful, why is it so much better to instead use the N-word phrase ad nauseam to make that point. For me, intellectuals comfortably tossing around the N-word phrase is no better than hip-hop's use of "nigga."

"Nigger" transformed into the N-word during the O. J. Simpson trial in 1995.[51] It was by no means the first time we had heard the term, but it was the first time it got prominent widespread usage. And that's because of a racist cop named Mark Fuhrman. Fuhrman's "nigger"-spouting tapes along with attorneys questioning his use of the word were front and center in the courtroom during the trial. Some have argued that Fuhrman's fondness of the word is what began to tip the trial in O. J.'s favor.[52] Whatever its significance may have been legally, the effects on language were immediate. All that "nigger" talk in the courtroom forced the media to figure out how to talk about what was going on without spouting the racist epithet themselves. The N-word thus became the go-to choice. And just like that, the word "nigger" went from being a word avoided at all costs in polite discourse to being casually uttered by anyone everywhere.

I tried to do a news search to see how often the N-word phrase appears in the media, but I discovered it is too many times to count. Literally. Nexis will not do the search because the phrase has more than 3,000 references, the automatic stopping point for the electronic database. And that doesn't count how many times the euphemism appears in each news story, just the number of stories that used it at all. When I limited the search to just the past year, for English-language U.S. publications, it still didn't help. No other evil word that we are supposed to hate so much gets such a pass with an acceptable substitution that is used so commonly and freely.

In February 2007 the New York City Council officially banned the use of the N-word in the city.[53] It prompted a wave of similar bans passed by municipalities across the country. Of course, I find these bans outrageous. My objections as a journalist are probably obvious for the ban's infringement on free speech. We journalists are kind of no-exception sticklers for that. (Maybe that is why, personally, I am a let's-say-what-we-mean type of girl. I much prefer a "nigger" to the face than a whispered N-word any day.) However, it is my objections as a black woman that I wish were obvious, too. N-word bans, as they are called, take aim at a symptom of illness rather than the cause, like handing out Band-Aids for a knife wound. It is patronizing. And that such a move of utter inaction can make us feel better means our expectations are much too low. Just because our history is ugly doesn't mean we should ignore it. If we really want to get rid of a hateful word, instead of making it forbidden, we should focus on getting rid of the hatred that the word embodies because then there would be no reason to ever say it.

But who am I kidding? These bans are really about the "nigga" talk amongst ourselves and not the "nigger" talk of burning crosses. Apparently my expectations are indeed too high. Of course, we should not allow this "nigga" talk in our communities. But is that behavior we need the government to legislate, or should that be something that we as a society should be handling ourselves? I would rather the government use its efforts to take care of our schools and roads and institutions and health and safety. When our city councils start trying to institute values by legislating behavior, we have in effect given up all responsibility as a society. If you really want to change behavior, that starts in our homes, our blocks, our neighborhoods, and our communities. Our silence around behavior we don't like is an endorsement. So speak up.

My other objection is that when these bans come up it creates a whole lot of discussion amongst grown folks using the N-word phrase over and over again. And that is just as dangerous. Our media becomes inundated with a lot of blah-blah N-word talk. Maybe it is just me, but whenever I hear someone use the N-word euphemism I feel like giggling. "Nigger" could never have that effect. But the N-word sounds childlike. How can we have a grown-up conversation about a word that we have given a nickname to? You give nicknames to pets, children, and lovers. Not despicable, offensive, vile language you hope to rid from use.

According to the New York City Council resolution, the first documented written use of the N-word was in 1786 by slave masters to denote African slaves. Actually I must assume that esteemed city council members were actually referring to the word "nigger." That's because the two-page resolution doesn't actually ever use the word "nigger" once. Instead "N-word" is used thirteen times.[54] That means even in the resolution's tracing of history the New York City Council relied on the N-word euphemism instead. In the council's retelling: In 1906 Booker T. Washington deliberately embraced Negro over the "N-word." Then the film *Birth of a Nation* helped cement in American culture caricatures of black people as "lazy, ignorant, stupid," with its use of the "N-word." By the 1960s the "Black Power Movement" and James Brown "denounced the use of the N-word" in favor of "brother" and "sister." The document continues by explaining that in the 1970s some African Americans started using the "N-word" to refer to themselves during the cultural era known as Black Exploitation, and, lastly, the term was also adopted during the beginning of the 1990s in the cultural era known as hip-hop. The document adds that hip-hop culture removed the "-er" from the end of the word and added an "a."[55] Again, since the resolution only uses "N-word," which has no "-er," assumptions have to be made.

And here's the kicker: "Resolved, That the Council of the City of New York declares a symbolic moratorium on the use of the N-word in New York City."[56]

If only!

A governing body is trying to legally ban something and cannot name it?! This is not the land of Harry Potter. To quote Samuel L. Jackson: SAY IT! (All caps because he yells it, of course.)

Because if we do say the word, it wouldn't be so easy.

And that is the point.

Then instead of having a public debate about whether a movie's use of the N-word is too much, a reporter would be grown-up enough to ask a question and realize that even one utterance of the word "nigger" is too much, especially when paying money to be entertained.

Getting back to New York's resolution, consider the damage that our addiction to using the N-word phrase has already done. The city council's historical journey of "nigger" is like Black history month on speed sprinkled with some Disney PG pixie dust. The document is

almost comical in its lack of respect for history. It's more like a Way-
ans' brothers spoof without even trying. Just reading the phrases "the
N-word" and "*Birth of a Nation*" (a film whose racism was so vivid
that it became a recruitment tool for the KKK)[57] in the same sentence
is horrifying in the reality that is hidden. As a journalist I find this
sanitized retelling of history particularly troublesome, since part of
the job of a journalist is to simply report, to create a record of what
is happening. It is why historians often turn to newspapers at the
beginning of research to re-create our past. But what is happening?
Tarantino's script, for instance, did not use the N-word 110 times, it
used the word "nigger" 110 times. There is a difference.

To some it may seem petty to harp over word choice when it is
the essence that matters. But that is only because we are in the luxury
of being in the N-word moment, so there is no misinterpretation of
meaning. But, hovering around forty years old, I am already part of
a generation that has not actually heard the word "nigger" hurled in
anger that much in its lifetime. Please note that I cannot say "never,"
but have carefully settled on not "that much." Many of us have stories. For me there was the time walking late on campus in college in
Connecticut with a group of fellow black students when a car full
of "nigger"-yelling morons drove by. My husband was first called
"nigger" at his private middle school in Pennsylvania. Still, I would
argue, with my generation, for the first time, for many the hatred of
the word is actually more learned than experienced. That can't be said
for my parents' generation and certainly not for my grandparents'
generation. So what happens with each generation that moves further
and further away from that experience, when "nigger" was spouted
regularly from our lips in anger? My future grandkids or their future
grandkids? If those kids read a document like the New York City
Council resolution of 2007, will they understand the reality that a
euphemism, by definition, tries so hard to hide? Apparently, my generation must not, or we would never call each other "nigga."

Ironically, the NYC resolution, and the similar ones it inspired
across the country, were all symbolic and so hold no real weight.
The First Amendment took care of that. So you can't be arrested for

calling me a "nigger." Your kids can't be fined for calling each other "nigga." And, unfortunately, I can't call 911 when the N-word is hurled back and forth on MSNBC.

———

It is interesting driving with kids in a car. There is this world in the backseat that you hear but can't see as you are concentrating on the road. I often think that my kids' chatter from the backseat is the best glimpse I get of who they really are. They talk as if they are encased in a bubble of privacy that prevents their voices from penetrating the airspace of the front seat. My son is the talker in the family. He can talk to himself for hours in his deep, yo yo Brooklyn voice. When he was a toddler, women on the street would actually stop me to comment on his deep voice. My husband and I often joke that my son is an old man trapped in a little body. That is because his talk so often sounds like a little old man. Driving with my kids one day I heard from behind me my seven-year-old daughter complaining about an itchy rash she was battling. "Outchie, outchie," she whined. To which my little old man, who was four, drops this:

"That's what life is," he tells her in his deep Brooklyn tenor. Full pause. "That's what life is."

That's why saying the N-word instead of "nigger" will never work. Hatred should not be sugarcoated. Because when it is, it becomes too easy to ignore. But life is ugly. It is messy. It is hard. And it hurts.

That's what life is.

JOHN

Nigger, please!

Randall Kennedy's "national bestseller" *Nigger: The Strange Career of a Troubling Word* was published in 2002, when I was just about two years out of graduate school. The book is one law professor's attempt to narrate a version of American history by unfurling some of the legal cases linked to the language of racism, linked to one of America's most infamous words. I plowed through the book as soon as it came out. It was a breeze to read, relatively short and sweet, but that brevity helped to win it as many detractors as fans, at least among academics.

The book's large-fonted accessibility reeked of public intellectualism, what the least generous academics still dismiss as pandering, dumbed-down nonsense, a superficial offering that shouldn't "count" as real scholarship. (Ivy League law professors don't really need to write books for tenure. Their bread-and-butter are law review articles, so Kennedy probably wouldn't have cared much about the critique anyway, even if he might have disputed its characterization of his efforts.) That book was popular, aroused so much interest, positive and negative, because everyone understood the provocative nature of the word at its thematic core, and Kennedy was trying to find a compelling way of both explaining the term's overwrought social significance and challenging the N-word's ability to make everyone shrink in terror before its seemingly boundless rhetorical powers.

And there was a related critique of that book, one often voiced by African American scholars in particular. For some, the problem isn't public intellectualism per se. Black scholars have a duty, they might argue, to speak beyond the academy, to produce research that matters to the masses. By some accounts, that might even be their first order of business. But certain forms of public scholarship get cast as more important and sincere than others, more committed to uplifting black people versus uplifting the black author. *Nigger* would have been dismissed in some quarters as a sensationalist and even gratuitous effort to cash in on the publishing industry's race/racism market by providing a relatively light treatment of a serious issue, its succinctness adding to its suspiciousness. (And incidentally, the book you're currently reading would get hit with a similar indictment, and even harder.)

You might chalk that criticism up to envy and playa hating, but some of the most famous and best-known black scholars are often mocked in academic contexts for the scholarly equivalent of "jumping the shark," crossing a line between genuine intellectual effort and the hucksterism of snake-oil salesmen. In whispered tones, they get likened to a slick-talking and nonbelieving preacher who cons his congregation out of its hard-earned money. These are scholars who are revered by some and lampooned by others, dismissed and deified at the same time, depending on the audience and the atmosphere.

When Kennedy's book was released, I remember one of my academic colleagues talking about the book as a bald-faced attempt to join the group of high-paid black academics that political scientist Adolph Reed once disparagingly called "The Superfriends." And he asked me, playfully but with a masterful poker face, if I wanted to contribute a piece to the anthology he was planning to publish in response to Kennedy's new offering. The book was going to be called *Nigger, Please!*

"Nigger, please!" is a phrase that black folks have been known to use whenever a black person they are talking to says something particularly crazy, bizarre, or self-evidently inaccurate. The offending comment is met with a simple and decisive, "Nigger, please!" Which means, "I don't believe a word you are saying, and there is even something about what you just said—and your very existence in this moment—that is an affront to everything I stand for and know to be true in this world."

Usually bandied about in a playful and communal kind of way, a hand wave of dismissal between friends, it can sometimes, more rarely, take on a hostile tone. "Nigger, please!" can also be a precursor to something more confrontational or violent, especially among strangers. "I am so offended," it portends, "I may have no choice but to beat your ass."

"Nigger, please!" is the quintessential black rejoinder to any and all would-be nonsense. For example:

"Man, I could take Mike Tyson if I had to!" (A common street-corner boast heard circa 1992.)

"What did you say? Mike Tyson?! Nigger, please!" (The "he'd kill your black ass" is left implicit.)

And there are many things that are said in the public sphere these days (by pundits, elected officials, academics, journalists, entertainers, tweeters, everybody) that could justifiably be met with a decisive "Nigger, please!"—and in a postracial kind of way that opens the derision up to more than just black folks.

"Forty-seven percent of Americans vote for Obama because they want handouts?" Nigger, please!

"You got tricked into taking steroids by somebody?" Nigger, please!

"You got caught ranting about 'niggers' on video, but you're not really a racist?" Nigger, puh-leeeze!!!!

For the academic who cleverly offered up that colloquial phrase as a sequel to Kennedy's book, it was a concise way of invoking the critique about black scholars privileging larger monetary advances and broad-based popularity over a rigorous intellectual and policy-based agenda, another way of bemoaning the fact that yet another elite academic got an agent to help him exploit the race market.

Any talk of the N-word can be lucrative, but that's not all it can be. It depends on the specifics. Local newspapers started reporting about the possibility of kicking Eagles wide receiver Riley Cooper off the team once his N-word rant got caught on videotape. And Southern chef Paula Deen has only recently stopped hemorrhaging advertisers after admitting during a deposition that she has used "the N-Word" in the past. As I'm typing this, I just got a news alert on my cell phone telling me that a Republican named James Lee Knox has withdrawn from the mayoral race in Winston-Salem, North Carolina, after admitting that he used the N-word back in 2012 to describe a black election worker with whom he had a disagreement. The N-word can be very costly. On the other hand, CNN just aired a news special on "the N-Word," and it tripled the number of viewers that the network typically gets in that time slot. So, people do and don't want to hear the word. As usual, it depends on who is saying it to whom—and with what kind of emotional and personal investment.

"Nigger" can be playful in some circles and profitable in others, but it is usually the kiss of death in mixed racial company. Comedian Michael Richards's infamous onstage meltdown (where he called black hecklers "niggers" and seemed to offer a heartfelt paean to the time when blacks could have been beaten or lynched for disrespecting whites) is just one of the more high-profile and relatively recent N-word "gotcha!" moments. And we all know that there have been many. It has become a kind of cottage industry in our new media moment, with spinoffs like catching famous people saying everything from "Hymie-town" to "Jew Bastards" to "macaca."

"Nigger" is a distillation of all that the history of American racism and chattel slavery represent. The Southern slave master's ability to spit out—with mouthwatering relish—all the venom humanly possible into two tiny syllables is legendary. There could have been no transatlantic slave trade, no legalized segregation, no Civil War without the word "nigger"! Racism had to create its catchphrase, a neologism for carrying all the hate and anger and fear and lust that the institutionalizing of white supremacy demanded.

The word has so much power, seemingly as much as any string of consonants and vowels can possibly hold. In a multiracial America, one that wants to envision itself (or at least its future) as postracial, no other term comes loaded down with nearly as much angst and foreboding. Others might come close, but "nigger" hits the sweet spot of American racial trauma. It is the term that all of our PC infrastructure is hell-bent to suppress. The third rail of American crossracial dialogue.

Even still, it is said far more often than many of us admit or realize, starting with the more or less sanctioned and stylized offerings of pop culture. I haven't counted them (though I'm sure somebody has), but I'd bet the N-word mentions in Quentin Tarantino's films must number in the millions. It probably already passes that mark if we only stick to those lines he's written for Samuel L. Jackson.

Radio host Howard Stern had bad-boy musician Kid Rock in his studio last year admitting that he has used the word, but Rock argued that he only says it to his close friends as part of the excessive and politically incorrect ribbing and joking that they all do with one another. He didn't talk about using it in anger, just good-humored and intimate interracial play. "Shock jock" Stern had already declared to his listeners (on several occasions) that he doesn't use the N-word (except when quoting a news story or mocking someone else's usage), but he concluded that he would give Rock a pass on account of the fact that the rock star has a "mixed-race son." But even in that conversation, the two men seemed conscious of the fact that they were entering tricky territory—and that they needed to tread lightly.

Some of the biggest hip-hop artists in the world challenge Tarantino in terms of how much they use the N-word in their work, but Eminem, a hugely successful white MC known for poetically peppering his lyrics with some of the most vulgar and profane language he can come up with, steers clear of the N-bomb in his songs. Even a well-respected white rapper with the street cred that comes from creative lyricism and a social clique that includes Dr. Dre and 50 Cent doesn't have carte blanche to throw around the N-word like that.

But that's just what happens in public, what we are privy to via mass media. I don't have any statistics on this, but I suspect that young black people use the term a lot. I would also guess that there are whites who offer up far more "niggers" when there aren't any ostensible niggers around. People talk in very context-specific ways, and in the context of white-only social circles (of which there are many, especially the most intimate ones), I'd wager that the frequency of "nigger"-hearings is higher than in mixed racial contexts. And I would imagine that the numbers are even higher when the context is, say, a heated discussion about a black person who just cut said white person off at an intersection or stole a pocketbook or got the promotion at work that others were gunning for. Ironically, it is probably a kind of cathartic term in the latter situations, a way to dabble with a taboo and let off some steam.

So, I have a modest proposal that I want to suggest, something I call (reframing that famous "Nigger, please!" phrase) The National Nigger Please Service (NNPS). As I envision this, it would be an effective way to deal with many social issues at once, some of them quite intractable, but let me briefly describe the plan before I try to delineate what I see as some of its amazing social benefits.

NNPS would be a government-sponsored program that allows whites to pay blacks for the right and privilege of saying the N-word in their presence. That's it. Simple. But with so much potential—for everyone.

If a white person wants to say "nigger," he or she isn't relegated to conversations with white friends under the protective cover provided by the exclusivity of dinner tables or bedrooms. That's just another form of repression, not a fully cathartic release. Instead, they can say it to a bona fide, would-be nigger. Just take out your wallet, pay the appropriate fee, and let it rip. When the process is complete, everyone feels like they are the better for it. A white person gets the N-word off his or her chest (and probably even more therapeutically than ever, since they are actually saying it to a member of the targeted race). And the black person gets cold, hard cash.

Why not use neoliberalism to really end the country's racism problem, or at least to monetize it? Given the high rate of unemployment (even higher among blacks than anyone else), this would undoubtedly pour more money directly into poor black people's pockets. I think it was Ben Bernanke or another high-level government official who argued that we might want to think about just dropping wads of cash out of helicopters to make sure that allocated recovery money actually makes it into the hands of everyday Americans (not just the coffers of multinational corporations)—so that those average Americans can spend more and further fuel the economic recovery. This seems like an even more inspired idea, no? And at least as direct.

The cost structure needn't be that complicated. As I see it, there are several factors that would impact pricing. For one thing, there should be a scale linked to people's income, both the name caller and the name callee. The wealthier the white person deploying the word, the more expensive the service. And you pay per usage. So you can pay for a lone "nigger," carefully unfurled with just the right amount of gusto, or roll off a string of them in rapid-fire succession. Just add the N-words up and write the check.

There could also be a block-time model. Where you can pay for fifteen minutes or an hour to shower as many N-words on the recipient as you'd like. There could even be competitions to see who can squeeze the most N-words into a specific time window. Mo' money, mo' money, mo' money. The government would take 25 percent off the top (to help offset the price of the program and pay down the national debt), but the rest goes to the recipient without any further tax obligations. Win-win.

That's the basic service, simple math, but we might need fancier algorithms to add important wrinkles to the pricing structure. I could be convinced of that. For instance, if we do connect N-word costs to the income of the recipient, how does that work with the speaker's income? So there would have to be an equation that seems to come up with the N-word rate as fairly and elegantly as possible, given the specific income and wealth of both parties. And I think that it should probably cost the wealthier more money to say the N-word as linked to the poorness of the expletive's target, with the lower middle class our fee baseline. The basic premise is that it would take a lot to entice wealthy black people to subject themselves to such name calling. Indeed, in the current economy, only the truly wealthy could afford not to participate. And then only a really wealthy white person could afford that rate. Or a ton of poorer whites could pool their money together to watch one of their own unleash the N-bomb on, say, the regional manager of a fast-food chain.

At the same time, there are a lot of reasons for a poorer black person to take cash for being subjected to the N-word, but there have to be allowances for the fact that these folks would have been most prone to kicking the perpetrator's ass outside the context of NNPS. Therefore, there is an added fee for poorer blacks to passively allow such an affront without any hostile and physical response.

In order for this all to work, we have to be talking real money. One middle-class white person calling one middle-class black person "nigger" one time should be in the ballpark of, say, $250. A nice, even number. To really unleash the power of the market, it might make sense to allow the price of the N-word to function as a kind of government commodity that fluctuates with demand and interest—kind of like an N-word stock market. Hell, could we find a way to trade it on the actual stock market as NNPS? The only issue would be that we wouldn't want to price people out of the market, just allow the market to help determine the cost of a "nigger" (and take it out of the hands of the government). Let's find out what the N-word market will bear. We can talk about it like a conversion rate between international currencies. "The N-word is up $5 dollars today; experts say it is either because of the anniversary of the Zimmerman verdict, or O. J. Simpson's upcoming parole hearing."

There is also the question of how to design the mechanics of the program. Maybe we should all be able to apply for NNPS nano chips, which would be inserted just under the skin. We have the technology. Just inject something in our palms that can fuse with our individual palm prints and allow us to transfer the NNPS cash and credit with a handshake. Better yet, a high five!

With this new system, any white people who wanted to safely use the N-word beyond the sanctity of their own homes (again, which is more fun, anyway) could do so. And we should make allowances for first timers. What about the driver who doesn't yet have the chip but wants to use NNPS in a heat of rage for the jackass who just cut him off in traffic? Screaming the word to himself in the front seat of his car isn't enough. It would be so much more satisfying to (safely!) say it right to the person's face. Even without the requisite chip, they should be able to signal the offending driver (with an NNPS light, like a bat signal for racism, something we can have factory-added to our vehicles). Better yet, with Bluetooth. It dings, and if the black driver who swerved has his Bluetooth NNPS hood-mounted device on, he can be notified that "one NP request has been made. Do you accept?" If accepted, they pull over and do their business.

We could even have N-word kiosks stationed like Starbucks on sidewalks and at highway rest stops, and on a whim—without any provocation—whites could step up and scream the magic word to the black person who happens to be manning the booth. Mo jobs! Mo jobs! Mo jobs! Even if people go off the books and do unsanctioned or ad hoc N-word transactions, we are still using the word to bring resources to those who need it.

There could also be group rates, if one wanted to hurl a certain number of N-words to a group of black folks. Say a basketball team. Or inside an inner-city rec center. The groups can preexist or be cobbled together based on specific directions/instructions from the requester. Either way, there would be special rates and complicated ways of determining them. Different blacks in the same group could get the same amount or negotiate different N-word fees for the same group event. Let the market do its thing. The less governmental tampering, the better.

By the way, no one would have to say "please" when they offered up their N-words. It is implicit in the process of creating a safe space for a contractually agreed upon N-word encounter. And "Nigger, please!" could be marketed with a national media campaign, even if that campaign has to plaster its print ads with signs that read "N$%#!&, please!" for the sake of the kids.

I've already hinted at some of the reasons why NNPS would be an amazing boon. In effect, it is an antipoverty program, a deficit-reduction program, an antidiscrimination program, and a form of psychotherapy all at the same time.

It will deliver cash to the poor. That's for sure. A small number of whites would even be willing to cruise around slum areas looking for poor blacks to "nig-quest." Or blacks would be able to go to major shopping centers on the hunt for willing whites with cash to burn for their N-word habit. Christmastime would be insane! And none of this would be any more demeaning than panhandling, and should be quite a bit more lucrative. It could even be much better than an entry-level, service-sector job. An employment program for the poor that would beat McDonald's—and could be boosted by individual initiative. And it isn't the same thing as a government handout, either. This isn't just getting money for nothing. It is building people's interpersonal skills and potentially increasing their proficiency in math. The right wing should be firmly onboard.

At first glance, it might seem like the NNPS is much less effective against American debt than it is at dealing with national poverty. But how many whites are there in America? The number is shrinking every day, but there are still a ton. Even if only one-tenth of that group occasionally used the service twice a year, even at the bare minimum of $200 a pop, we are talking about hundreds of millions of dollars a year. Okay, on second thought, given the multitrillion-dollar national debt, maybe this would only be a drop in the bucket, but it would still be able to fund a few more government programs. Free iPods for all third graders.

There might very well be people who are squeamish about all this when the NNPS program is launched. At a certain level, it seems bizarre, right? Paying people to call them names. But a few folks will certainly be early adopters. And not all of them will be Klansmen. And if things work out, some of the sting of the N-word would dissipate as well, but hopefully not too much. Because then the program would have a finite shelf life. In fact, the key would be to hire an undersecretary in charge of NNPS who could help make sure that the system doesn't get so flooded (or N-words so cheap) that the program becomes a liability in need of a government bailout. We know that slippery slope.

In terms of helping Americans deal with their angst about the N-word, this is all a delicate balancing act. NNPS only works for as long as the word maintains its taboo status. If we so routinize and domesticate it that it loses its hypnotic power over us, N-word rates would plummet. The N-word market would crash. That might just be a perfect way to end the program, making the word obsolete because it doesn't have the seemingly oversized cultural power that it once boasted. We'd lose this new cash cow, but we might gain a version of our postracial souls. That's ridiculously wishful thinking, I know, but such pipe dreams might beat allowing any single word to hold us all hostages forever.

JOHN

Is half as good better than nothing?

A young child scribbling away on a blackboard perched on an easel in the hallway of a two-bedroom apartment, just at the entrance to our kitchen.

That's one of the earliest memories I can conjure up. I'm standing there writing my ABCs and spelling out three-letter words, fingertips and palms caked white with chalk. Everyday, starting from about the time I was three years old, this was part of my afternoon routine, a ritual mandated by my stepfather, who periodically made surprise stops at that chalkboard, ever so briefly, on his way out the door, or to the bathroom, just to confirm that I was demonstrating the kind of progress in my "lessons" that he expected.

The idea was that I had to be better prepared for school than all the other kids on the block. More to the point, he had convinced himself that I already was. And the chalkboard was just sealing the deal, speeding things up. The man loved to pump me up with positive reinforcement about my exceptional intellectual abilities, my God-given gifts—only further enhanced by the judicious enforcement of my daily chalkboard regime.

"This boy is a smart one," he would boast, almost daily, declaring this to me and anyone else within earshot, family or not. It was a belief that he faithfully espoused since as long as I can remember, since before he had any real data to go on. "He is a bright one. Bright,

bright, bright!! If he hits those books like I ask him to, he can do anything. Sky's the limit."

I can actually recall him invoking just those words, "Sky's the limit," on more than one occasion, which is a common enough phrase, I know, but for some reason, it always sounded a little weird coming from him. Like no matter how many times he repeated the phrase, it would always be foreign to his West Indian tongue. But I got the point. He had high hopes for me, high expectations, and whenever I fell a little short of them, even early on, if I couldn't distinguish, say, C-A-T from C-O-T on that tattered and peeling blackboard, he had little patience for it—and no qualms about showing his disappointment to me in actions and not just words.

By the time I started kindergarten, given my at home pre-K regimen, I was more than prepared for a public school curriculum. And I did well, both at the original elementary school I attended (with mostly Afro-Caribbean and African American classmates) on 55th Street, a few blocks from Church Avenue, in Brooklyn, and at the second one (with a majority of Jewish and Italians kids) just a fifteen-minute drive south in Canarsie, a lower-middle-class neighborhood in the same borough. We moved into that New York City housing complex down in Canarsie, the Bayview Houses, when I was still in the second grade, a move prompted, at least in part, by the perennial parental search for safer neighborhoods and better public schools.

I practiced spelling much more than math on that rickety old chalkboard, but I started to do some basic math once I got to school, and my stepfather expected me to devote as much attention to that as I had always done to reading and writing. And my first few years of school showed the bountiful benefits of all that at-home preparation. School was all mostly just review for me over the first few years, especially since the chalkboard drills didn't stop once I got to kindergarten. I was supposed to finish my homework and then further practice that material—and more—at the board. (I didn't move on to using composition notebooks exclusively until well into the third grade, my chalkboard finally stored in the back of a closet until my sister, five years younger than me, would be ready to start the same at-home program.)

With all of my monitored board writing at home, above and beyond homework, I continued to do well in my classes, so much so that the principal of PS 272 gave my parents the option of allowing me to skip the second grade altogether, and my junior high school, John Wilson, was poised to place me in an accelerated program that would condense three years of middle school work into two, which would get me off to high school a year earlier. My parents said no to both ideas, not really giving either serious consideration. "Let him just stay on schedule," they said. And so I did, having my early schoolwork monitored periodically at home and my recreational activities directly and proportionately linked to study time.

For every hour of reading I got through, I could watch thirty minutes of television. And I absolutely *loved* TV (and still do), so I was committed to reading—only so that I could watch as much TV as possible, overdosing on situation comedies but organizing my 1980s around hour-long-detective shows like *Remington Steele* and whatever that Bruce Willis and Cybill Shepherd one was called. I wanted to be Michael J. Fox from *Family Ties*, and I risked life and limb in high school by rummaging through my stepfather's closet every morning (he had to be at work by six a.m.) and wearing his fanciest and most colorful sweaters from the tenth grade on (trying to put them back in his closet, just so, as soon as I got home). Those sweaters being the sartorial influence of both Michael J. Fox and, no doubt, *The Cosby Show.*

I read and read and read, and so I watched more and more TV. Honestly, I don't think I ever really enjoyed reading, maybe specifically because it was simply a paperly means to a televisual end, but I did it. And it wasn't like anybody just took my word for it about what I'd read. My parents recognized that I wasn't above trying to game the system, so I had to write out fairly detailed summaries of everything I'd read each day and leave them on the kitchen table for my folks to peruse at their leisure. And my stepfather would always look at them, no matter how late he got home, even once in a while waking me from my sleep to get clarification on a passage. He hated bad handwriting or sentences that weren't well proofread. "Write this over. It is too sloppy. And please take your time, John. When you rush, you make mistakes."

Sometimes, he or my mom would even go back to the book I'd read, which I always had to leave on the kitchen table alongside my recaps, and quiz me further about specific parts of the reading (usually only if a summary seemed underwhelming to them, like the superficial by-product of mere skimming). All of this helped to keep me safely at or above grade level during those early years. And during parent-teacher conferences, teachers would corroborate my stepfather's assessment. I was a smart kid, they said. Make sure he keeps it up.

And there were other incentives besides TV shows and the flattery of grade-school teachers. If I came home with a 100 on a test, I would be rewarded with a dollar. Or maybe an extra thirty minutes to play outside. There were inducements all over the place. Positive and negative.

When I received a score in the 90s on something, I would hear tongue-in-cheek (mostly) questions about why I hadn't gotten the full 100, since 100s were the goal, with the occasional 104 or 105 (from successfully answered extra-credit questions) sometimes bringing even more bonuses. And anything less than a 90? Well, I didn't bother to bring those home, or if I did, they just stayed in my bag, since dipping below that 90 cutoff was considered a kind of household failure, and my stepfather's response could get pretty dark pretty quickly. And I got the point. I had to be the best. I was supposed to be the best. I was supposed to outcompete everybody in all of my classes.

"What did the chiney girls get?" he'd say.

My mom married a charismatic immigrant from Trinidad and Tobago who was raised in a culture where all Asians were called "chiney" and who had little more than a high school education himself, the latter being part of the reason, I think, why he focused on my early schooling like a dog with a bone. He valued the importance of education and knew how relatively difficult it was to get ahead without it. He was going to make sure that I didn't fall into the trap of dropping out early. And the real working assumption was that I couldn't just get average grades if I wanted to be successful. I had to be at the top of my class. A standout. The exception. There certainly wasn't any extra household money squirreled away for college tuition, so I had better show these schools that it was worth their while to pay my way.

He expected me to perform at my best. To be the best—at every subject. If my scores weren't always perfect, they had to be far, far, far above average. Anything else was unacceptable, and he made that crystal clear through the end of junior high school. With stern, silent looks and the baseline threat of corporal punishment. So, I knew I had to do well, for a lot of different reasons.

When I was growing up, we never really talked about racism in my household, and certainly not as the reason for why I had to work hard. In fact, I never heard my parents talk about race at all. When we moved to Canarsie, there were ample opportunities for them to wax xenophobic—or at least frustrated and incredulous—about the ethnic whites in our housing project complex or in the coveted brick houses just across the street. But if they did, I wasn't privy to it. Or at least I didn't take enough note of those comments to recall any of them these many years later. They didn't have any white friends, mind you, not as far as I can tell. Coworkers they were cordial with, sure, but nobody they went out with or had over for dinner. They didn't have many *black* friends either (based on the criteria of having people over for dinner and stuff), but they didn't go out of their way to talk about white people one way or the other.

When Cora and I agreed to write this book together, I made a pact with myself, for better or worse, not to do what scholars are wont to do: cite studies ad nauseam on every point. If you want to see my skills of citation, you can check out my other books. Here, let me just say that many academics have written about the differences between how African Americans and black immigrants from the West Indies or Africa deal differently with race and racism in the United States—with various theories for why those differences exist and how they impact black people's lives and life chances. Many of those studies would find this relative lack of race talk predictable, given that my mother and stepfather were both from the Caribbean, but I clearly grew up thinking of myself as an African American as much as a second-generation Afro-Caribbean, and not just because my biological father and his family were from the American South. For most of the black kids I went to school with, West Indian or not, we were raised on NYC hip-hop music, and mostly ignored its fundamentally transnational roots, so our sense of self was American, urban, and generally countercultural. America was our reference point, and though the extent of our race talk generally consisted of little more than repeating the jokes that Eddie Murphy and Richard Pryor told about differences between how blacks and whites behave in similar circumstances, we read ourselves quite fully into the saga of America's sordid racial history.

So, my parents didn't spend a lot of time schooling us on race in America. They didn't seem to talk about it much. Probably still don't, though the subtle invocations are much easier for me to see as a grown-up, or maybe I just missed them as a kid, which is still telling. And although my stepfather didn't talk about race, to my young eyes he had a kind of natural fearlessness, an aura of invincibility, that I believed would have met racism—and any would-be racist—with a swift kick in the ass (or just a couple of lashes from his belt). But it was clear to me, even early on, that I didn't have the luxury, as far as he was concerned, of being mediocre. He couldn't intimidate some admissions officer into punching my ticket for Harvard or Yale. And part of his strict mandate about studying and getting high grades was about his assessment of the difficulties that growing up as a young black man in America was going to entail.

Some African Americans still wax nostalgic about how much harder black people used to work. It is a subplot in the story about segregation's golden age of black-on-black harmony and mutual benevolence. Racism was so awful and humiliating, they claim, that blacks had no choice but to stick together and give every action their all, to work as hard as they possibly could. Being unexceptional—or not working your hardest—was the kiss of death as a black person in a white man's world. Even when you worked hard, chances were that you got little in return, especially compared to whites. Those who were exceptional might still not get much more than the white world's castoffs. But underachieving—or just plodding along in uninspired mediocrity—was hardly an option.

Not every black person in 1960s America heroically marched with Martin Luther King Jr. or achieved singular greatness thanks to strong black social ties and the neighborly supervision of other people's children. Black people could always be mediocre; the only issue was that in a white supremacist state, mediocre blacks "proved" the rule of racial inferiority. They made the race look bad. Mediocre whites were individual underachievers, but racism demanded that mediocre blacks stand in for the inherent, God-given limitations of their entire race. Plus, whites controlled most of the important social and economic institutions in the country, and the weaker members of their social networks could still benefit from those connections. Blacks didn't have nearly the same kind of social power or even access to it, so they didn't have the luxury of being average if they still wanted a chance to thrive and succeed. "We had to be twice as good as whites," some elders explain, just to get the jobs that white Americans didn't even want.

My stepfather never said that I had to be twice as good as whites. His racial references for achievement were my "chiney" classmates, those "model minorities." In fact, he didn't really talk much about white people at all. He wasn't much of a talker in general, but he especially didn't seem to have much to say about white people (at least not around me). But his assumptions about what I would need to commit to as a young person seemed to pivot on that belief that I had to constantly push myself, that I had to keep working harder. I might have been smart, in his estimation, but that alone didn't guarantee a thing, which is why he was such a stickler about me and my chalkboard time. If I lost my focus, if I slipped in terms of my disciplined approach to learning, all the natural ability in the world wouldn't matter. I would be in trouble, especially since I had no powerful social network to fall back on.

I have to admit that I didn't (and still don't) feel exceptionally bright. As a teenager, I remember thinking that all parents must believe their kids are budding geniuses. I didn't think I was stupid. But some of my classmates seemed no less intelligent, including some of the ones who didn't pass many of their classes—or even attend them on a consistent basis. What I had mastered was how to get good grades from teachers, though after I successfully passed the test to get into Brooklyn Technical High School—one of New York's selective public high schools—my parents exhaled ever so slightly, and I was able to coast a bit, which meant that the 100s were fewer and farther between.

The "twice as good as whites" rhetoric was about recognizing that American society was a place where whites and blacks could perform the same actions and come out with very different results. That's one textbook definition of racism. "Twice as good" implied that mediocrity meant different things for blacks and whites.

But there is another (related) argument afoot in certain sections of the black community, some of its biggest proponents being various black neo-cons and comedian Bill Cosby. But it isn't just them. I hear versions of the claim whenever I speak to black audiences about my anthropological research on class differences in contemporary Harlem, and not just the older audience members who lament the state of black youth today: exhibit A is the most misogynist and violent forms of hip-hop music they can find. The claim is simple, and it turns "twice as good" on its head. Some people believe that there is a new mentality on the rise in black America, a mentality oblivious to the pitfalls of black mediocrity, a mentality that couldn't be more different from everything "twice as good" was supposed to represent and inspire.

There was a time when blacks championed high achievement, the argument goes. They didn't have what they deserved, so they fought harder to get it. Nowadays, African Americans have grown quite comfortable with having less, content in their generally second-class citizenship, less angry about their social marginalization. They once fought tooth and nail for equal rights, now they seem to embrace their own continued inequality. They once protested and marched and faced down dogs for the right to vote. Now they seem to have lost just about all of that reverence and respect for the ballot, even in an Obama era when more young blacks were convinced to head to the polls.

We might call this a version of the "culture of poverty" argument, the notion that poor people of color possess a belief system that promotes underachievement and dysfunction, placing a premium on behaviors that are maladaptive and self-destructive. These cultures reward bad behavior with social legitimacy, street cred, and underachievement. The "code of the street" in black neighborhoods, they argue, is an even more warped version of mainstream American avarice, selfishness, and ignorance.

What's the logic of their argument? Blacks think they should be handed everything. Forget about being twice as good. For the twenty-first-century black person, "half as good" is more than enough. The country doesn't deserve any more out of them. They are so busy focusing on race and what racism did to them and their forefathers (and what it continues to do), they won't pull themselves up by their proverbial bootstraps and take responsibility for their lives. They are constantly on the lookout for scapegoats, for external forces that justify and explain away their underachievement. I didn't get good grades because the test is biased. I didn't get the job because the employer must be racist. The bank won't give me a loan because the loan officers are racist. It is raining in my neighborhood, because the clouds are bigots. It isn't me; it's them.

Now, there are all kinds of statistical regressions that folks have used to show that other things being equal, there are still a ton of ways in which racism accounts for differences that it shouldn't. Think of the audit studies where, say, identical résumés get black- vs. white-sounding names at the top, and the Biffs end up getting called in for job interviews much more often than the Leroys (with the same qualifications), in ways that are statistically significant and hard to explain by chance alone—or by invoking any factors other than race.

This position (that blacks have gone from promoting the idea of "twice as good" to embracing the notion of only being "half as good," that less should be more than enough) is absurd and brilliant at the same time. First of all, it tends to claim that to talk about racism at all is to use it as a crutch. People who see racism must be the "half as good" blacks, the ones looking for a handout, celebrating their victimhood. Critical analysis and social critique be damned. To see race or racism is to be lazy. And racist. Period. And ostensibly the only real racists left, to hear some right-wingers tell it. It means just trying to kick back on your heels and wait for the white man to give you everything you want. "Why should I have to work hard?" the thought-bubble in black people's heads is supposed to be saying. "My forefathers built this country. They worked enough for all of their offspring. We are owed our forty acres and a mule. Our reparations. So, I am not going to do a hard day's work until I get what's already long overdue."

Proponents of this position might argue that few people speak so self-consciously and in such crystal-clear terms about their own motivations and social traits. Culture doesn't work that way. I'm an anthropologist, so I should know that. The "half as good" position is just something blacks have come to take for granted. It informs their actions even when they can't articulate their commitment to it. They know that they don't want to work, but they still need money and food and fancy TVs and everything else that takes money. They want their bling, but they don't want to do a thing to earn it. This belief is exactly why there is such a hyperdemonization of "the welfare state." The culture of poverty folks have long argued that food stamps and welfare and other government handouts help to grease the wheel for this mentality, for this "half as good" mind-set, without even knowing it. Those programs are Trojan horses of psychological self-destruction. With Affirmative Action and other governmental efforts to reward blacks for not doing anything, they don't have to be nearly as good as their white counterparts to get the job or the college seat or the government contract or anything else. According to this theory, blacks are smart enough to know that they don't have to be as good as whites to succeed, and they have thoroughly internalized this realization.

So, the argument closes, if these blacks think they should get everything without doing anything and you combine that with Americans' penchant for lavishing praise on their children for mediocrity, for even just average accomplishments, then you get a perfect storm of racial underachievement, lowered expectations, and do-nothing entitlement.

There is hardly a public intellectual around who hasn't weighed in on this debate from the right or the left, either taking the position of bootstrapologist or dismissing the argument as another attempt at "blaming the victim," making blacks the too-easy cause of their own social marginalization. But I don't think blacks are clamoring for "half as good" success, even if many self-respecting self-help gurus might say that the name of the game is precisely to get more while exerting less energy. By that logic, if "half as good" were true, it might even be a rational response to America's racial lineage. But as I see it, blacks are not clamoring for half-as-good opportunities. If anything, they feel that twice as good might get you even less than it used to.

Just take my own tribe: black academics. A few years ago I wrote a piece for *The Chronicle of Higher Education*'s online site that absolutely terrified me. A series of odd coincidences and scheduling serendipity found me breaking bread with some of the most successful blacks in the academy over the stretch of a few weeks, scholars at the very top of their fields in the humanities and the social sciences who have won all kinds of awards. Their work has been cited liberally within their disciplines and beyond. They are tenured at some of the most prestigious institutions in the country. And every single one of them felt underappreciated, disrespected, and dismissed as scholars. They had achieved everything that they could have in their chosen fields, and they felt like their white colleagues treated them with little more than contempt, envy, or utter indifference. It was disheartening to hear. These senior scholars of color described themselves as ignored by administrators, maligned by colleagues in their fields, and somewhat alienated from the centers of their disciplines—even when *they* were arguably the centers of their disciplines.

The first time I heard such a tale, over lunch at a coffee shop in California, I tried to dismiss it as an isolated incident, one person's idiosyncratic experience. Maybe he was just being hypersensitive. Or I could have caught him on a bad day. But then I sat across from a few more senior and very successful scholars (in Michigan and Massachusetts, in New York and North Carolina) with similar stories to tell (of humiliating slights that they interpreted as race-based disrespect), and I had to admit that something more was going on than what some might dismiss as thin-skinned bellyaching.

Most of these scholars were sharing their stories with me (as their junior colleague) for my own good, in hopes of steeling me for a similar (potential) future of professional discontent. Their point: no amount of publishing productivity or public notoriety exempts one from the vulnerabilities and burdens that come with underrepresentation in the academy. Being twice as good as most of their white colleagues (by objective and generally agreed-upon criteria) still wasn't enough to spare them from the sting of race-based stigma.

These scholars weren't lamenting the stain of "affirmative action," the fear that their successes were tainted by other people's assumptions that their achievements were based on something other than purely meritocracy. That's the Clarence Thomas critique of affirmative action. Only one person seemed plagued by such a concern. The others were arguing something close to the opposite: that they had genuinely succeeded at a game decidedly stacked against them, that most people in their fields knew and understood that, but that the thanks they received was a tacit (or not so tacit) attempt to ignore them anyway, to demean them with cool disinterest and a series of daily exclusions from important departmental discussions or real leadership roles at their respective universities. What explains all that? And am I doomed for the same discontent?

My stepfather might have given me my early taste of academic success, but my mother gave me my temperament, a mix of smiling (often), being nice to people, and trying not to let others get under my skin. Or at least not letting on that they have when they do. Young black boys love their mamas, and I am certainly a version of that cliché. And her everyday sensibilities rubbed off on me much more than my stepfather's did. He was gruff and stern, always in a glare that hinted at a hot rage just beneath the surface. I tend to be much more open-faced than that. That's my mother's influence. She is still very quiet and deferential and polite. Always polite. And seemingly as invested in other people's happiness as her own.

Long before anyone told me about inspirational speaker Earl Nightingale's take on the seemingly endless powers of a "good attitude" and before Wharton professor Adam Grant's counterintuitive claim that even in business (as it has always been in matters of spirituality, at least as far as Christianity is concerned) it is better to give than to receive, I have always tried to be a generous and empathetic person. At least I want to think I am. And if anything, that is one of the things that separates me from some of my colleagues. There are at least two kinds of academics when it comes to empathetic impulses. Most faculty can have empathy for students that they think of as being just like them. Maybe based on their ethnic affiliation, their regional background, or any number of other factors, they see themselves in those students—rightly or wrongly—and can be more than willing to give them the benefit of the doubt on things, in subtle ways, maybe even without knowing it. To lobby for them to get a second chance. Or some special scholarship. I have seen that at just about every single place I've ever taught. And it doesn't matter if the academics in question are left-leaning, right-leaning, male, or female. Everyone does it. But only a smaller subset seems to muster the same kind of empathy for (and investment in) folks they see as different from them in some substantial way. Clearly, race is one of those rubrics, but it isn't the only one. They are sometimes a little less likely to go the extra mile for these students. More prone to matter-of-fact pronouncements. Doing things "by the book" instead of thinking off script about what these students need, in more humane and creative ways, something many people are much more likely to do with folks they consider to be just like them.

And I do think that more than being twice as good as whites (or only benefiting from affirmative action in ways that allow blacks to get away with being "half as good" as white scholars), what modicum of professional success I might have is almost exclusively a function of the fact that I try (though I don't always succeed) to take everyone I meet very seriously. It is an anthropological disposition, I'd argue. All human beings are more than adequate ambassadors of their cultural worlds. It doesn't matter how smart they are or aren't; if you listen long enough and carefully enough, an anthropologist can always learn something by listening and looking. If not, the failure is the anthropologist's, nobody else's. And I think that sometimes people just respond generously to that. To the sense of being listened to.

I always tell myself that I smile too much. That I wish I had more of my stepfather's colder stare. But I also realize that smiling, genuinely and warmly smiling, is a kind of magic bullet, especially for black men in America.

Not too long ago, I did a kind of experiment. I am constantly telling students that "everything is ethnography," that an anthropologist is always on the clock, seeking out new ways of spying and interpreting cultural practices and processes. So, I went against the grain of my general tendencies and tried not to smile. Just to see how it would affect my social interactions. I conducted this little experiment as part of a job interview. I didn't really know anyone on the search committee, at least not very well (academic jobs are usually vetted by a committee), and I decided that I would actively try not to oversmile during our session. I wouldn't scowl, but I would try to stay emotionally and facially neutral. I couldn't help but forget for a second or two (during the thirty-minute interview) when a smile or two broke out across my face at a couple of different points, but I tried to suppress them immediately. I did all I could to look serious. Not angry, but not smiling, either. I crossed my right leg over my left. I sat back calmly. I wanted to perform a kind of calm self-confidence. I answered their questions soberly but substantively (I thought), and then I left. I don't know how I was read. I suspect as arrogant.

Maybe even a little standoffish and "uppity." Who knows? It wasn't a controlled scientific experiment, so I can't isolate all the variables and search for some statistically significant correlations between features of my performance/personhood and the committee's decision that I wasn't a good fit for the job. I could feel their coolness during our conversation though, and I wished that I could go back in again and test that response against the one that my more smiley self might have garnered.

I want to think about my liberal use of smiles as an example of interpersonal empathy and generosity, but maybe I am reading myself too generously. When I am being more cynical and self-critical, I call it the postmodern version of "shucking and jiving," doing what I have always done in all-black spaces, but now doing so in all-white or mixed ones: trying to do whatever I can to put people at ease, to listen to what they have to say, to shower them with inviting (and unself-conscious) smiles. The twenty-first-century equivalent of the Yes Man? Even if one positions one's smiles around an actual "no" to the powers that be?

I must not have wanted that job if I was willing to do what I just described. But it still stung when I didn't get the nod. When I was told that I wasn't right for the post, I thought of my more senior black colleagues and the disrespect they'd talked about. Like everyone else, my world is full of tiny and not-so-tiny slights, major and minor humiliations just about every single day, a barrage of looks, comments, emails, reactions, decisions, and personal or professional rejections—intended and inadvertent—that belittle at every turn. At least it feels that way, like my daily life is organized around the reeling dash from one disrespectful dismissal to another. The world's playlist constantly ending up back on a version of the same tune, "John, don't believe your own hype. You're not as good as people pretend you are. And don't forget it." This little ditty does battle with my stepfather's earlier accolades, his talk of my exceptional brightness. It is probably an outgrowth of my skepticism about those very accolades, a skepticism noxiously nurtured by my nasty little subconscious.

I spent my twenties and thirties hoping that I could credentialize myself into a kind of protective cocoon against such onslaughts. I may not have been twice as good as anybody, but I was going to try my damnedest to have the discipline to reach my goals: BA. MA. PHD. Tenure. Named professorship. None of it is foolproof. And at the end of the day, it might all be reducible to how much you smile, to whether or not a black man is twice or half as good at that.

CORA

Mediocrity Nation?

It never occurred to me that there weren't twice as good thinkers out there until I started teaching. When I was on maternity leave and needed some stimulation for my brain, I started teaching college journalism part-time. My house is free of babies now, but surprisingly I am still not free of the teaching, and I continue to try to teach one class a semester if my writing schedule allows. Being around twenty-year-olds on a regular basis has been and continues to be a constant reminder of how much the world has changed. And the disappearance of twice-as-good thinkers is one of those reminders. By "twice as good" I, of course, mean the age-old saying of successful black households that you have to be twice as good, work twice as hard for the same results as your white peers.

If you talk to highly successful black faces of a certain age the belief instilled by their parents that they have to be twice as good is at the center of what drives them. During my years covering the business world I don't think I came across a single high-powered black executive—from Ken Chenault, CEO of American Express, to Dick Parsons, former CEO of Time Warner and chairman of Citigroup, to Sam's Club CEO Rosalind Brewer—who did not evoke this lesson as a foundation for their success. Denzel Washington once caused a stir when he dipped his foot into the colorism debate and told his daughter Olivia that if she wants to act that she would have to be a triple threat (or three times as good) because she was dark-skinned, black, and a woman. While his honest nod to the hurdles of skin color is what made some uncomfortable, his twice-as-good thinking about race (or even gender) did not make anyone blink—it is like telling your kids to look both ways before crossing the street.

In fact, "twice as good" may have started as a model of success for Black America, but it was then adopted by waves of immigrant groups, people of color at large, and any other marginalized community that was trying to climb. So, in my high school around college application time, the Asian kids would complain that they had to be twice as good. When I started working and was in newsrooms where women editors on the business desk were still rare, there were murmurs in the ladies' room about having to be twice as good. When it was clear that Latinos would take over as the face of diversity, you started to hear a lot more "blacks *and* Hispanics have to be twice as good" groans during discussions of inclusion. Some uber-successful even take race out of the advice entirely and just argue that anyone should strive to be twice as good to make it to the top.

Regardless of how it has been adapted or watered down, twice as good has a history that is rooted in Black America. It was concrete advice that comes from our segregated past. Black parents did not hide behind the explicit racial lesson—there was no question that it was the reality. When doors started to open not everyone was going to be let in; you had to be twice as good to take that journey. Once you made it in you had to be twice as good in order to stay. And you had to be twice as good so that others that looked like you could follow. It is the survival guide for integration.

When President Obama gave the commencement address at Morehouse, much of the focus from the outside world was on his "personal responsibility" nagging. What went pretty much unnoticed was his pledge to the "twice as good" camp. "Every one of you have a grandma or an uncle or a parent who's told you that at some point in life, as an African American, you have to work twice as hard as anyone else if you want to get by," he told graduates in the rain.[58] Forget the personal responsibility double standard, the fact that even the president of the United States believes that our best and brightest black children still have to be twice as good in 2013 should make us all question how far we've really come.

Interestingly, a month before Obama's speech *Southern Living* magazine ran a Q&A with Condoleezza Rice conducted by former first daughter Jenna Bush Hager. Mixed into chitchat about favorite Southern dishes (fried chicken) and favorite Southern expressions ("Mama an'em") was also "twice as good" talk.

> JENNA: Your parents were both teachers. What did they teach you?
> CONDOLEEZZA RICE: They would say, "Condi, you'll have to be twice as good." That was their answer for overcoming prejudice. I still say it to my students now. Even if you don't think you'll face prejudice, being twice as good is a good way to be prepared for life.[59]

That this particular Democratic president and Republican former secretary of state, who are polar opposites in their world views, could agree without hesitation on the need to be twice as good shows how engrained the adage has been to the black belief system about success.

More significant than that they agree, is that both figures are preaching this lesson to students. I think they are doing that, in part, because this is a lesson that young folks aren't embracing as much anymore. I say this not to disparage my students. When I am on campus it is one of the key differences that I see between their generation and my own. And I am beginning to think that maybe that is not a bad thing.

Unlike Condoleezza, I am not old enough to know legal segregation firsthand. There were no whites-only water fountains, church bombings, or burning crosses outside the tenement buildings on the Lower East Side of Manhattan where I grew up. Instead, in post–civil rights America (or post–post–civil rights America) our nation's racism and discrimination is more undercover. So there were code words like "welfare queens" and "state's rights," and attacks on affirmative action became personal. Make no mistake, coming of age during the Reagan 1980s it was clear that black folks were under attack. (George

W. Bush wasn't the first president not to care about black people.) But there is a difference between underground and overt. Derald Wing Sue, a social psychologist at Columbia, writes a lot about "racial microaggressions" or the "brief everyday slights, insults, indignities, and denigrating messages sent to people of color, women, LGBT populations, or those that are marginalized by well-intentioned people who are unaware of the hidden messages being communicated." Sue's research finds that we are "better able to handle overt, conscious, and deliberate acts of racism than the unconscious, subtle, and less obvious forms." As a result, Sue argues that daily bombardment of microaggressions can be even more harmful (psychologically and physically) than obvious racist discrimination because of their invisibility.[60] To me it makes no sense to quibble over what generation has suffered more when everyone is suffering. Depending on who you are, a lot of Sue's research can come across as "well, duh!" chatter or "give me a break" blabber. Still because we, as a generation, were dealing with perceptions, subtly, and the invisibility of the attack, sometimes the twice-as-good lesson was learned in different ways. In my husband's house it was something that his mother would say to him over and over again. In my house it was never explicitly said but something that I still learned over and over again.

Either way, the thinking that you must be twice as good is engrained in the successful black America of my peers—the generation that was lucky enough to stand on the shoulders of those who opened doors and so we thought if we jumped we would reach the sky. Personally, among my friends and colleagues I can think of no one who does not function that way.

"The first time I remember that [twice-as-good] lesson was when I was in Head Start, so I was four years old," the email read from Mike, someone I went to college with, whom I had not spoken to since graduation, but he was still quick to respond to an informal shout-out email I sent to the email addresses in my address book asking for twice-as-good stories. "I really loved books, but I wanted someone to read them to me. My mom told me that I needed to learn to read early just so some prejudiced people wouldn't be able to put me in the special-ed class."

For Deesha, also from college, the "twice as good" words were not exactly uttered but the lesson was still clear. "My mother and grandmother did implicitly teach me something similar, and that is that white people could 'get away with' things that I, as a black person, could not. This teaching made me not take my educational opportunities for granted, and I worked hard to make sure that the sacrifices my family made for me to go to college would not be in vain. I realize now that while my mom and grandmother based their perspective on race, this is about class privilege (or lack thereof) as much if not more than it was about race. I agree that class and race privilege are real, but I know that they are not always and everywhere insurmountable."

And my favorite twice-as-good memories come in from my friend Dionne, whose Brooklyn sarcasm makes no apologies.

ME: Did your parents or grandparents teach you that you had to be twice as good?

DIONNE: My parents, mostly my dad, his parents and his entire family had that stenciled onto the blankets we all wore home from the hospital. It was THE guiding principle.

ME: How old were you the first time you heard it?

DIONNE: The first time I remember being conscious of it as a THING, may have been as young as 6 or 7, first or second grade. Certainly by the time I was in third grade, it existed alongside "eat your vegetables" and "say your prayers." There was no first time because it was always there.

———

I wish I could share the rest of our colorful email conversation, which involved references to Garveyism, Black Jesus, *Soul on Ice*, *Manchild in the Promised Land*, Black Star certificates, and a "5 x 7 block of wood painted red, black, and green on which the words 'Blacks Will Be Free' prefaced a bullet, an actual bullet, attached to the wood." But I don't want to get off track too much since the point is really the end of Dionne's response: "It was always there."

That's my circle. And those who may not have subscribed to the twice-as-good mentality by college were quickly converted once they hit the workplace. So when I come across young black folks who clearly don't function that way it shocks me. It is their boldness in their rejection that stuns me most.

I teach part-time at a competitive private university. The students remind me all the time how just by attending they must be the best and brightest. I have to remind them that I will make that judgment based on their work. The first lesson I learned when I started teaching is that apparently a B is the old C. When I give out Bs it drives students to tears. Literally. Every semester I have had at least one student come to office hours in tears over a B. And before you get trapped by gender biases, these crying students have not all been women. My classes are small seminars of about fifteen students, so at least one crying incident a semester is significant. Giving out Bs apparently makes me a tough grader in this day and age. Just add it to the list of things that have changed. One morning during midterms some students were chitchatting in our classroom before class began. Although I was in the room their talk was as if I was not. They were complaining about the workload of another class and worried about its upcoming midterm. That's when the only black student in the room piped in with advice: "As long as you do the reading you can still get a B." Given the stigma of a B these days, I was stunned. In fact most in the room pushed back because they did not want just a B. She stood firm that a B is enough. I don't think I will ever be able to shake those "you can still get a B" words. Of course, she is not the first mediocre black student. Nor is she the first mediocre black student on a mostly white campus. What I found so shocking was her bold embrace of being just fine with being a mediocre black student on a mostly white campus. That combination shook my twice-as-good mind-set to the core.

The incident got me wondering. Are we not teaching this lesson anymore? I started trolling through parenting web forums. I informally polled friends and colleagues. I'd bring it up, impolitely, in conversation whenever I was talking to black parents.

I was reassured by Keith, a former colleague, who discovered that his twice-as-good mentality became even more empowered as a parent, particularly as his oldest son began high school in a mostly white affluent Connecticut suburb. "He's a black kid growing up in a world where people seem intent on bringing about a false construct of postracialism, and I don't think that would serve my sons well. They will still face a world where race, and cultural attributes attributed to race, will be very much in play in terms of how people judge them and what opportunities they are afforded. So while I don't want them growing up 'racist,' as in shunning white kids as friends or hating anyone on the basis of skin color or culture, they need to understand that there is a healthy, skeptical instinct that they need to develop in order to survive and excel in a world that co-opts, but doesn't fully accept or actualize, those who are different."

Keith's a writer so, understandably, he knows how to use words. But, although his eloquence makes his words stand out, he was not alone in what he is saying. None of these conversations would pass as formal reporting in my class, but sometimes informal pulse-taking can still offer insight. I don't think black families are not teaching the credo anymore, but perhaps it is not being learned. There is a difference. Instead, I think young people are *choosing* not to believe in the mantra, not because they don't have the talent or intelligence, but instead boldly and unapologetically rejecting the notion that they should have to be twice as good.

Something we don't respect enough is that every generation has their own race story. The times that we come of age in help shape our experience with race. My students were barely in high school when a black man was elected president. But even when changes to our national race story are subtle they are still significant. So while many of my generation will firmly commit to the twice-as-good belief system, perhaps we are no longer teaching these lessons explicitly enough, because our race experience is one where the battles are often not as explicit anymore. That doesn't mean the battles are not there, but when the fight shifts from battling hoses and dogs and opening doors to battling words and actions with double meanings and how high you rise once you are through the door, your survival tactics shift and can be more subtle. As a result, we may think we are teaching the need to be twice as good by infusing our children with pride in self and their culture and pushing them to always do their best but that is different from explicitly telling a five-year-old she "must be twice as good as white folks," as Condi's parents did. There is no questioning the meaning of that statement. As a result, we are raising a generation of young people who are coming up with their own survival tactics. And increasingly shedding themselves of the twice-as-good burden is part of their fight.

Personally, I still believe as a black woman I have to be twice as good, always. Those who do not subscribe to that notion will always puzzle me. A *generation* that doesn't subscribe to it worries the hell out of me. ("Still a B" will never be as motivating as "Twice as good.") But, maybe, the fading of the mantra is progress for people of color and the nation. It might mean that we are finally living in a moment when those on the margins are feeling true equality and acceptance. Instead of feeling the need to be twice as good, part of becoming mainstream American is the right to be mediocre, too.

JOHN

No more Sojourners.

My mother's mother, Petrova, died young. Of a broken heart, some family members say. And so her three daughters had to be sent for. Flown, all by themselves, from Barbuda, a small island in the Caribbean, to New York City, the Big Apple. They would start new lives with extended family in the Bronx and Harlem—continuing motherless but together.

I know very little about Petrova, my grandmother, the one I never got a chance to meet, except through the tiniest slivers of half-told stories. Her children's father, my grandfather (whom I did know, at least a little), emigrated in search of all those opportunities to be found abroad, in search of the promises that many Americans dream about, leaving the four of them alone on that little island, in a small shack that several people pointed out to me, in all its weed-filled and cinder-blocked emptiness, when my mother first took us to visit the place where she grew up. I was about ten years old. And we would go back almost every other summer after that until I went off to college.

I used to love those visits to Barbuda, the smell of fresh baker's bread in the morning, so different from the aromas that the oven produced in our Brooklyn apartment, and those trips to the beach at Coco Point, where my mother would spend just about the entire time, sometimes hours, standing in the water, submerged to her chin (she can't swim), her skin pruned almost to the point of being unrecognizable once she finally did get out.

279

Whenever I'd walk around the island on my own, adults would stop me to ask what brought me there. Who brought me there? "Ethlyn," I'd answer. "I'm her son. She's Petrova's daughter." And then they would smile, and see the resemblance to some other long-dead relative. They'd share some brief story about that person and then proceed to explain to me how we were related to one another, how everyone on Barbuda was related. It was such a tiny and insular island (with a population well under 2,000 people) that I was ostensibly kin to everyone I ever met there. "Me and you are family," they'd always say, filling in those branches of the family tree that connected us. "Welcome home."

I didn't realize it at the time since I was only a kid, but my mother probably really needed those brief trips back home to Barbuda. For herself. Sure, she wanted us to see where she grew up and to meet some of the people she knew as a child, but she also made good use of that stint away from the hustle and bustle of her life in New York City.

My stepfather never came with us, so she got a break from him, too.

And someone else could pick up the slack at work, look after her caseload, and worry about her elderly "clients" for a little while. For two weeks, one of her coworkers was deputized to run around the city, trying to make sure that my mom's charges had money and clothes and meals and shelter. Those clients always seemed on the verge of getting evicted. Or the sheriffs had already arrived to remove their belongings from their homes, and my mom had to help find them a new place to stay as quickly as possible. It must have been really stressful, though she never bothered us with any of that. But going back to Barbuda was one of the ways that she rewarded herself. I think it helped to keep her saner than she otherwise might have been.

And she actually seemed like a new person when we were down there. It was a subtle thing, but there was a difference. She was more relaxed, like she was letting out one long exhalation that lasted for our entire vacation. She would literally let her hair down. And just laugh.

Really laugh. The kind that brings tears to your eyes and forces you to reach for a couch before you pass out. It isn't that she didn't laugh in New York. She did. But with so much going on, you couldn't really luxuriate in such frivolity, not the way she did "back home." I loved watching her laugh as she shared childhood stories I'd never heard before, that she'd almost never think of relaying to us in Canarsie. Maybe they were harder to recall from afar. But she was soaking in so much more than the sun during those visits—and storing it all up for later, for when she got back to the city.

It has always been particularly difficult to be a black woman in America, carrier of the double burden of race and gender, the dual stigma of blackness and femininity. I know that because I know my mother. And because of all the other black women in my life, including my wife, my sister, my daughter. And so I can glimpse some of what anthropologist Zora Neale Hurston means when she has a character talk about the particular vulnerabilities of black female life in her most famous novel, *Their Eyes Were Watching God*:

> Honey, de white man is de ruler of everything as fur as Ah been able tuh find out. Maybe it's some place way off in de ocean where de black man is in power, but we don't know nothin' but what we see. So de white man throw down de load and tell de nigger man tuh pick it up. He pick it up because he have to, but he don't tote it. He hand it to his womenfolks. De nigger woman is de mule uh de world so fur as Ah can see.

From the slave women who had to deal with the trauma of separation from their families and the insatiable sexual appetites of their enslavers, to the contemporary double standards that allow black women to be painted as "welfare queens," expert emasculators, "nappy-headed hoes," and all of the other dismissive characterizations, black women have to negotiate a world overstuffed with material and symbolic assaults.

In many professional contexts, any black woman who isn't demonstrably demure gets cast as "the angry black woman." Black women get read as "hostile," as being particularly loud and prone to public displays of unhappiness that nobody else wants to hear. I know of one black female academic, a senior scholar, who applied for an administrative post at her university and was summoned into her dean's office and questioned about how she might react if, in some hypothetical scenario, she had suggested a course of action to the dean that the dean decided not to follow. Would she go all "angry black woman" on her, or not? It was such a surreal meeting, she said. Like nothing she'd ever experienced before. So insulting and infantilizing.

Black women may not be able to boast a lot of collectively sanctioned authority at work, or may not be trusted to work politely without "going postal," but they are believed to have taken on a disproportionate amount of responsibility in heading up their families and maintaining their households, especially with the relative absence of black men in their homes. There has long been a debate in the social sciences and the popular media about "the black family" in America as "matriarchal," headed by the "strong black woman," the motherly or grandmotherly "superwoman" who tries valiantly to keep kin together and protected in the face of massive centrifugal forces (structural, cultural, and psychological) threatening to rip them apart. Many feminists and womanists have described "the strong black woman" (meant as a compliment, a way to recognize the seemingly preternatural feats of black women) as a kind of trap—both a backhanded justification for continued black male irresponsibility (with a superwoman at home, the kids will be okay no matter what) and as a kind of deal with the devil, a Faustian bargain that will provide only heartache and pain in the end.

R&B singer Karyn White's '80s lament, "Superwoman," just so happened to be a big hit on black radio during my very last precollege trip to Barbuda, and its chorus started with a spirited denunciation of that role: "I'm not your superwoman," she croons. "I'm not the kind of girl that you can let down and think that everything's okay."

Black women have to be super, the argument goes, because the men they are relying on prove to be anything but. The superwoman motif is often in symbiotic relationship with the "demonized black male" discourse. Alice Walker's Pulitzer Prize–winning novel *The Color Purple* is in essence the classic example of a superwoman story, full of superwomen with different kinds of superpowers. Long-suffering Celie, the main protagonist, withstands decades of physical and psychological abuse from her husband, "Mister," only to tame him in the end and have the last laugh. Nettie, Celie's sister, creates a truly transnational life for herself by finding her way to Africa. Shug Avery, the blues singer who helps Celie get access to her sister's letters, actually ends up doing much of the heavy lifting to bring those sisters, that family, back together again. And the book was controversial in certain quarters because some black male readers interpreted it as yet another attack on black men—the book's many awards, a consequence of society's insatiable need to perpetuate negative images of black manhood. If we can make a case that the three main women of the book were arguably different kinds of superwomen, they needed Mister's non-super (or even inhumane) antics for their own exceptionality to shine. To accept Superwomandom, though, is to enable and perpetuate a set of gender relations (and long-standing assumptions about gender roles) that ultimately have a debilitating effect on black women's lives. For my mother, I think, submerging herself in those Barbudan waters was one small way of slowing down some of that debilitation.

A few years ago, anthropologist Leith Mullings called the particular health-related impact of black women's attempts to navigate racial oppression the "Sojourner syndrome," named after nineteenth-century activist Sojourner Truth.[61] Truth withstood all the horrors of slavery (including family separations and sexual assaults) before escaping to freedom and becoming one of the most famous and inspirational abolitionists in the nation. Her name, Sojourner Truth, which she took on in the 1840s, was meant to express her intentions: to travel the country speaking the truth about slavery's and sexism's many evils.

The Sojourner syndrome maintains that social factors like "class exploitation, racial discrimination, and gender subordination—as expressed in environmental racism, employment insecurity, and problematic housing conditions" combine to impact the health of working-class and even lower-middle-class black women. In the early 1990s, psychologist Sherman James began to talk about what he called "John Henryism," which is the idea that many of the coping strategies and behaviors that black men devise to deal with social problems in their everyday environments might make them more prone to developing chronic health issues such as hypertension.[62] John Henry, legend has it, was a nineteenth-century black man who tried to outperform a mechanical steam engine with his arms and his trusty hammer. As the tale goes, he won that match against the machine but dropped dead from exhaustion and overexertion right after the competition was done. That little story encapsulates the intuitive premise of John Henryism and the Sojourner syndrome. The kinds of herculean feats that black men and women might devise to deal with the vulnerabilities of social marginalization may be a blessing and a curse at the same time, allowing them to win some small (or not so small) material and psychological victories, but potentially just killing them quicker in the end.

The Sojourner syndrome, Mullings writes, "is a survival strategy, which may have both short-term and long-term benefits," like keeping women's families' fed and housed, allowing them to negotiate hostile work environments, making sure their children are getting their work done in school, protesting to improve the community, and dealing with all the everyday structural issues that threaten to consume them. The Sojourner syndrome is the combination of all the ways black women try to negotiate a landscape that has long been tilted against them. It is an amazing adaptation to the precarious nature of social life. "But it has many costs," she cautions, including those that potentially impact the longevity and quality of black women's lives for the worse, physically and psychologically.

In some ways, it is hard for women *not* to embrace the kinds of strategies and tactics that make up the Sojourner syndrome. They don't really have a choice. The only other option would be to quietly accept the unjust consequences of a social deck stacked against you, which would be a very different kind of martyrdom—without any chance of small victories or overcoming obstacles.

Whereas John Henry had something to prove, something profoundly and existentially important, like his value and humanity, Sojourner Truth was doing something that had to be done lest she and her children perish. Part of the point Mullings wants to make is that for black women, being a Superwoman can literally make you sick.

To be poor and black and female is to be a mule of the world. It means you have to carry your load and everyone else's, too. That kind of double duty has consequences, even for those who seem to bear the extra burden effortlessly—and without a single complaint. Sometimes without seeming to break a sweat. But it takes a toll on the body, a toll that can mean high blood pressure pills, obesity, and a series of other potential health challenges.

The Sojourner syndrome and its consequences might just be the price of the ticket for black women's admission into contemporary American life, but it is an added fee that demonstrates just how much more work needs to be done to make contemporary America the fully inclusive democracy that it wants to be.

Sojourner Truth may be an inspirational figure, but the racist and gendered stereotypes that, in turn, demonize and supernaturalize black women can actually make them feel ashamed as much as anything else—or can be about trying to find a vaccine for that sense of shame. Political scientist and TV personality Melissa Harris-Perry argues that "the Superwoman" is a kind of "myth" that black women invoke to deal with a society that tries to demean them at every turn, to embarrass and dehumanize them with tales of their supposed promiscuity and hypersexuality, of their seemingly irrational anger and hostility, and of their mammy-like devotion to white people's interests over their own.[63] The Strong Black Woman, that reincarnation of Sojourner, tries to disprove society's common stereotypes of black women. But Harris-Perry also argues that its embrace comes with strings attached, the demand that black women put their families' needs, their neighborhood's needs, and their racial community's needs before their own, still bearing those burdens alone and in relative silence.

But some of this stuff is generational, to be sure, and there are versions of the Strong Black Woman that certainly can speak—and speak loudly. I knew a lot of self-described Strong Black Women as an undergraduate at Howard University, an HBCU, like others, where they outnumbered black males at a pretty good clip. The Strong Black Woman was out in force, even just when invoked as a way to pep talk oneself into a kind of stopgap defense against existential attacks.

It is hard out there for a black woman. Hard for everyone, sure. But any way you slice it, black women are usually getting the short end of the ever-shortening stick.

For Petrova, the Barbudan grandmother I have only ever known secondhand, it meant being left alone with her children while their father found a new life—and started a new family—in a faraway country. In that scenario, the Strong Black Women are supposed to soldier on. Through sheer strength of will, they put those children through school, keep them clothed and fed and happy. Most days, they don't let on that the slightest thing is wrong. One might get a hint of sadness, now and then, but it is so fast you can miss it—or imagine you were just seeing things.

This Superwoman doesn't worry about that *other* family. The new one her husband has started somewhere far away. She can't worry about it. That's for him and his God. She simply sojourns on—soldiers on—and takes care of her own, and her part of his. And she works hard. All the time. At home. On the job. She puts out big and little fires as they appear. People know to come to her as soon as the embers start to glow. She wears a mask, which so many superheroes don, but this one "grins and lies," as nineteenth-century poet Paul Laurence Dunbar once put it. She tries, valiantly, to shelter and save her small patch of the world.

What else can she do? What's the alternative? Dying from a broken heart and hoping that the rest of your world will figure things out without you?

THE CONCLUSION

I'm done talking

Why? Do you think you've said too much?

Yes and No

All that talk was more draining than I thought it would be.

For me, it was like I was having a conversation not just with you or with readers but also with myself. That was the taxing part for me. Feeling like half the stuff I was saying had another part of me saying. No you didn't just write that.

NNPS??? Nigger, Puleeeze! :)

What topic was hardest for you to talk about?

Sex and religion. Hard to be 'impolite' without being patently offensive with those two. You?

OMG the exact same 2! Sex I was feelin lil' bit like a hypocrite cuz I couldn't shake the thought that my mom will be reading this! Religion also felt like my non-conventional religious upbringing by nature offends some. Does it make me a little of a poser to talk on such things.

I think we all pose. It's all about which one you strike and why.

That sounds like some Mr. Miyagi wisdom.

Is that how you spell miyagi? Did you have to look that up? Or was it already in your mental Rolodex?

Oh pleeze I am the WORST speller in history. I look everything up constantly. Before there was spellcheck I carried around an electronic Franklin speller

The hardest essay for me to read was your Jazz piece.

Really? That wasn't hard to write at all, mostly because I know any real jazz heads will just dismiss me as crazy and go on about their business.

Your dad would have probably done that, no?

My dad would have dismissed most of what is said today as crazy including my talk. My bro on the other hand not sure. The big sis in me took it much more personally than I expected.

Make sure he knows I still would go see him play anytime. And without earplugs.

LOL look at you trying to be so polite.

Just want to make sure I don't piss your brother off so much that he makes you unfriend me. We like hangin w/you all in BKLYN

I'm not on facebook so much harder to unfriend you. :)

:)

What about what u read?
Anything get to you that I said?

Hey since you aren't on Fbook, you haven't been seeing all this BTHS 25th Anniversary Reunion stuff. Have you? We have to go!!! Though none of the names or faces look familiar to me.

Hey I better finish editing my last chapter

No prob. 25th reunion sounds crazy and depressing.

And we will talk about this reunion again.

AUGUST 14, 11:37 AM

So you never answered my question. If sex and religion were your hardest essays to write, what essay was your hardest to read? what was Jazz for you?

If u say I never pissed u off then u are being too polite.

Or maybe I was being too polite. :(

That's a hard one.

Probably Praying, Mobility, and Mama's Fault. All for different reasons.

Different how?

I've known you a chunk of this time. Just always feel a little implicated in the moves you make.

LOL funny when I was reading your essays I often thought about how even tho I know u so well I really didn't know much about your life. I think cuz we both don't dwell backwards always fwd. I honestly thought u had erased BKLYN from your memory.

I know what you mean. i think we are both about kim: keeping it moving.

I did try to erase some of BKLYN. It just keeps bubbling back up.

LOL That's how BKLYN is, hard to shake. Guess that's why I'm stuck here.

It was funny because growing up not having any Caribbean in me, which now makes me definitely a minority among black folks in nyc, always assumed us/ them was so different. Your home sounds so West Indian to me but at the same time so familiar. Your trinidadian step dad and my dad from the south side of chicago were so alike in some ways even when they weren't.

Btw, My stepdad loved his Calypso and Soca music, but he also really respected Jazz. I can see the album covers in my head now.

Another thing: now that we are parents (crazy cuz I can still look at you and see u as 15) I can't even imagine how our dads could do the belt thing.

This stuff can feel so hard sometimes. Remembering can be like juggling fire.

I can imagine, especially when mine have turned their 'listening ears' all the way off. I just know I can't do it. My stepdad wouldn't even have to ask us to turn our listening ears on. He'd dare us to take them off. Like Dirty Harry. Make my day, he'd say.

LOL there is no way my bro and I would have been able to get away with an ounce of the crap that my kids do. We wouldn't even have the guts to even think it.

The day I lost my virginity I came home and my dad was waiting for me. Sitting at the kitchen table which cuz our apt was so small was basically the apt. He was ridiculously calm, which was unnerving cuz he was typically a yelller, and said: "I know what you've been doing." It still haunts me. I often thought I could start a novel with that scene but couldn't figure out where to go from there. Remembering is like playing with fire.

Wow. That was the other thing it looks like both of them shared. This superhuman ability to know shit they ostensibly shouldn't. How could he have known? Was he following you?

No way he followed me. They just knew shit. Or at least knew how to scare us into believing they knew shit. I've convinced my 4 yr old that I have X-ray vision. I've heard him telling his friends. We'll see how long that lasts.

Deb has our little ones unsure about if she can see them upstairs from downstairs. You all are impressive.

I was proud of myself

Are you nervous about folks reading our book?

Definitely. And for so many different reasons. Personal and professional.

You?

Actually more nervous writing it than I am now. Once it is on the page I don't have any regrets. But I found myself more nervous trying to get stuff on the page. For you not me tho. I felt more responsibility. I worried I was saying something that could cause u professional trouble, ya know since you're the big time Prof.

AUGUST 17, 9:09 AM

I can't believe we are almost done. I honestly didn't think we would finish the manuscript especially with you writing on trains, plains, automobiles, and camels. :)

I'm sorry I had you stressed out the bulk of the time.

If we had written a black women's guide to stress relief that'd be a bestseller

:)

Did you ever think we wouldn't finish?

What do you mean? We had tons of bus rides in South Africa. I just dusted off my legal pads. Even took notes on iPhone. Everything.

Did being in Africa during a big chunk of writing affect your thinking on these issues?

Totally. America just felt so far away sometimes. Tho towns in /near Jo'burg had us thinking we were in BKLN too. Crazy! On Nostrand or Church Ave. I swear!

Is there anything else you wish you had written about? That you just didn't? Or couldn't figure out the best way of doing?

LOL told u BKLYN is hard to shake. What's that lil Kim line bout BKLYN. We don't run we run shit.

Put your lighters up!

:) we are so old

Hmmm. Never thought of what more to write. There is always more to say I suppose. The journalist in me often worries that what I've already said will be old news by the times folks get to read it.

What about you? What do u wish u'd written on?

Maybe. I would have wanted to write a piece about academia, but couldn't get traction. Plus only academics would even care. And even they prob wouldn't

LOL I think that you went out on a ledge by doing this kind of writing as an academic. says a lot even if you didn't get to do a formal essay.

Speaking of getting old, we gotta go to that BTHS reunion. It is only depressing with the wrong outlook. Besides, old is the new young.

Hope that ledge will hold me.

Should we pray on it. :)

:) couldn't hurt

Who would I talk to at the reunion besides you?

We could co-write a great essay on it. And that would be a nice reason to talk to EVERYBODY!! Get all the stories

Appealing to my reporter instinct. How to Be Impolite at your High School Reunion

Hey do you think it is weird that I sent my Philly Inquirer piece to the Atria folks and never heard back? Not even acknowledging receipt. Bad omen?

love that title btw

I think folks were on vacation when u sent it so it probably got lost in the shuffle. Don't worry. It was a great piece.

cool you're right. You know abt black folks feeling DISRESPECTED

For someone who is hit or miss with responding to emails I get indignant when mine are ignored. One of my double standards.

I do sometimes fear tho that my J-school prof was right that no one will read any of this because they think it is just about Black folks.

Same issue w/film funding. They assume nobody will go see it.

About to take the kids to Please Touch More in a bit . . .

LOL Please Touch More definitely needs a new title sounds crazy out of context

Never even thought of that

BTW, I meant Please Touch Museum not More. Damned autocorrect.

Out for now

So R U done talking?

For now

See ya at the reunion :)

ACKNOWLEDGMENTS

Forgive this moment of politeness. Books do indeed take a village. Here's ours:

Thanks to our agent for this project, Nicholas Roman Lewis, for his advice, support, and never-waiving faith in our work. Thank you to the Atria Books family at Simon & Schuster for giving *Impolite Conversations* a home. In an age when serious books often go unnoticed, we were lucky to find a publisher that never made us feel overlooked. Many thanks to our editor, Malaika Adero, for supporting our vision no matter what. You are the type of editor who writers only dream about. Thank you to Malaika's assistant, Todd Hunter, for all his behind-the-scenes hard work taking care of the day-to-day and making the day-to-day such a breeze for us.

And most of all, we would like to thank you, the reader. Of all the obligations and distractions in life, thank you for taking the time to sit down and read us.

CORA: Thanks to the Arthur L. Carter Journalism Institute at NYU for taking me in and its support of this project without question, to Mary Quigley for being the best non-boss boss I've ever had, to Marcia Rock for making me feel like I am part of a great creative team, and my students who challenge me in ways I never realized I needed. This will sound over the top, but I would also like to thank the field of print journalism. This project marked a move for me from the discipline of reporting the news to the freedom of commentary. It was a difficult adjustment, but it is my foundation as a journalist that holds up the type of work I tried to do here making me question everything around me, and I hope kept my words grounded. And no matter how much folks hate reporters, I will always be proud to be one.

Thank you to Mike Brown, Candice Frederick, Deesha Philyaw, Paul Fauntleroy, Keith Reed, Sheryl Tucker, Michelle Patterson, Kimberly Seals Allers, Dionne Grayman, and Janene Outlaw—just some of my twice-as-good crew who did not hesitate to share when I asked for sharing.

A heartfelt thank-you to my coauthor and dear friend, John. This now makes the third time I am shouting you out in book thank-yous. If this were the Oscars—or rather the Emmy's, given your lovefest with TV—celeb watchers would notice, so hopefully you have too. Your friendship means more to me than you can imagine. Thank you for taking this crazy adventure with me without hesitation and without holding back. Thank you for pushing me to do the same. Without getting mushy, working together has been a special ride.

Thanks to my mama for being the most supportive mom a daughter could ever hope for, doing everything and anything I could ever want and need, making everything and anything I do possible. Listening to your passion while talking politics taught me to talk passionately. Thanks to my lil' bro Mr. O, who is my conscience and helps keep my talk honest. Thanks for being such a good friend. Thanks to my dad, who I continue to miss, who taught me never to fall into the trap of caring what anyone thinks. Without that thinking this book would never exist.

Thank you to my husband, Rondai, my friend, my partner, my support, my love. Thank you for this wonderful conversation we've been having since the moment we met twenty-plus years ago. Thank you for reading all my words and for always listening. And a big thank-you to my children, Maya and Kaden. Thank you for teaching me what it means to talk honestly and openly, always. You are the inspiration for this book and so much more. I love you both this, this, this, this, much.

JOHN: I want to thank my friends and family, who have always been so supportive, including the ones who have asked to read portions of the manuscript or simply commented on its themes in ways that were insightful, funny, inspiring, and incredibly generous (without even trying), especially Ezekiel Dixon-Román and Fran Markowitz (both of whom I should have thanked in *Thin Description*), Marla Frederick, Carolyn Rouse, Kamari Maxine Clarke, Shaun Harper, Noah Feldman, Salamishah Tillet, David Kyuman Kim, Devin Fergus, Monica Miller, Charles McNeal, Mark Anthony Neal, Marc Lamont Hill, Andrew Janiak, Chaz Howard, Khadijah White, C. Riley Snorton, Jasmine Cobb, and Jasmine Salters.

I want to thank my friends and colleagues at Penn (who make teaching there so fulfilling). This is just a partial list of that group: Michael Delli Carpini, Richard Perry, Paul Messaris, Greg Urban, Adriana Petryna, Kathy Hall, Lyndsey Beutin, Lee Baker, Charlie Piot, Tudor Parfitt, Tsitsi Jaji, Guy Ramsey, Emily Ladue, Corrina Laughlin, Sharrona Pearl, Barbie Zelizer, Carolyn Marvin, Marwan Kraidy, Philippe Bourgois, Janet Monge, Rose Halligan, Joe Diorio, Deb Porter, Deb Williams, Larysa Carr, Amy Gutmann, Vince Price, Anita Allen, Lubna Mian, Betsy Rymes, Lynn Lees, Raisha Price, Salamishah Tillet, Sue White, Richard Leventhal, Joanne Murray, Alison Berstecher, Hermon Mebrahtu, Asif Agha, Yogi Sukwa, Emily Plowman, Richard Cardona, Waldo Aguirre, Cory Falk, Matthew Tarditi, Kate Zambon, Debora Lui, all of my other Penn colleagues in Africana Studies, Anthropology, Annenberg, GSE, SP2, and all across campus. And I could go on and on and on. There are so many folks I left out, but I hope to make up for that by thanking some of them in person. Maybe even over a meal.

My mom, brother, and sister (and stepdad) are with me every single day, even though I don't call them nearly enough. I love you all more than a thousand books could ever capture. And love to all the nieces and nephews who make our lives so much larger. There are so many extended family members I haven't spoken to in forever—cousins, aunts, uncles. I won't write another book before I start to fix that.

I want to thank Andrew Stuart, my agent; Sar Ahmadiel Ben Yehuda, a model of scholarly seriousness and commitment; Louis Massiah, an inspired filmmaker and media-institution builder; Kathy

Newman, my fearless and wildly supportive advisor; Ben Vinson, Martha Jones, Prudence Carter, Roxanne Varzi, Bayo Holsey, J.R. Jarrod., Khari Wyatt, Jafari Allen, and Kristen Drybread, the folks in my grad school crew who seem to have not totally given up on me yet; Netflix, for all those binge-based distractions.

I honestly don't know what to say to you Cora. Where to even begin? I've known you longer and better than just about anybody else on this planet who isn't one of my family members. And after writing this book with you, I can honestly say that I hardly knew you at all. :) I learned so much from you (and about you) during this process. And I'm glad we decided to finally do it. You are such a special human being. Thanks for teaching me what genuine friendship looks like.

To my wife, Deb, all I can say is thank you, thank you, thank you for making my world so precious and special and safe and satisfying. You are the sexiest and smartest woman in the world. Period. End of discussion. You read every single word of this manuscript, when you had looming deadlines snapping at your heels and caught so many more typos than I did. Thanks, sweetie. And as the little ones would say, I love you TTHHHIIISSSSSS MMMMMUUUUUUC-CCCCHHHHHH!!!!!!! Infinity plus infinity plus infinity plus five thousand million and pi!!!!!

And I want to take a second to recognize the people who "hate on *us*," all of us, because we're *fabolous*. Thanks for the fuel.

ENDNOTES

SEX

Sexually Active Daughters

1. "Having the Sex Talk with Your Kids," Dr. Laura Berman, *Oprah*, March 26, 2009.
2. ABC News, "Female Orgasm May Be Tied to Rule of Thumb," Susan Donaldson James, *New York Times*, September 4, 2009, and "A Critic Takes on the Logic of Female Orgasm," Dinitia Smith, *New York Times*, May 17, 2005.
3. "Joycelyn Elders Puts Congress on Blast," Cynthia Gordy, *The Root*, April 18, 2011.
4. Mt. Holyoke College alumni gallery website. The college has some of her original Valentine's Day cards on display: http://www.mtholyoke.edu/news/stories /5684261.
5. "Student debt delays spending, saving and marriage," Blake Ellis, *CNNMoney*, May 9, 2013.
6. "A Religious Portrait of African Americans," Neha Sahgal and Greg Smith, Pew Research Center's Forum on Religion & Public Life, January 30, 2009.
7. "What the Bible Really Says About Sex," Lisa Miller, *Newsweek*, February 6, 2011.

Conspiracy Hypersexualize Black Boys

8. This entire chapter and its title are a riff on Jawanza Kunjufu, *Countering the Conspiracy to Destroy Black Boys* (Sawk Village, IL: African American Images, 1985).
9. This is part of the reason why rapper Jay-Z's collaboration with openly gay singer-songwriter Frank Ocean on the song "Oceans," about celebrity, the transatlantic slave trade, and selling drugs, is such an important intervention. Of course, for the conspiracy theorists, it just demonstrates his Illuminati-related attempt to destroy God's creation any way possible, including by promoting homosexuality within the black community.
10. "Mugabe chides homosexuals again," http://www.newsday.co.zw/2013/07/25/ mugabe-chides-homosexuals-again/.
11. I would argue that these rapes are less about an extra sensitivity to lesbianism over male homosexuality, and more a cover for the sexist impulse to control women and their bodies.
12. A discussion of "hypersegregation" can be found in Douglas Massey and Nancy Denton, *American Apartheid: Segregation and the Making of the Underclass* (Cambridge, MA: Harvard University Press, 1993).
13. Richard Majors, *Cool Pose: The Dilemmas of Black Manhood in America* (New York: Touchstone, 1993). For three recent scholarly discussions about black masculinity

that I have found particularly insightful, see C. Riley Snorton, *Nobody is Supposed to Know: Black Sexuality on the Down Low* (Minneapolis: University of Minnesota Press, 2014), Mark Anthony Neal, *Looking for Leroy: Illegible Black Masculinities* (New York: New York University Press, 2013), and Jeffrey Q. McCune, Jr., *Sexual Discretion: Black Masculinity and the Politics of Passing* (Chicago: University of Chicago Press, 2014).

MONEY

Mobility Myth

1. Jason DeParle, "Harder for Americans to Rise from Lower Rungs," *New York Times,* January 4, 2012.
2. Michael Moran, "In Connecticut, Two Sides of the Deep Divide," NPR/*GlobalPost* partnership, January 17, 2013.
3. Pew Charitable Trusts Economic Mobility Project, "Pursuing the American Dream: Economic Mobility Across Generations," July 2012.
4. Markus Jantii, "American Exceptionalism in a New Light: A Comparison of Inter-generational Earnings Mobility in Nordic Countries, the United Kingdom and the United States," Department of Economics and Statistics, Åbo Akademi University, Turku, Finland.
5. Pew Economic Mobility Project, "Pursuing the American Dream: Economic Mobility Across Generations," July 2012.
6. Ibid.
7. "Divided We Stand: Why Inequality Keeps Rising," OECD Publishing, 2011.
8. Annie Lowrey, "Income Inequality May Take Toll on Growth," *New York Times,* October 16, 2012.
9. Michael Moran, "The Great Divide, global income inequality and its cost, two sides of Connecticut's economic divide reveal price of inequality," *GlobalPost,* January 17, 2013, http://www.globalpost.com/dispatch/news/regions/americas/united-states/121226/connecticut-economic-divide-inequality?page=0,1.
10. Barack Obama, State of the Union address February 12, 2013, Whitehouse.gov.
11. Findings from Pew Commissioned National Poll on Economic Mobility, March 12, 2009.
12. Greenberg Quinlan Rosner, Pew Economic Mobility Project, "Findings from a National Survey & Focus Groups on Economic Mobility", March 12, 2009.
13. Ibid.
14. Pew Economic Mobility Project poll, "Economic Mobility and the American Dream: Where Do We Stand in the Wake of the Great Recession?," March 24–29, 2011.
15. Benjamin Zimmer, Linguistlist.org listserv, "figurative bootstraps" discussion, August 11, 2005.
16. Alexander Ewing, "On Bootstraps," *More Intelligent Life,* the additional online content for *The Economist's Intelligent Life* magazine, no date of posting available. http://moreintelligentlife.com/content/alexander-ewing/bootstraps.
17. *The Daily Show with Jon Stewart,* Wednesday, July 28, 2004.
18. Pew Economic Mobility Project, "How Much Protection Does a College Degree Afford?," January 9, 2013.
19. "New Report on Black America Reveals 'A Tale of Two Truths,'" *Tell Me More with Michel Martin,* NPR, April 10, 2013.
20. Pew Economic Mobility Project, "Downward Mobility from the Middle Class: Waking Up from the American Dream," Gregory Acs, September 2011.

21. The Heritage Foundation, "Defending the Dream: Why Income Inequality Doesn't Threaten Opportunity," David Azerrad and Rea S. Herderman Jr., September 2012.
22. DeParle, "Harder for Americans to Rise from the Lower Rungs."
23. Center for American Progress, "Our Working Nation in 2013: An Updated National Agenda for Work and Family Policies," Heather Boushey, Ann O'Leary, and Sarah Jane Glynn, February 2013.
24. "Our Family Myths: Q/A with Stephanie Coontz," *Atlantic Journal-Constitution*, March 26, 2006.
25. "Parents and the High Cost of Child Care: 2012 Report," Child Care Aware of America, August 2012.

Jazz

26. See Aaron James, *Assholes: A Theory* (New York, Doubleday, 2012).
27. For a canonical version of this critique on mass culture, see Theodor Adorno and Max Horkheimer, *Dialectic of Enlightenment* (Stanford, CA: Stanford University Press, 2002).
28. Ralph Ellison, *Living with Music: Ralph Ellison's Jazz Writings* (New York: Random House, 2001).
29. This is the very argument made in Steven Johnson's celebration of contemporary television, *Everything Bad Is Good for You: How Today's Popular Culture is Actually Making Us Smarter* (New York: Riverhead, 2005).
30. Elihu Katz and Paddy Scannell, eds., "The End of Television? Its Impact on the World (So Far)," *The ANNALS of the American Academy of Political and Social Science Series*, vol. 625 (September 2009).
31. Guthrie Ramsey, *Race Music: Black Cultures from Bebop to Hip-Hop* (Berkeley: University of California Press, 2004).

RELIGION

Hope

1. "Post-Election Partisanship Among Millennials Deepens, Harvard Poll Finds," release of spring 2013 survey conducted by Harvard Institute of Politics, April 30, 2013.
2. Ibid.
3. "For 'Millennials,' a Tide of Cynicism and a Partisan Gap," Sheryl Gay Stolberg, *New York Times*, April 29, 2013.
4. "Millennials Pessimistic About Future," One Young World press release, September 2011.
5. "'Nones'" on the Rise," Pew Research Religion & Public Life Project, October 9, 2012.
6. "Those without religion reshape America's faith landscape," Rachel Zoll, Associated Press, October 9, 2012.
7. Pew "'Nones'" survey.
8. Secular Student Alliance history (www.secularstudents.org) and "Teenagers Speak Up for Lack of Faith," Michael Winerip, *New York Times*, April 3, 2011.
9. David Silverman, president of American Atheists, makes this argument in *Forbes* magazine, "Unbelievable! Atheists to Rally in Record Numbers," Carol Pinchefsky, March 21, 2012. Silverman's quote: "Atheists are the fastest-growing religious subgroup in all fifty states. There are more atheists in this country than there are Jews, Muslims, Hindus, Buddhists combined and doubled."

10. "America's 10 Million Unemployed Youth Spell Danger for Future Economic Growth," Sarah Ayres, *American Progress*, June 5, 2013.
11. "One in Seven: Ranking Youth Disconnection in the 25 Largest Metro Areas," Measure of America, a Project of the Social Science Research Council, September 2012.
12. "Latinas, Black Males Most Disconnected," Rosa Ramirez, *National Journal*, September 27, 2012.

POLITICS

Republican
1. David Graeber, *The Democracy Project: A History, a Crisis, a Movement* (New York: Spiegel & Grau, 2013).
2. Stephen L. Carter, *Reflections of an Affirmative Action Baby* (New York: Basic Books, 1991).

American Dream
3. Steven Eisman, portfolio manager, FrontPoint Financial Services Fund, LP, New York, NY, speech, "Subprime Goes to College," given at the Ira Sohn Conference, New York City, May 26, 2010. Also parts read into testimony at full committee hearing held by the Senate Committee on Health Education Labor and Pensions. "Emerging Risk? An Overview of the Federal Investment in For-Profit Education," June 24, 2010. http://help.senate.gov/hearings/hearing/?id=464686ba-5056-9502-5d95-e21a6409cc53.
4. Anthony P. Carnevale, research professor and director of the Georgetown University Center on Education and the Workforce, discusses the findings in the Century Foundation's latest publication, "Rewarding Strivers: Helping Low-Income Students Succeed in College," June 16, 2010.
5. "Total College Debt Now Exceeds Total Credit Card Debt," Mark Kantrowitz, publisher, and Fastweb student loan debt clock, fastweb.com.
6. Fastweb.com.
7. "Burden of College Loans on Graduates Grows," Tamar Lewin, *New York Times*, April 11, 2011.
8. Complete College America, "Time Is the Enemy," The Completion Shortfall, 2011, National Report.
9. "Improving Student Transfer from Community Colleges to Four Year Institutions," College Board Report, July 2011.
10. Complete College America National Report.
11. Caitlen Dewey, "Worst college majors for your career," *Kiplinger,* September 6, 2012.
12. CCAP nonprofit DC-based education research center, which crunched Bureau of Labor Statistics data.
13. *Chronicle of Higher Education,* "Why Did 17 Million Students Go to College?", Richard Vedder, based on research by The Center for College Affordability and Productivity, October 20, 2010.
14. "Chasing the American Dream: Recent College Graduates and the Great Recession," study released by John J. Heldrich Center for Workforce Development at Rutgers, May 2012.
15. Ibid.
16. Ibid.
17. "Is College Worth It?", chapter 1 overview, Pew Research Center, May 15, 2011.

18. Brooklyn Community Board 3 social characteristics data drawn from the American Community Survey 2007–2009 found on NYC.gov.
19. "A History of College Grade Inflation," Catherine Rampell, Economix, *New York Times,* July 14, 2011.
20. "Rewarding Strivers: Helping Low-Income Students Succeed in College," Century Foundation, June 16, 2010.
21. "Part-Time Undergraduates in Post-Secondary Education 2003–2004, National Center for Education Statistics, U.S. Department of Education report, 2007.
22. "4 out of 5 in Community College Want to Transfer, Report Says," Lily Altavena, College Board Study, July 14, 2011.
23. "Rewarding Strivers: Helping Low-Income Students Succeed in College," Century Foundation, June 16, 2010.
24. Ibid.
25. Ibid.
26. Testimony of Steven Eisman before the U.S. Senate Committee on Health, Education, Labor and Pensions hearing on "Emerging Risk? An Overview of the Federal Investment in For-Profit Education," June 24, 2010.
27. Ibid.
28. "Burden of College Loans on Graduates Grows," Tamar Lewin, *New York Times,* April 11, 2011.
29. Ibid.
30. Wikipedia, University of Phoenix entry, http://en.wikipedia.org/wiki/University_of _Phoenix, accessed November 29, 2013.
31. Mamie Lynch, Jennifer Engle, and Jose L. Cruz, "Subprime Opportunities: The Unfulfilled Promise of For-Profit Colleges and Universities," report conducted by Education, a nonprofit research group, November 22, 2010.
32. "Rewarding Strivers: Helping Low-Income Students Succeed in College," Century Foundation, June 16, 2010.
33. Ibid.

Whites Whiter

34. Slavoj Žižek, *First as Tragedy, Then as Farce* (London: Verso, 2009).
35. Noah Feldman, *Cool War: The Future of Global Competition* (New York: Random House, 2013).
36. Pierre Rosanvallon, *Democracy Past and Future* (New York: Columbia University Press, 2006).
37. Shelby Steele, *White Guilt: How Blacks and Whites Together Destroyed the Promise of the Civil Rights Era* (New York: Harper Perennial, 2006).
38. Émile Durkheim, *The Division of Labor in Society* (New York: Free Press, 1984).
39. John Hartigan Jr., *Odd Tribes: Toward a Cultural Analysis of White People* (Durham, NC: Duke University Press, 2005). Also, Pamela Perry, *Shades of White: White Kids and Racial Identities in High School* (Durham, NC: Duke University Press, 2002).
40. Tim Wise, *White Like Me: Reflections on Race from a Privileged Son* (Berkeley, CA: Soft Skull Press, 2008).

Complacency (1st black presidents)

41. *Meet the Press,* January 27, 2013.
42. "NAACP President: Black People Worse Off Under Obama," Jessica Chasmar, *Washington Times,* January 28, 2013, editor's note with correction added.
43. "Obama and Black Americans: The Paradox of Hope," Gary Younge, *Nation,* June 6, 2011.

Mama's Fault

44. Robert Andrews, ed. *The Columbia Dictionary of Quotations* (New York: Columbia University Press, 1993), 364.
45. *The Works of John Adams, Second President of the United States: With a Life of the Author, Notes and Illustrations*, volume 9, John Adams (Boston: Little, Brown, 1854), 540.
46. "The Neighborhood Effect," Marc Parry, *Chronicle of Higher Education,* November 5, 2012.
47. "Link to Marathon Bombing Rattles City Known for Its Tolerance," Jess Bidgood, *New York Times,* June 5, 2013.

RACE

Haters

1. Adriane Raine, *The Anatomy of Violence: The Biological Roots of Crime* (New York: Random House, 2013).
2. Jane Goodall, *My Life with Chimpanzees* (New York: Aladdin Books, 1996).
3. Marshall Sahlins, *Culture and Practical Reason* (Chicago: University of Chicago Press, 1976).
4. Robert N. McCauley, *Why Religion Is Natural and Science Is Not* (Oxford: Oxford University Press, 2011).
5. Beverly Daniel Tatum, *"Why Are All the Black Kids Sitting Together in the Cafeteria?" and Other Conversations About Race* (New York: Basic Books, 1977).
6. Oscar Lewis, *Five Families: Mexican Case Studies in the Culture of Poverty* (New York: Basic Books, 1975).
7. Glenn C. Loury, *The Anatomy of Racial Inequality* (Cambridge, MA: Harvard University Press, 2002).

One Box Rules

8. "2010 Census Shows Multiple-Race Population Grew Faster Than Single-Race Population," U.S. Census Bureau press release, September 27, 2012.
9. Ho, A. K., Sidanius, J., Levin, D. T., & Banaji, M. R. (2011), "Evidence for hypodescent and racial hierarchy in the categorization and perception of biracial individuals," *Journal of Personality and Social Psychology* 100(3): 492–506.
10. Dorr, Gregory Michael, "Racial Integrity Laws of the 1920s," *Encyclopedia Virginia*, Virginia Foundation for the Humanities, October 15, 2012, accessed online July 24, 2013.
11. Ibid.
12. "One-Drop Rule Persists," Steve Bradt, *Harvard Gazette,* December 9, 2010.
13. Ibid.
14. Ibid.
15. Ibid.
16. "'They deserve a vote': Call and response in Obama's State of the Union," Susan Brooks Thistlethwaite, *Washington Post,* February 13, 2013. (Appeared only in the newspaper's online coverage.)
17. *The Daily Show,*"Speech Therapy—Post Racial," January 28, 2010.
18. Cora Daniels, *Black Power Inc.: The New Voice of Success* (Hoboken, New Jersey: Wiley, 2004), 5–6.
19. 1nedrop.com/about.

Color Wars

20. W. E. B. DuBois, "Back to Africa," *Century* 150, no. 4: 539–548 (February 1923).
21. Marcus Garvey: Amy Jacques-Garvey, ed. *The Philosophy and Opinions of Marcus Garvey, or, Africa for the Africans*, (Dover, MA: Majority Press, 1986).
22. Jennifer L. Hochschild and Weaver Vesla. "The Skin Color Paradox and the American Racial Order," *Social Forces* 2007, 86(2): 643-670.
23. Arthur H. Goldsmith, Darrick Hamilton, and William Darity Jr., "From Dark to Light: Skin Color and Wages Among African-Americans," *Journal of Human Resources* vol. 42, no. 4 (Fall 2007): 701–738.
24. Ibid.
25. "EEOC Settles Color Harassment Lawsuit with Applebee's Neighborhood Bar and Grill," EEOC press release, August 7, 2003, http://www.eeoc.gov/eeoc/newsroom /release/8-07-03.cfm.
26. Ibid.
27. EEOC Charge Statistics FY 1997 through FY 2011, http://www.eeoc.gov/eeoc /statistics/enforcement/charges.cfm.
28. Darrick Hamilton, Arthur H. Goldsmith, and William A. Darity Jr., "Shedding 'Light' on Marriage: The Influence of Skin Shade on Marriage for Black Females," *Journal of Economic Behavior and Organization* 72(1): 30–50.
29. DeNeen L. Brown, "The Legacy of Colorism Reflects Wounds of Racism That Are More Than Skin-Deep," *Washington Post,* July 12, 2009.
30. "Shedding 'Light' on Marriage."
31. Jennifer L. Eberhardt, Valerie J. Purdie-Vaughns, and Sheri Lynn Johnson, "Looking Deathworthy: Perceived Stereotypicality of Black Defendants Predicts Capital-Sentencing Outcomes," (2006), Cornell Law Faculty Publications, Paper 41.
32. Topher Sanders, "The Lighter the Skin, the Shorter the Prison Term?", *The Root,* July 5, 2011, http://www.theroot.com/views/lighter-skin-shorter-prison-term.
33. Marcus Garvey, "W.E. Burghardt Du Bois as a Hater of Dark People," *Negro World,* February 13, 1923, reprinted in *The Philosophy and Opinions of Marcus Garvey, or, Africa for the Africans,* edited Amy Jacques-Garvey (New York, Routledge, 1977).
34. W.E.B. DuBois Marcus Garvey: A Lunatic or a Traitor? *The Crisis,* 1924, reprinted in *Call and Response Key Debates in African American Studies,* edited by Henry Louis Gates and Jennifer Burton (New York: W.W. Norton & Company, 2010).
35. http://en.wikipedia.org/wiki/Afro-Brazilian. Entries about the Brazilian census are well documented in the Wikipedia entry through news stories in the Brazilian press.
36. "Brazil's Racial Identity Challenge," *New York Times,* March 29, 2012, http://www .nytimes.com/roomfordebate/2012/03/29/brazils-racial-identity-challenge.
37. "From Dark to Light: Skin Color and Wages Among African-Americans," Arthur H. Goldsmith, Darrick Hamilton, and William Darity Jr., *The Journal of Human Resources* vol. 42, no. 4 (Fall 2007), 701–738.
38. Joni Hersch, "The Persistence of Skin Color Discrimination for Immigrants," *Journal of Social Science Research,* December 23, 2010.
39. Ibid.
40. Study of Immigrants Links Lighter Skin and Higher Income, Travis Loller, Associated Press in the *New York Times,* January 28, 2007.
41. Joni Hersch, "The Persistence of Skin Color Discrimination for Immigrants," *Journal of Social Science Research,* December 23, 2010.
42. Ibid.
43. "U.S. Census Bureau Projections Show a Slower Growing, Older, More Diverse Nation a Half Century from Now, U.S. Census press release, December 12, 2012. http://www.census.gov/newsroom/releases/archives/population/cb12-243.html.

44. Carol Morello and Ted Mellnik, "Minorities Become a Majority in Washington Region," *Washington Post,* August 31, 2011.
45. Sabrina Tavernise, "Whites Account for Under Half of Births in US," *New York Times,* May 17, 2012.

F*ck the N-word
46. Jordan Zakarin, "Tarantino's 'Django Unchained' Reignites Debate over N-word in Movies," *Hollywood Reporter,* December, 15, 2012, http://www.hollywoodreporter.com/news/tarantinos-django-unchained-reignites-debate-402445.
47. *"The Howard Stern Show,"* http://www.youtube.com/watch?v=Bojzdu_AMQ8.
48. TMZ.com, December 29, 2012, http://www.tmz.com/2012/12/29/katt-williams-quentin-tarantino-django-unchained/#ixzz2GpiTdfeN.
49. CBS local affiliate in Houston, January 3, 2013, video: http://houston.cbslocal.com/2013/01/03/samuel-l-jackson-tries-to-get-film-critic-to-say-n-word-during-interview/.
50. Cora Daniels, *Ghettonation: A Journey into the Land of the Bling and the Home of the Shameless* (New York: Doubleday, 2007).
51. James Braxton Peterson, "How did ni**er become 'the n-word'?" *Grio,* June 12, 2012.
52. Fox Butterfield, "Behind the Badge: A Special Report: A Portrait of the Detective in the 'O. J. Whirlpool,'" *New York Times Book Review,* March 2, 1996.
53. Anahad O'Connor, "In Bid to Ban Racial Slur, Blacks Are on Both Sides," *New York Times,* February 25, 2007.
54. "Resolution calling on the Council of the City of New York to declare symbolic moratorium on the use of the 'N' word in New York City," RESOLUTION 0693-2007.
55. Ibid.
56. Ibid.
57. PBS WGBH Culture Shock companion website to the show, online entry for D.W. Griffith's *The Birth of a Nation* accessed November 29, 2013, http://www.pbs.org/wgbh/cultureshock/flashpoints/theater/birthofanation_a.html.

Mediocrity Nation
58. Remarks by President Obama at Morehouse College Commencement Ceremony, May 19, 2013; transcript provided by whitehouse.gov.
59. *Southern Living,* "Paper Napkin Interview: Dishing with Condoleezza Rice," Jenna Bush Hager, March 20, 2013.
60. Derald Wing Sue, PhD, "Racial Microaggressions in Everyday Life: Is Subtle Bias Harmless?", *Psychology Today,* October 5, 2010. Also an accompanying YouTube video by Dr. Sue linked to *Psychology Today* story that defines and illustrates the term "microaggression."

Sojourners
61. Leith Mullings, "Resistance and Resilience: The Sojourner Syndrome and the Social Context of Reproduction in Central Harlem," *Transforming Anthropology* 13(2): 79–91; also, Leith Mullings and Alaka Wali, *Stress and Resilience: The Social Context of Reproduction in Central Harlem* (New York: Kluwer Academic, 2001).
62. Sherman James, "John Henryism and the Health of African Americans," *Culture, Medicine, and Psychiatry* 18 (1994): 163–182.
63. Melissa V. Harris-Perry, *Sister Citizen: Shame, Stereotypes, and Black Women in America* (New Haven, CT: Yale University Press, 2011).